1940
Myth and Reality

CLIVE PONTING

Elephant Paperbacks
IVAN R. DEE, PUBLISHER, CHICAGO

1940: MYTH AND REALITY. Copyright © 1990 by Clive Ponting. This book
was originally published in 1991 by Ivan R. Dee, Inc.

First ELEPHANT PAPERBACK edition published 1993 by Ivan R. Dee, Inc.,
1332 North Halsted Street, Chicago 60622. Manufactured in the United States
of America and printed on acid-free paper.

Library of Congress Cataloging-in-Publication Data:
Ponting, Clive.
1940 : myth and reality / Clive Ponting. -- 1st Elephant Paperback ed.
p. cm.
"Elephant Paperbacks."
Includes bibliographical references and index.
ISBN 1-56663-036-3
1. Great Britain—Politics and government—1936–1945. 2. World War,
1939–1945—Great Britain. I. Title.
DA587.P58   1993
941.084—dc20   93-11244

Contents

1940:
Myth and Reality

1940:
Myth and Reality

Introduction: 1940 – The Myth

The year 1940 is a memorable one, a time of great events: Dunkirk, the fall of France, the Battle of Britain, the Blitz, and Churchill leading the nation through these troubled times. It was the year Britain stood alone against Nazi-dominated Europe and thereby ensured the preservation of freedom and liberty. Nothing can diminish that achievement. Yet the way in which Britain survived and the other stirring events of that year have become obscured by myth. The process began in 1940 itself and has continued ever since, through books such as Churchill's war memoirs and with the passage of time affecting personal recollections as people look back through rose-tinted spectacles.

I can still remember the impact that reading Churchill's history of the Second World War had on me many years ago; its wonderful language redolent of Macaulay and Gibbon, its dramatic story so clearly told, its moral message so apparent. Some years later, when I was reading the government papers of the time in the Public Record Office, I began to realize that the story was far more complex and that there was much that had been oversimplified or even left out altogether in Churchill's account. Despite all its virtues, his six-volume history is a politician's memoir designed to relate his version of events and to present the story as he wanted. On returning to the archives recently I was even more struck by how much the accepted story of 1940 differed from the picture that emerges from the government papers.

The current widely accepted view of what happened in 1940 could be summarized as follows. In the 1930s the British Empire was one of the strongest powers in the world, but through a misguided and craven policy of appeasement and failure to rearm it allowed the aggressor states (Germany, Italy and Japan) to expand until war became inevitable. Britain and France missed a golden opportunity to defeat Germany in the autumn of 1939 and then in April 1940 Chamberlain's incompetent direction of the war let Hitler conquer Denmark and Norway. Popular discontent with the government swept Churchill into the premiership as the war leader acclaimed by all. The old policy of appeasement and British weakness disappeared under Churchill's inspiring leadership. Immediately on taking office he had to face the collapse of France caused by the numerically superior and highly mechanized German army using waves of modern tanks in a new style of *blitzkrieg* warfare. The British army, let down by the French and betrayed by the Belgians, fought its way back to the coast, where it was evacuated by a fleet of small boats from the beaches of Dunkirk. Left alone, the British government, refusing even to entertain the possibility of peace with Germany, decided to fight on to final victory. Facing a determined threat to invade Britain, brilliant direction of the RAF defeated a German air force that held all the advantages in the Battle of Britain. Morale in Britain remained high, as the country, united as never before and inspired by Churchill's regular radio broadcasts, was guided by a benevolent government which had great faith in the strength and steadfastness of the British people. The Blitz, one of the heaviest bombing campaigns ever mounted, began when Hitler started the policy of bombing major cities. Well-prepared and efficiently organized emergency services ensured that there were few problems in dealing with the results of the Blitz. Churchill, working closely with his friend President Roosevelt and taking advantage of the strong identity of interest between Britain and the United States, brought the Americans to the brink of entering the war. By the end of 1940, Britain was still a great power and firmly established on the road to victory.

When we examine the historical record, however, not one of these statements turns out to be true.

The purpose of this book is to strip away the myth and examine the events of 1940 from a different perspective. The result is a radically different, less comfortable view of Britain's 'Finest Hour'. This book goes behind the scenes to examine many of the facts and episodes that were kept carefully concealed at the time. The fact that the emphasis is on high government policy and not on the details of military campaigns, nor on feats of individual courage and heroism, nor on the human suffering of war, is not to deny or denigrate them in any way. The choice was made deliberately to deal with those aspects of 1940 so often neglected or played down by other books. We must never forget those who died or suffered in the Second World War in order to defeat a vile and evil system. At the same time, there is no need to ignore some of the hard facts and less well-publicized lessons of that war. After fifty years it is time to face up to reality.

1

22 August 1940

The date 22 August 1940 is one of the most significant yet least famous in British history. It is the day on which the war cabinet faced the fact that Britain would shortly cease to be an independent power in the world. Whatever the outcome of the battle being fought by the Spitfires and Hurricanes of RAF Fighter Command ir the skies over Kent and Sussex, within three or four months either Britain would become a dependency of the United States or it would have to seek peace from a victorious Germany. The reality of Britain's position in the summer of 1940 was very different both from the contemporary rhetoric and the subsequent mythology.

This complete collapse of British power was well hidden from the public behind an outward show of independence and determination. Britain had stood alone against Germany and Italy for just over two months following the conquest of Norway and Denmark in April and the collapse of Holland, Luxembourg, Belgium and France in May and June. Britain had no allies in Europe and most of the rest of the continent was rapidly learning to accommodate itself to German domination. Churchill's speeches, with their self-consciously archaic style and mixture of historical and biblical references, romanticized Britain's isolation and near defeat as its 'Finest Hour' and compared it to the days when Drake faced the Spanish Armada in 1588 and Napoleon waited to cross the Channel in 1805. The will to fight on had been shown in one of the most tragic episodes of the war when Britain turned on its defeated ally and sank part of the French fleet at Oran at the beginning of July. But determination would not be enough on its own. The military situation facing the isolated British government was grim and its ability to survive, let alone go on to victory, widely doubted in the rest of the world. The threat of invasion had mounted steadily but the British army, after the escape from Dunkirk, was still ill-equipped, untrained and unready to meet any serious attempt to cross the Channel. Survival therefore depended on the maintenance of air supremacy over south-east England to deter the Germans from attempting an invasion. That air battle had begun in earnest on 13 August with the heaviest fighting two days later, when the Luftwaffe lost seventy-five aircraft in a day (the highest loss of the battle) and the RAF thirty-four (the second highest of the battle). On 20 August Churchill had already immortalized the conflict in his speech in the House of Commons with the words: 'Never in the field of human conflict was so much owed by so many to so few.'

22 August was a quiet day in the Battle of Britain; the RAF lost five aircraft and the Germans two in a series of minor raids across southern England. The brilliant sunshine of May and early June (which in retrospect is now believed to have lasted through the summer) had long since gone. Typical English summer weather – low cloud and rain – had restricted operations to small-scale raids since 19 August. Both sides were using the lull to regroup and assess tactics before what was to be the most crucial phase of the battle in the last week of August and early September.

The crucial events of the day took place at 10 Downing Street, where the war cabinet met at noon. Winston Churchill had just got out of bed to chair the meeting. He had taken over as Prime Minister on 10 May but only during the last six weeks had he begun to dominate the government and assume the mantle of national leader. Four other members of the six-strong war cabinet were present: the aristocratic figure of Lord Halifax, the foxhunting highchurchman who had been Foreign Secretary since 1938 and who could have been Prime Minister in May had he wanted the job; Lord Beaverbrook, the blunt, egocentric Canadian newspaper magnate and long-time crony of Churchill who had been Minister of Aircraft Production since May where he had, by various unorthodox methods, turned out the fighters to win the Battle of Britain; Clement Attlee, the reticent MP for Limehouse who had become leader of the Labour Party in 1935 only because there was nobody better available and who was now deputy Prime Minister; and Arthur Greenwood, the deputy leader of the Labour Party whose addiction to alcohol meant that he could not be given a job of any importance. The missing member was Neville Chamberlain, Prime Minister from 1937 until his replacement by Churchill and now a trusted and valued member of the new government. He had just undergone an operation for cancer, but at Churchill's insistence was still receiving cabinet papers at his country house.

Seven other ministers were seated around the rectangular table in the cabinet room overlooking Horse Guards Parade: Kingsley Wood, a Chamberlain protégé who had changed sides and supported Churchill and had been rewarded by being made Chancellor of the Exchequer; Anthony Eden, Secretary of State for War, whose rapid political rise had ended with his resignation as Foreign Secretary in 1938 and who was now making his way back to the top under Churchill's guidance; A. V. Alexander, the uninspiring Labour MP who was First Lord of the Admiralty and almost incapable of controlling the admirals under him; Archie Sinclair, leader of the tiny independent Liberal Party, Churchill's second-in-command during his spell in the army in the First World War and now Secretary of State for Air; Herbert Morrison, the boss of the London Labour Party machine who had reluctantly accepted the post of Minister of Supply; Duff Cooper, the reactionary womanizer who had resigned over Munich and been rewarded by Churchill by being made Minister of Information where his incompetence and laziness were to finish his political career; and Lord Caldecote, a minor Conservative politician who had been Minister for Defence Co-ordination before the war (a post Churchill had wanted) but who was now fading into obscurity as Dominions Secretary. Apart from the secretaries, there were four other officials present: Sir Richard Hopkins from the Treasury; Sir Alexander Cadogan, the head of the Foreign Office; Sir Cyril Newall, Chief of the Air Staff; and Sir Robert Haining, Vice Chief of the Imperial General Staff.

The agenda for that day was not crowded but it illustrates the multitude of problems facing the war cabinet in the summer of 1940. The minor items were a report on the previous day's air battles, which had been no more than raids by individual aircraft; a report from Yugoslavia of a possible Italian attack from Libya into Egypt and another discounting rumours of a similar attack on Greece. Instructions for the Governor of Singapore about the action to be taken to intern Japanese civilians in the event of hostilities or warlike action by Japan were agreed, as was the text of a message from Churchill to President Roosevelt about the exchange of old United States destroyers for bases in British colonies in the western hemisphere. They even found time to discuss the setting up of 'hospitality committees' by MPs for the armed forces of the various governments-in-exile now in Britain.

But the main item on the agenda was a Most Secret seven-page paper circulated the day before by Kingsley Wood entitled 'Gold and Exchange Resources'.[1] The number of copies was highly restricted and even the ministers present had to surrender their papers before leaving the meeting. It was perhaps the most sombre and devastating paper ever taken by a British cabinet: it forecast Britain's imminent financial collapse and inability to continue the war.

The background to the paper had been familiar to ministers for more than a year as they grappled with the problem of mobilizing the nation's resources for total war. British industry was incapable of producing the range and quantity of armaments required to win the war. Even those items that could be manufactured domestically were heavily dependent on imports of raw materials and products such as steel. Most of these imports came from the United States and had to be paid for either in gold or in dollars. Under American legislation Britain was prohibited from raising loans in the United States as it had done to pay for goods in the First World War. There were large investments (over £3.5 billion) in the Empire and other countries, particularly Latin America, but even if these were sold they would not provide dollars and so they were, therefore, irrelevant. As new orders were placed in the United States Britain's financial resources would steadily decline until a point was reached when no more could be paid for in cash.

Britain's potentially weak financial position had been recognized within Whitehall before the war began. In April 1939 the Treasury warned: 'If we were under the impression that we were as well able as in 1914 to conduct a long war we were burying our heads in the sand.'[2] In July they pointed out that from an economic point of view sustaining a three-year war (then Britain's military assumption) 'is very likely much too optimistic'.[3] By February 1940, the Treasury thought that British resources might last between two and three years if they were carefully husbanded.[4] That estimate turned out to be over-optimistic under the mounting pressure of war. The demands of the armed forces were higher than expected, the mass of equipment lost at Dunkirk had to be replaced and when France had gone out of the war their orders in the United States were taken over by Britain.

On 22 August Kingsley Wood had to break the news that the day of reckoning was rapidly approaching. From a total of £775 million at the beginning of 1940, Britain's gold and dollar reserves (together with saleable investments in the United States) had fallen by over a third to £490 million. Earlier estimates had suggested that the reserves might last until June 1941, but massive new arms orders had been placed earlier in the summer. As a result the rate of decline was rapidly increasing, and the reserves had fallen by £80 million in the last month alone. Wood now estimated that they would last another three or four months at most. By the end of 1940, therefore, Britain would be unable to carry on the war by its own efforts.

The only alternative to a compromise peace with Germany was open-ended American assistance, in the form of military equipment, raw materials and food, on whatever conditions the US government was prepared to make them available. In May and June the government had decided to fight on rather than make peace in the knowledge that future US help would be essential. The problem was that on 22 August the government had no idea whether or not the Americans were prepared to save Britain. None of the rhetoric about 'Their Finest Hour' could provide an escape from this awful situation.

The US administration had been told of the precarious British position in July when a senior Treasury official, Sir Frederick Phillips, had seen the US Secretary of the Treasury, Henry Morgenthau. Despite requests for help, no promise of assistance had been obtained. The reason was simple: the United States was in the middle of a presidential election campaign in which President Roosevelt was attempting to secure an unprecedented third term. With sentiment in the country strongly against direct involvement in Europe's quarrels, there was no question of Roosevelt taking difficult decisions before the election on 5 November. Britain's survival therefore depended on the vagaries of American domestic politics, as Wood pointed out: 'We are faced with the immediate practical problem of holding out till well into November in the case of a Democratic victory, or until after the 20th January, when the new President takes office, in the case of a Republican victory.' Given the state of Britain's reserves, it seemed likely that a victory by the Republican candidate, Wendell Wilkie, would mean that any assistance might come too late to save Britain. Even if US assistance were forthcoming, Wood warned his colleagues that Britain would have no say over the terms and conditions under which Britain would be allowed to continue the war: 'The United States will no doubt settle both the extent to which and the conditions under which we can enjoy the products of American industry and agriculture, and in that way may materially influence the character of the war.'

In the war cabinet discussion no one dissented from Wood's conclusions that Britain would simply have to wait, Micawber-like, to see what turned up from the other side of the Atlantic.[5] Churchill read out Chamberlain's view that 'it would be necessary for us to gamble to some extent on the willingness of the United States to give us financial help on an extended scale'. A more aggressive view of the possibilities open to Britain came, not unexpectedly, from Beaverbrook, who argued that the rate of ordering in the United States should be stepped up. There was a curious logic in his view. Placing more orders with US industry, which was only beginning to invest in new plant and generate employment after the long slump of the 1930s, would increasingly tie them to the completion and continuation of British contracts and put pressure on the federal government to ensure that Britain did not collapse militarily or economically. More orders would also create the public impression that Britain was stronger than was in fact the case. If Britain could not afford to pay even for its current orders within a few months, it would make little difference whether these unsustainable obligations were increased. At worst Britain would only default on even more contracts and at best the US government would probably pick up the bill.

The war cabinet also considered what might be done to try and boost Britain's declining gold reserves. The Indian and South African governments held about £130 million of gold but this was needed to fund purchases from countries other than the United States. The European governments-in-exile held about £350 million in London and might be persuaded to part with this if Britain promised to repay it after the war. The Vichy French government also owned £200 million of gold stored in Canada, but this would have to be seized illegally. The problem was that even if all these resources were somehow made available they could put off the evil hour only for a few months. When they were exhausted Britain would still face the same dilemma of choosing between dependence on the United States or peace with Germany. The last resort would be to requisition all gold objects, including wedding rings, in Britain. At most this would raise £20 million and, as Churchill commented, 'this was a measure to be adopted at a later stage, if we wished to make some striking gesture for the purpose of shaming the Americans'. But he also recognized that it might be necessary to go even further and to hand over the ownership of the whole of British industry to the Americans in order to try and ensure the delivery of the necessary arms and materials: 'If the military position should unexpectedly deteriorate, we should have to pledge everything we had for the sake of victory, giving the United States, if necessary, a lien on any and every part of British industry.'

The war cabinet meeting ended in time for a late lunch after ministers decided that they could do no more than wait and see whether the United States would save Britain. There can have been few, if any, among the ministers and senior officials present who did not realize that Britain's time as an independent power was coming to an end. The immediate threat of invasion might recede and the RAF might repel the assault of the Luftwaffe, but that victory would be pyrrhic. The insidious, hidden financial threat working to undermine Britain was inevitable and would strike a fatal blow at its prestige and place in the world. The country no longer had the resources to continue the war. Its fate would be decided by another nation.

Behind the Churchillian rhetoric and the subsequent mythology of 1940 lay a stark reality: the disintegration of British power. How had Britain arrived at a position of such devastating weakness?

2

Façade of Power

The collapse of British power in 1940 was so extensive that by
the end of the year the nation could no longer ensure its
continued independence by its own efforts and from its own
resources. This situation did not emerge suddenly because of the
rapid German conquests and the collapse of France, Britain's only
ally. The crucial events of 1940 were a culmination of a combination of trends, all working to reinforce British weakness. Some of
these were long-term, dating from the last part of the nineteenth
century; others had developed since the end of the First World
War or even later, in the last few years of peace before the
outbreak of war in 1939. The two decades before 1940 witnessed
the gradual coalescence of a multitude of adverse factors: too
many world-wide commitments, inadequate resources to defend
these commitments, a failure to reduce the number of potential
enemies, a lack of powerful allies, a weak industrial base and
enfeebled finances. The governments of the 1920s and 1930s tried
but failed to deal with this daunting array of problems; indeed
they were probably insoluble. Without an understanding of the
underlying problems, the way in which they developed and the
attempts at finding a solution made in strategic, foreign, economic,
financial and industrial policy in the previous decades, the events
of 1940 lose all perspective and meaning.

The victory parade through the streets of London in 1919, with
its colourful military contingents from every part of the Empire,
may have lacked some of the pomp and self-confidence of the
parades marking Queen Victoria's Golden and Diamond Jubilees
in 1887 and 1897, but that could be explained by the after-effects
of the most dreadful war in modern history. To most of the
public, the British Empire was at the apogee of its strength, the
greatest power in the world. With the peace treaties that ended

the First World War, the British Empire reached its widest extent. German colonies such as Tanganyika and South West Africa passed into imperial control and the collapse of Turkey in the Near East established British rule over Palestine and Mesopotamia. The Empire consisted of over 450 million people in every continent on the globe, a quarter of the earth's population. It was the largest the world had ever seen. Imperial territories gave Britain access to a vast range of resources: seventy per cent of the world's gold production, sixty per cent of rubber production and fifty per cent of the rice crop. The informal empire, achieved through economic domination rather than political control, was just as powerful in areas such as Latin America, with its major British investments in railways and cattle ranching.

At the core of the Empire were the self-governing white dominions of Canada, Australia, New Zealand and South Africa, although in importance they were matched by the Indian Empire that embraced all of present-day India and Pakistan. In the Far East, apart from the colonies of Malaya and Borneo, lay the great trading settlements of Hong Kong and Singapore, together with the extensive 'concessions' in China such as Canton and Shanghai that gave Britain control over much of the trade of the area. In Africa, Cecil Rhodes's dream of a continuous band of British territory from the Cape to Cairo was at last realized with possession of Tanganyika, complemented by the colonies of tropical west Africa: Nigeria, the Gold Coast and Sierra Leone. In the Middle East, Britain was the dominant power and directly controlled Egypt, Palestine, Transjordan, Iraq, Kuwait and the coastal states along the Persian Gulf. In every ocean of the world there were the island colonies ranging from the West Indies across the Atlantic (Ascension, St Helena and the Falklands) to the Indian Ocean (Mauritius and the Seychelles) and the Pacific (Fiji and Samoa). British military forces could be found on every continent and the Empire was linked together by naval bases such as Gibraltar, Malta and Aden for the world-wide deployment of the Royal Navy. In 1919 the Empire had just won the most terrible war in its history, one in which troops from the white dominions and India had fought alongside the British on the western front, in the Balkans and in the Middle East. The strategic effort of the Empire had been directed from London by an imperial war cabinet that seemed to be the first step towards integrating the resources of the Empire. To the superficial observer in 1919, British power must have seemed firmly established and likely to endure for decades to come.

In reality the strength of the Empire resembled a Potemkin village. Behind the grandeur of the façade was a lack of substance. The Empire, and in particular Britain, suffered from debilitating political and economic weakness. One fundamental problem was the lack of a coherent political and administrative structure. Little attempt had been made to integrate the various territories and it remained a motley collebtion of self-governing dominions, colonies of various types at different stages of evolution, and territories, such as Egypt, under indirect rule. The white dominions had made it clear before 1914 that they preferred to move towards a looser structure with greater independence for themselves, and the British government had little option but to accept this trend. The expansion of the Empire in the latter part of the nineteenth century brought with it a steadily increasing military burden for defence without bringing either a corresponding increase in internal organization or the resources needed to meet the threat. The Empire contributed little towards imperial defence and on balance was a drain on British resources. The 'jewel in the crown', the supposed keystone of the Empire, was India. Maintaining control of the sub-continent and its borders absorbed a third of the British army directly and considerably more when combined with the perceived need to control the lines of communication to India through the Mediterranean, the Suez Canal and the Near East. Yet India contributed little in return. Similarly, defending the dominions, especially Australia and New Zealand, against any threat on the other side of the globe from Britain was a major commitment, yet their governments provided no ships of any consequence to aid the Royal Navy. The new areas acquired after the war only added to the weakness of the whole structure. Control of Palestine in particular gave Britain a major problem of internal security in trying to contain the growing Arab revolt over Jewish immigration.

The vast extent of the British Empire was, therefore, a source not of strength but of weakness. It left Britain with the task of defending vulnerable territory in every area of the globe. And Britain, a small island off the coast of Europe, with a population of just forty million and dependent on imports for most of its raw materials and half its food, simply did not have the resources to undertake such a vast task. As the first country to industrialize, Britain had become the dominant economic power in the world by the middle of the nineteenth century, but that domination was short-lived. Relative economic decline had set in from the 1880s. In 1880 Britain had produced twenty-three per cent of the world's manufacturing output, fifty per cent more than the United States and three times the level of Germany. By 1900 Britain had been overtaken by the US and by 1913 its share was thirteen per cent, whereas the United States had thirty-two per cent and Germany fifteen. The same trend could be found in the key economic indicator: iron and steel production. In 1890 British output had been twice that of Germany and only just below that of the US. By 1913 Germany produced nearly twice and the US four times as much as Britain. At the same time, British technology was failing to keep pace with foreign developments. Key industries such as chemicals were falling far behind their rivals and productivity levels were also lower in most other sectors of the economy.

Until 1914 growing economic weakness had been partially disguised by financial strength. London was the world's pre-eminent financial centre and sterling the accepted medium for international trade and exchange. To a large extent British wealth had been used, not for investment in domestic industry, but for investment overseas. In 1913 Britain had over £4 billion of overseas investments − forty-three per cent of the world total. These resources provided not just an annual income to offset an unfavourable trade balance but also a store of assets. The strain of financing the military effort made in the First World War, however, forced Britain to liquidate many of these assets, thereby permanently weakening London's role as a financial centre and significantly altering Britain's relationship with the United States.

In August 1914 a small expeditionary force was sent to fight alongside the French and Belgians, but under pressure from its allies Britain was soon committed to the creation of a huge army on a continental scale. The equipping and supplying of such a large army proved to be beyond the capabilities of British industry. In the autumn of 1914 Britain started to place arms orders with American firms and, as the demands of the new army in France for munitions − in particular shells − rose dramatically, so did British orders in the United States. In 1914 Britain estimated that the American orders might cost a maximum of $50 million, but by early 1917 expenditure was running at about $80 million a week and during the first two years of the war orders amounted to $20 billion. Additional strain was placed on Britain's resources by the financial weakness of its allies. From September 1915 Britain was responsible for the US purchases made by Russia and Italy and, after May 1916, for those of France as well.

These large-scale American purchases could be financed only by transferring gold to the US, by selling British-held securities in US companies or by raising loans in the United States. By the autumn of 1914 the pound was already slipping in value against the dollar. One year into the war the first US securities were sold, followed in the autumn of 1915 by the first loan raised in the United States. More loans were necessary throughout 1916 but were obtained only at escalating rates of interest. By the autumn of 1916 the situation was becoming serious. Forty per cent of the British war effort had to be financed in the US, but the supply of securities that could be sold was dwindling, stocks of gold were running low, and without backing from the US government, it was becoming increasingly difficult to raise further loans. Doubts were growing concerning Britain's ability to continue the war and Reginald McKenna, the Chancellor of the Exchequer, warned his cabinet colleagues that: 'by next June, or earlier, the President of the American Republic will be in a position, if he wishes, to dictate his own terms to us'.[1] By the spring of 1917 the situation was desperate. Britain had just $219 million of gold and securities in the US and about $530 million of gold held in the UK. With spending running at about $80 million a week, it was enough to finance the war for less than ten weeks. The Allies were saved from having to negotiate a compromise peace with Germany by the US entry into the war in April 1917.

The declaration of war by the United States provided only a temporary respite for Britain. In July 1917 McKenna had to tell the Americans that Britain was on the verge of disaster: 'Our resources available for payments in America are exhausted. Unless the United States government can meet in full our expenses in the United States ... the whole fabric of the Alliance will collapse.'[2]

The crisis was resolved because the United States, now an ally, was prepared to take a more active role in solving Britain's financial difficulties. First, the UK borrowed about $180 million a month from the US government from the middle of 1917 onwards. Second, the American administration set up a War Industries Board to direct US economic mobilization and by forcing the Allies to become a subsidiary part of it, decided how much of the US war effort would be allocated to each ally.

By the end of the war Britain was no longer the predominant financial power in the world; the focal point of the system had shifted to New York. The UK itself emerged significantly weaker in relation to the United States. It had a total debt to the Americans of £1,365 million and a national debt of £7,435 million (compared with only £650 million in 1914), a huge financial burden on the country. Interest on the national debt accounted for about forty per cent of the budget after the war. By the 1920s, therefore, Britain possessed an Empire that was a strategic liability and its ability to offset this through financial strength had been permanently damaged. In the immediate post-war period these weaknesses led to a decisive shift in British strategic policy that was to have a fundamental impact for the next twenty years and produce a dilemma that successive governments, including Churchill's in 1940, were unable to resolve.

Since the 1890s Britain had accepted that a war with the United States was unthinkable because of American economic strength and the vulnerable imperial territories in the western hemisphere. After the First World War the British had to come to terms with growing American power in other areas too. By 1918 the US navy had a battle fleet of sixteen Dreadnoughts, equivalent to the combined fleets of Italy, France and Japan, and was planning on a fleet of thirty-nine that would dominate both the Pacific and the Atlantic and dwarf the Royal Navy. At a series of agonizing meetings Lloyd George's cabinet was forced to accept that Britain simply did not have the resources to match the US fleet, and that to attempt to emulate the Americans would certainly be economically disastrous, and probably politically disastrous as well. Reluctantly, they had to concede that the Royal Navy would no longer be the largest in the world.

It was not surprising, therefore, that the UK government readily accepted the US invitation to attend the 1922 Washington Conference. This was a gathering of all the major naval powers to agree on naval arms limitation. The outcome was an agreement on parity between the US and UK navies and Japanese acceptance of an inferiority of three to five in major warships compared with the two principal navies. On the surface the Washington treaty seemed satisfactory from Britain's point of view. In fact Britain was forced, by nascent American power, to make a concession which increased the vulnerability of the Empire. The United States insisted that the Anglo–Japanese alliance should not be renewed. Britain had been allied with Japan since 1902 and during the war the Japanese navy had cleared the Indian Ocean of German ships and even patrolled the Mediterranean, thereby releasing Royal Navy ships for home waters. The alliance had also provided protection for British possessions in the Pacific, in particular Australia and New Zealand, and enabled Britain to avoid some of the cost of their defence. Despite dominion pressure to renew the treaty, the British felt they had no option but to follow US wishes because the Americans were, in the last resort, more important to Britain than the Japanese. Yet the alliance with Japan had been a key point in imperial defence and the Washington treaty was to create fundamental problems for the next twenty years.

Although the Japanese had accepted overall inferiority in naval strength compared with Britain, the agreed ratio of forces was enough to give them local superiority in the Pacific. Should they assert themselves militarily it would cause acute problems of regional defence for British interests in the Far East and for Australia and New Zealand. Any threat from Japan would, the British military planners assumed, be mainly naval and would have to be countered by sending part of the fleet to the major base at Singapore, then in the early stages of construction. The problem was how much of the fleet could safely be sent to the other side of the world. The new treaty limitation on the size of the Royal Navy, coupled with the lack of any US commitment to help Britain in the Pacific, meant the British would have to send the major part of the fleet to the Far East to provide an effective counter to any Japanese hostility, a move which would leave home waters dangerously denuded against any threat from a European power. In the event of simultaneous hostilities in Europe and the Pacific (or even the threat of such hostilities) Britain's responsibility for the defence of Australia and New Zealand might be impossible to fulfil. Nevertheless, a central feature of British policy until 1939 was that the fleet would be

sent to the Far East, if necessary, even at the expense of other
interests. While the threat to British interests in the Far East from
Japan seemed no more than theoretical, it was tempting for the
cabinet to accept Churchill's reassurance, given in 1925 when he
was Chancellor of the Exchequer: 'I do not believe Japan has any
idea of attacking the British Empire, or that there is any danger of
her doing so for at least a generation to come.'[3]

The world in the early 1920s held other possible long-term
threats to the British position. The United States, whose intervention had been crucial in bringing about the defeat of Germany,
refused to join the League of Nations and turned away from
political and military commitments in Europe. Russia, the other
potential major power which had been a substantial threat to
Germany before 1914, turned in on itself. It was only slowly
rebuilding its shattered economy after the chaos of the Bolshevik
revolution and was shunned by most of the other powers for
ideological reasons. This left a power vacuum in Europe. Although
weakened and disarmed by the Versailles treaty, Germany
remained a potential threat: it still had a population a third bigger
than that of France and possessed three times its iron- and steel-
making capacity. The French strategic position was weaker after
the war than in 1914. It had lost 1.5 million dead and a million
wounded (a quarter of all males under thirty) and now had to rely
on the newly created, weak states of eastern Europe to try to
provide a counter to any revival of German power. Such a revival
would directly involve British interests by upsetting the fragile
balance of power in Europe and once again threatening the
domination of the continent by a single country.

Like the United States, Britain too turned away from Europe
after the post-war settlement. In 1922 the cabinet agreed that the
main roles of the army should be internal security and imperial
defence and that no preparations should be made for the despatch
of an expeditionary force to Europe. In 1925, rather like his
predecessors in the nineteenth century, Austen Chamberlain, the
Foreign Secretary, told his colleagues that the only threat he
could foresee to British or imperial security was in India and
Afghanistan, from the Soviet Union. A year later the Chief of the
Imperial General Staff told his fellow chiefs of staff that 'the
priority in regard to Army commitments was India'.[4] No forces
were provided for fighting a European war and the 1926 annual

review by the chiefs of staff stated that 'so far as commitments on the Continent are concerned, the Services can only take note of them'.[5]

Until the beginning of the 1930s the weakness of the British strategic position remained well concealed. Britain had an enormous interest in preserving the status quo; as the First Sea Lord, Admiral Chatfield, told the head of the Treasury, Warren Fisher: 'We have got most of the world already, or the best parts of it, and we only want to keep what we have got and prevent others taking it away from us.'[6] During the 1920s the international situation seemed to favour Britain retaining that position. In Europe, Germany, under the Weimar Republic, appeared to be increasingly integrated into the structure of the post-war world. Italy, under Mussolini, posed no threat in the Mediterranean and Japan in the Far East was equally quiescent. Yet within a few years Britain was to face the nightmare threat of having to fight all three countries, supported only by a weakened France and unable to draw on the economic resources of the United States. It was impossible to defend the Empire against all these threats simultaneously and the danger was that a conflict with even one enemy would weaken Britain's defences elsewhere to such an extent that it would tempt one of the other powers into aggression. The only possible solution was to try and reduce the number of potential enemies by diplomatic means. But this would be difficult to achieve without making fundamental concessions that undermined British power and prestige. All British governments in the decade after the early 1930s had to combat this formidable combination of multiple threats and inadequate resources. No government could escape from the problem as Churchill, for all his criticism of government policy in the 1930s, was forced to concede in January 1942 when the Japanese overran the Empire in the Far East:

There has never been a moment, there never could have been a moment, when Great Britain or the British Empire, single-handed, could fight Germany and Italy, could wage the Battle of Britain, the Battle of the Atlantic and the Battle of the Middle East – and at the same time stand thoroughly prepared in Burma, the Malay Peninsula, and generally in the Far East ...[7]

The first signs of a worsening international climate became apparent in September 1931 with the Japanese invasion of Manchuria, the ousting of the Chinese, the establishing of a puppet regime and the defying of the League of Nations. The deterioration in the international situation could not have come at a worse time from an economic and financial point of view. Britain's relative economic decline had continued unabated since the First World War. By the 1930s Britain's share of world manufacturing output was well below Germany's and only a third of the US level. Its share of world trade had fallen from fourteen per cent in 1913 to less than ten per cent in 1937. By the late 1930s Britain was attempting to control about a quarter of the globe with only ten per cent of its manufacturing strength. That disparity is the fundamental measure of British weakness; it meant that Britain did not have the resources available to mount the required defence effort if imperial territory was to be adequately defended.

The situation in early 1932 was bleak when the cabinet met to consider a review of imperial defence prepared by the chiefs of staff. Following the crash of 1929 the world was slipping deeper into depression and financial crisis. By the early 1930s the British economy was feeling the effects not just of relative decline but also of a collapse in world demand. In the UK, shipbuilding output was at seven per cent of its 1913 level, textile production (responsible for forty per cent of exports) at a third of its level in the 1920s, steel production had fallen by forty-five per cent and coal by twenty. Britain's balance of trade was also slipping into the red. Pressure on the overvalued pound in the summer of 1931 led to the collapse of the minority Labour government when it could not agree on a package of public expenditure cuts. It was replaced by a coalition government that was unable to keep Britain on the gold standard and one of the last remnants of Britain's domination of world trade – the belief in free trade – was also soon to be abandoned in favour of tariffs and preference for goods from the Empire. Against this background the chiefs of staff asked for the end of the 'Ten Year Rule' and the beginning of rearmament. The rule had been adopted in 1919 when the armed forces were told to plan on the assumption that Britain would not be involved in any major war for ten years. Defence spending had been cut back accordingly, most enthusiastically of all by Churchill when he was Chancellor of the Exchequer from

1925 to 1929, and in 1928 the cabinet, under Churchill's prompting, had converted the rule into a rolling assumption that there would be no war for at least ten years. In 1932, under the growing threat from Japan in the Far East, the cabinet agreed to scrap the ten-year assumption but, because of the precarious economic situation, refused to agree to any rearmament programme. It was not until 15 November 1933, eleven months after Hitler came to power, that permission was given for work to start on assessing what needed to be done to improve Britain's defences.

The work was undertaken in the Defence Requirements Committee (DRC), composed of the three chiefs of staff, the heads of the Foreign Office and Treasury and the Cabinet Secretary. The first problem to resolve was which threat should take priority. The cabinet had agreed on an assumption that France, the United States and Italy should not be regarded as potential enemies but the military could not agree about the relative weight to be attached to the threats from Germany and Japan. The Royal Navy favoured Japan because in this theatre they would be predominant. The army was still obsessed with India and put Europe a long way down its list of priorities, while the RAF opted for Europe, where their bomber force would have a major role to play. The argument was resolved by the three civilian members of the committee, who forced through the only sensible conclusion: that Germany was the 'ultimate threat' against which rearmament should be directed because only Germany could defeat Britain itself rather than conquer imperial territory. Since German rearmament was not yet under way on a significant scale, there was still time to take some additional measures in the Far East to try and restrain Japan. Even on this basis, however, the three chiefs of staff were unable to produce a coherent defence programme and could only advise roughly equal increases in spending on all three services to put right the worst deficiencies.

As a result, when the DRC report was considered by the cabinet in March 1934, it offered no clear strategic thinking on a programme of defence preparations. A small group of ministers, dominated by the Chancellor of the Exchequer Neville Chamberlain, was asked to sort out the confusion. They accepted the DRC's conclusions about the threats facing Britain but established prorities in the rearmament programme. Their report, agreed by the cabinet in June 1934, decided that naval preparations against Japan should continue and that the building of the Singapore base to accommodate and maintain the fleet, if it were sent to the Far East, should be completed by the late 1930s. Proposed spending on the RAF was increased, with the emphasis placed on home-based squadrons, but reserves were cut back. The aim was to build, as rapidly as possible, a front-line bomber force which it was hoped would impress the Germans and act as a deterrent. The main reductions affected the army, where spending was half that recommended by the DRC. A 'field force' (the name was carefully chosen to distinguish it from an 'expeditionary force') of five divisions was to be created by 1939, but the low priority given to its armament and the failure to build in any capability to reinforce it through the Territorial Army meant that its usefulness in any European conflict would be strictly limited. Ministers also agreed that all these defence preparations should be complete by the beginning of 1939, after which it was assessed Germany would be ready for war.

The policy adopted in 1934 was essentially defensive, concentrating on deterring any threat to Britain while avoiding any commitment to fight a war on the continent with an army on the scale of that involved in the First World War. It set out the priorities for British rearmament until the spring of 1939, but the programme expanded steadily under the pressure of a deteriorating world situation. Expenditure on the naval programme, which until 1938 absorbed more money than either the RAF or army, was expanded further when the cabinet agreed a 'new standard' of naval strength of twenty capital ships, which would allow the despatch of a deterrent force to Singapore while leaving enough ships in home waters to meet any threat from Germany. But this fleet would not be available until the early 1940s. As German rearmament progressed, RAF rearmament was also accelerated and expanded during the mid-1930s until a scheme for a force of 1,000 bombers by April 1939 was agreed. Until 1938 the emphasis in air rearmament was on bomber strength, in line with the RAF's accepted doctrine that a strategic bombing force would be able to devastate the territory of an opponent and by its sheer presence act as a deterrent to aggression. Alarmed by the increasing cost of the rearmament programme and the difficulty of financing a larger navy, an increased air force and even a limited army, the cabinet agreed, in mid-1937, that the Minister for the

Co-ordination of Defence, Sir Thomas Inskip, should conduct a full-scale review of defence effort and strategy. The results of the review reinforced the doubts already expressed in 1934 about sending an army to the continent. In November 1937 the Secretary of State for War, Leslie Hore-Belisha, told the Prime Minister, Neville Chamberlain, that 'our Army should be organized to defend this country and the Empire, that to organize it with a military prepossession in favour of a Continental commitment is wrong'.[8] A month later the cabinet endorsed the results of the strategic review by Inskip. The priorities for British policy were now to be air defence of Britain, followed by trade and imperial defence, and then: 'Our fourth objective, which can only be provided for after the other objectives have been carried out, should be co-operation in the defence of the territories of any allies we may have in war.'[9]

The 1934 decision, which left open the possibility of sending a small army to Europe, was thus rescinded three years later and the cabinet agreed that no preparations would be made for an expeditionary force. They had now opted for a strongly isolationist policy; it carried the risk that if Britain's only likely ally on the continent, France, did insist on the commitment of a British force as part of any joint defence effort against Germany, then a major army would have to be improvised at short notice.

Although rearmament was under way by 1935 the British dilemma — too many commitments and too few resources — remained unresolved. The world situation was continuing to deteriorate. Japan had taken over Manchuria and seemed likely to move further south into China proper, where there were substantial British trading interests. The Disarmament Conference at Geneva had failed and previously clandestine German rearmament had been openly avowed in defiance of the restrictions in the 1919 Versailles treaty. It now seemed clear that Germany under Hitler was embarked on a course designed to reassert its role as a major European power. That in itself was not necessarily a cause for British hostility, but the possibility of changes in European boundaries achieved by the threat of force and the ultimate threat of domination of the continent by Germany posed a direct challenge to Britain.

The objective of seeking to reduce the number of Britain's possible enemies was the course strongly supported by the Treasury. In 1934 both Neville Chamberlain and the head of the Treasury, Sir Warren Fisher, argued that with no allies, with the probable exception of France, and only limited resources, 'we cannot provide simultaneously for hostilities with Japan and Germany'.[10] Supported by a few other ministers, they favoured trying to reach a non-agression pact with Japan which would, in effect, restore the 1902 alliance. The problem was that although this approach might provide protection for Australia and New Zealand, a newly militaristic Japan would want tacit acceptance of its expansionist aims in China and this would be strenuously opposed by the Americans. Under pressure from the Foreign Office, the government decided that it could not afford to risk alienating the United States, and so the policy agreed at Washington in 1922, of no deal with Japan because of US sensitivities, was continued even though there was no evidence that the Americans would support the British position in the Pacific. Having ruled out an agreement with Japan as a policy option, the alternative was to try to reach an accommodation in Europe that might provide some room to deal with the Japanese threat. The Anglo–German naval agreement of 1935, which limited the size of the German navy to thirty-five per cent of the Royal Navy, provided a limited measure of reassurance. As long as the Germans kept to the terms of the treaty (which they did until 1939), it allowed the British to calculate the force needed in Europe to contain the Germans and therefore the size of the fleet that could be sent to Singapore to counter the Japanese should this become necessary.

This marginal improvement in the increasingly gloomy strategic outlook for Britain was almost immediately outweighed by developments in the Mediterranean. There Mussolini, deluded by dreams of imperial Roman grandeur, decided in 1935 to conquer Abyssinia. The Italian invasion placed Britain in an awkward position. As a prominent member of the League of Nations, and under strong pressure from public opinion, it felt obliged to back collective action and limited sanctions against Italy following its violation of the League's charter. It was reluctant to do more since it had no direct interests in Abyssinia and had a strong interest in keeping on friendly terms with Italy. In the end Britain finished up with the worst of all worlds. The international sanctions that were imposed were enough to alienate the Italians without being sufficiently strong to halt the aggression, and the attempt to reach a secret deal with Italy (in the Anglo–French Hoare–Laval plan), which had to be abandoned under public pressure, cast doubts on Britain's commitment to collective security. The result of the affair was that Italy moved away from its old friendship with Britain and France and towards Germany. This posed the threat that Italy too would have to be added to the list of Britain's potential enemies. It left Britain with the prospect of having to deal with three enemies and for the first time the possibility of a direct threat to British interests in the Mediterranean. These fears led the Defence Requirements Committee to warn, in November 1935:

> It is a cardinal requirement of our national and Imperial security that our foreign policy should be so conducted as to avoid the possible development of the situation in which we might be confronted simultaneously with the hostility of Japan in the Far East, Germany in the west and any power on the main line of communication between the two.[11]

As the problems facing Britain mounted so did the difficulties of finding a diplomatic solution. In the Far East the situation worsened rapidly after the middle of 1937 when the Japanese began a full-scale attack on China. This posed a direct threat to the trade and other interests of both Britain and America and caused Anthony Eden, the Foreign Secretary, to object to what he described as 'upstart' nations encroaching upon 'white race' preserves.[12] However, although the cabinet seriously considered sending the fleet to the Far East after an accidental Japanese attack on British and US gunboats in December 1937, it proved impossible to agree on joint British and American action to restrain Japan, though low-level, secret staff talks were held on possible future moves. In the Mediterranean the Italians were conducting a propaganda campaign against British rule in the Middle East and actively supporting Franco in the Spanish Civil War. Yet no deal with Mussolini was possible unless Britain recognized the Italian conquest of Abyssinia. Germany, which had occupied the demilitarized zone in the Rhineland while Britain and France were embroiled with Italy over Abyssinia in early 1936, was rearming rapidly and seemed about to enter a more assertive phase, posing a direct threat to its immediate neighbours Austria and Czechoslovakia.

In this situation the chiefs of staff, at the end of 1937, demanded a diplomatic solution:

> We cannot foresee the time when our defence forces will be strong enough to safeguard our territory, trade and vital interests against Germany, Italy and Japan simultaneously. We cannot, therefore, exaggerate the importance, from the point of view of Imperial defence, of any political or international action that can be taken to reduce the number of our potential enemies or to gain the support of potential allies.[13]

It was comments like this that caused Eden to complain privately to Chamberlain (who had become Prime Minister in 1937): 'I cannot help believing that what the Chiefs of Staff would really like to do is to reorientate our whole foreign policy and to clamber on the bandwagon with the dictators, even though that process meant parting company with France and estranging our relations with the United States.'[14]

Nevertheless both men believed that some diplomatic action would have to be taken, although Chamberlain wanted to move further and faster than the Foreign Secretary. As he wrote privately in January 1938, 'in the absence of any powerful ally, and until our armaments are completed, we must adjust our foreign policy to our circumstances'.[15] A deal with the Japanese was ruled out because of American sensibilities and in any case they posed a less immediate threat to British interests. This left the possibility of an accommodation with either Italy or Germany. Eden favoured a cautious approach, with the emphasis on dealing with Germany. The Prime Minister, who wanted to try to get an agreement with Italy first, opened his own private line of communications with the Italians behind the back of Eden, who resigned when this emerged in February 1938. Chamberlain was able to reach an outline deal fairly quickly by trading British recognition of Italian rule in Abyssinia for a generally more co-operative approach from Italy, but it proved impossible to turn this into a comprehensive, long-term agreement.

Reaching any sort of agreement with Germany was to prove even more difficult. Had Chamberlain been negotiating with a rational and reasonable statesman he probably could have concluded a deal re-establishing a strong German position in Europe, restoring some German colonies and conceding German economic domination of central and south-east Europe, where Britain had only limited interests. Instead he had to deal with Hitler, whose aims were so grandiose, shifting and ultimately unacceptable to the rest of Europe that no agreement was possible. By 1938 Hitler felt strong enough to move from the phase of consolidating power in Germany, rearmament and reasserting absolute German control in the Rhineland to a more aggressive phase of redrawing the international boundaries agreed in 1919. In each case he was able to build on a legitimate grievance stemming from the Versailles treaty. In 1919 German and Austrian unification had been forbidden, the German population of the Sudetenland placed under Czech rule to give the new state defensible frontiers, and East Prussia separated from the rest of Germany by a Polish corridor to the Baltic at Danzig. After Hitler had reunited Austria with Germany in the Anschluss, his next target was clearly Czechoslovakia and control of the Sudetenland. At the end of March 1938 the chiefs of staff told ministers that: 'No pressure that we and our possible Allies can bring to bear, either by sea, or land or in the air, could prevent Germany from invading and overrunning Bohemia and from inflicting a decisive defeat on the Czechoslovakian Army.'[16] It would then be necessary, they argued, to continue the war to defeat Germany in order to restore Czechoslovakia and this would involve a substantial risk that Italy and Japan would join in the war with potentially catastrophic consequences for Britain. Chamberlain embarked on a dangerous course to try to resolve the Sudeten question and avoid a European war. He refused, until the last possible moment, to give any undertaking to France, which was bound by treaty to aid Czechoslovakia, to provide any assistance if it was attacked by Germany, thereby increasing the French pressure on the Czechs to settle. He also sent a British diplomatic mission to Prague in an attempt to solve the Sudeten problem by persuading the Czechs to make concessions. This mission failed, as did his attempt to negotiate personally with Hitler and get him to accept the idea of a referendum in the disputed territory. Eventually a disgruntled Hitler, deprived of the war he wanted, accepted a last-minute Italian proposal at the end of September 1938 for a four-power conference in Munich.

The conference, without consulting the Czechs, agreed on the transfer of the Sudetenland to Germany within a week. War was avoided, but the Munich agreement did not provide any long-term settlement with Germany.

By the end of 1938 the pressures on Britain were mounting rapidly. The widely scattered Empire still faced three potential enemies, since no agreement had proved possible with Germany, Italy or Japan to reduce that threat to more manageable proportions. Britain's weak economic and financial base was also under strain as rearmament, focused as it was on the Royal Navy and RAF, gathered pace. Yet within six months of Munich the situation was made immeasurably worse. Britain's only ally, France, demanded that the UK make the effort to build an army to fight on the continent. When the British finally agreed to the French demands, this new rearmament burden, together with the other pressures, began to raise serious doubts as to whether Britain had the economic or financial resources to sustain such a course for long or fight a lengthy major war if diplomacy failed.

Like the British, the French were suffering from strategic and economic weakness in the 1930s. They lacked the manpower and industrial strength to match Germany, which had a larger population and whose industrial production was twice as big as France's. France had to adopt a forward defence strategy because its major industrial centres were near the German and Belgian borders, but in 1936 the Belgians abandoned the French alliance, adopted a policy of neutrality and refused any staff talks with the French on possible joint action if Belgium were invaded by Germany. The French, who had an obvious interest in fighting Germany in Belgium if possible, felt unable to extend the defensive Maginot Line, designed to compensate for inferior French numbers, along the Franco–Belgian frontier. The French economy in the 1930s suffered from the depression for longer than almost any other European country. In 1938 national wealth was still eighteen per cent less than in 1929 and industrial production was below 1928 levels. Exports were falling, imports rising and France's share of world trade steadily declining. The franc was badly overvalued and its eventual devaluation in 1936, followed by further devaluations, left the French heavily dependent on British and American financial assistance. Debt and pension liabilities from the 1914–18 war took up half of public expenditure and left little room for rearmament spending. Nevertheless, a heroic effort was made in the 1930s to rebuild French defences. By 1938 defence spending was taking up over eight per cent of national wealth, a higher proportion than in Britain and over twice the level in 1913, before the First World War. Indeed in 1939 arms spending was even higher than in the last year of the First World War.

The French strategic position was made worse by the collapse of Czechoslovakia, which had provided some counterweight to Germany in the east. After Munich the French were beginning to feel the full weight of German military preparations. Although in the last week of September the British had finally agreed to assist France in the event of a German attack, they still refused to commit any land forces to fight alongside their ally. The French, with considerable justification, felt that the British expected them to hold the western front and provide a major air effort while the British concentrated on home defence. In the autumn of 1938 the French began to make it clear that they expected the British to play their part and provide a major land effort on the continent if the alliance were to have any meaning. Lord Halifax, the Foreign Secretary, was worried that without such a commitment the French might give up altogether and seek a rapprochement with Germany at Britain's expense. Others, such as Sir Samuel Hoare the Home Secretary, were more sanguine, arguing that 'whatever the French might think their interests were so bound up with ours that they could not afford to stand aloof'.[17] In January 1939 Halifax's view prevailed. Ministers agreed that the expeditionary force of four divisions (which until then had been equipped only for a limited war outside Europe), together with its supporting formations from the Territorial Army, should be equipped for a European war – although the French were told to expect only a token force of two divisions. This was not enough to satisfy them. When the European scene darkened still further in March, after the Germans seized the remnants of the Czech state, the French government put more pressure on the British. Chamberlain was determined to try to avoid introducing conscription but felt the need to make a placatory gesture. At the end of March a doubling in the size of the Territorial Army was announced. The decision, which made no military sense, was taken by ministers without consulting the army. This temporizing measure bought only a month's delay; Chamberlain was then forced to bow to continued

French pressure and announce the first ever introduction of conscription in peacetime. With that announcement, at the end of April 1939, went the decision to equip an army, of up to thirty-two divisions, to fight on the continent: it marked the end of the policy adopted since 1934 of trying to avoid a continental commitment.

Britain was now engaged in the creation of a full-scale army, a major air force and navy and the defence of world-wide commitments. Doubts about its ability to fund and maintain armed forces on this scale had been growing since the start of rearmament. Costs had been escalating at an alarming rate. In 1933 defence spending was just over £100 million. The first rearmament programme agreed in 1934 to put right the 'worst deficiencies' was estimated to cost a total of £70 million, a sum the Cabinet Secretary Sir Maurice Hankey thought was 'staggering'. Within fifteen months the cabinet had agreed a new programme costing over £1 billion between 1936 and 1940. In early 1937 the government's white paper forecast expenditure of £1.5 billion by 1942, but a year later the planned programme was accelerated to provide for expenditure of nearly £1.6 billion by 1941. From 1935 defence expenditure rose rapidly at about forty per cent a year, so that by 1939 spending was over £700 million, a seven-fold increase compared with the 1933 figure. As a proportion of national wealth, defence expenditure rose from three per cent in the early 1930s to eighteen per cent in 1939. This was a prodigious effort by any standards, especially since Britain also had to cope with the highest per capita debt in the world, caused by the First World War. Income tax rose from 22½p in the pound in 1934 to 27½p by the spring of 1939.* In addition, a special defence loan was introduced in 1937 and expanded to £800 million in the autumn of 1938. Rearmament caused other problems for the economy. As industrial capacity was increasingly devoted to armaments, that available for exports declined and armament production itself required more raw materials and therefore increased imports. The first signs of balance of payments problems came in 1936 with a small deficit of £18 million, but this tripled to £55 million in 1937 and reached £250 million in 1939.

The rearmament programme rapidly began to show up both the deficiencies of British industry and Britain's dependence on over-

* All figures have been converted into decimal currency.

seas sources of supply, another manifestation of fundamental strategic weakness that was to be of vital importance in 1940. In two crucial areas – steel production and machine tools – Britain had a grossly inadequate industrial base. The official history of munitions production in the First World War identified this weakness when it concluded that: 'It was only the ability of the Allies to import shell and shell steel from neutral America . . . that averted the decisive victory of the enemy.'[18] The situation was no different in the 1930s. Eighty per cent of British blast furnaces were obsolescent, with an average output per furnace lower than the United States achieved in 1910. In the late 1930s British steel output was at half Germany's level yet, unlike that of German industry, UK production was almost at full capacity. Thirty per cent of all special steels had to be imported from the United States and the armour plate for warships from Czechoslovakia. (During the war twenty-five per cent of the UK's requirements had to be imported and steel was the largest single import in 1940.) The situation in the machine tool industry, the key to modern production, was even worse. Britain produced only the simpler sorts of machine and even then half the requirements had to come from abroad. As rearmament took off the level of imports rose by over four hundred per cent between 1935 and 1937. For specialized machine tools Britain was totally dependent on imports. The production of Merlin engines for the Spitfire and the manufacturing of various types of valves and fuses depended on US machine tools. Some types of bomb and shell manufacture even depended on machine tools from Germany.

The aircraft industry provided even more examples of inherent weakness. The industry was good on design but weak on production, where its small scale and fragmented structure were major handicaps. This was compounded by a lack of skilled manpower, the result of inadequate industrial training: in 1937 70,000 workers were needed but only 4,500 could be found. Again imports played a major role. Altimeters, instrument panels and machine guns came from the United States, fuses from Switzerland and the revolutionary chain of radar early-warning stations depended on Dutch and American valves. The Spitfire was an overly complicated aircraft to build, taking three times the man-hours of the equivalent German fighter, the Me 109. It was a year late into operational service, and in early 1938 only five per cent of the expected number of Hurricanes had been delivered. Not until 1939 did British aircraft production match German levels and even then much of it comprised obsolete models such as the Battle, Blenheim and Whitley.

Given Britain's weak position, the problem that faced the government from the start of rearmament in 1934 was to reconcile the military requirements with the economic and financial capacity of the country. This required a fine judgement about the time when Britain should be ready for war. The choice of too early a date would result in obsolescent forces when war did begin and too late a date would mean inadequately equipped forces. The government got this decision right; as early as 1934 they chose the beginning of 1939 as the date and did not change that conclusion. Just as difficult was to decide the level of forces that could be provided. If this judgement were wrong, then force levels would peak in 1939 at a level the economy could not sustain in the long term, leading to fairly rapid reductions, with damaging effects on diplomacy and deterrence. Concern about the sustainability of the continually expanding rearmament programme was voiced in early 1938 when the Treasury cautioned that if the international situation did not improve 'we shall be faced within two years with a choice between defence programmes which we cannot afford, and failure to make defence preparations on an adequate scale'.[19] After Munich, and the decision to expand the RAF's fighter force by thirty per cent, the Chancellor gave a further warning: 'The Air Ministry's programme is . . . so costly as to raise serious doubts whether it can be financed beyond 1939–40 without the gravest danger to the country's stability.'[20]

The decisions taken in the spring of 1939 to introduce conscription and build up a major army only made the situation even more alarming. This major new commitment could not be financed by normal peacetime methods, nor could it be carried out without taking drastic controls over the economy to ensure the necessary allocation of raw materials, resources and manpower. Until 1939 the government had refused to take any powers to direct industry into armaments manufacture or to negotiate with the trade unions over labour problems, hoping instead that the operation of market forces would suffice. In the spring of 1939 a Ministry of Supply was established, but its powers were limited and the nettle of controls was not grasped. Nevertheless the Treasury made it clear that by the autumn wartime financing and controls would be essential whether or not Britain was actually at war. If war did not come in the autumn the government would be faced with some very difficult decisions.

By the spring of 1939 Britain was committed to a massive rearmament programme that was beyond the resources of the country and on the brink of full-scale mobilization. Moreover it still faced the problem of too many unsustainable world-wide commitments. This meant that a difficult choice had to be made about the relative priorities to be assigned to defence against Germany, Italy and Japan. Given Britain's limited resources, this meant that major risks would have to be run in at least one area. The overwhelming need to provide for the defence of the UK against the German threat meant that either the Mediterranean or the Pacific would have to be left virtually defenceless. The problems involved in making that choice were never resolved before the final collapse of the Empire in 1942. Italy had been deleted from the list of friendly countries in 1937 but at that stage had not been added to the list of potential enemies. The subsequent failure to reach a long-term agreement with Italy and the inability of Chamberlain and Halifax to change the situation during their visit to Rome in early 1939 meant that Britain was forced into planning on the possiblity of Italy entering a future war at some point.

In the Far East, continued Japanese expansion posed an increasing threat to British interests. Until 1939 the priority in British strategy lay in the Far East. In 1937 the dominions had been reassured that: 'The very existence of the British Commonwealth of Nations as now constituted rests on our ability to send our fleet to the Far East ... no anxiety or risks connected with our interests in the Mediterranean can be allowed to interfere with the despatch of a fleet to the Far East.'[21] The Singapore base was designed to hold out for seventy days until the fleet arrived and in 1937 the plan was to leave four capital ships in Europe to counter Germany and send eight to the Far East, a number inferior to the Japanese fleet but enough, it was hoped, to deal with any threat. By 1939 this plan was beginning to change under the pressure of events as Italy became more of a threat and Britain's only ally, France, harboured dreams of knocking out Italy quickly in the event of war. The commitment was modified:

the period for the relief of Singapore was extended to ninety days and the number of ships to be sent to the Far East reduced. A sub-committee of the Committee of Imperial Defence reported in April 1939 that it was 'not possible to state definitely how soon after Japanese intervention a Fleet could be despatched to the Far East. Nor is it possible to enumerate precisely the size of the fleet we could afford to send.'[22] Australia and New Zealand were not informed about this change of policy.

One possible way to make up for British weakness was to try to involve the United States in a more active policy in the Pacific. In April 1939 the Americans were persuaded to transfer their fleet from the Atlantic to Pearl Harbor, a move which it was hoped might act as a deterrent to Japan, and low-level Anglo–American naval staff talks were reopened. But the British rapidly realized that the United States was not prepared to defend imperial interests in the Far East and that no reliance could be placed on help from that quarter. In June, when the Japanese blockaded the British concession and assaulted Britons at Tientsin in northern China, ministers did consider sending a fleet to the Far East. Because of the situation in the Mediterranean they felt that only two ships could be spared to go to Singapore, a number clearly inadequate to cope with the Japanese fleet. As Chamberlain told his colleagues, a diplomatic solution was essential: 'We could only send an effective Fleet to the Far East at the cost of abandoning our naval position in the Mediterranean. This was conclusive in favour of making every endeavour to reach an early settlement of the dispute at Tientsin.'[23] A month later, however, when ministers considered whether to adopt a strategy of trying to knock out Italy as quickly as possible in any war, with the risk of losing two or three major warships, they agreed with the chiefs of staff that such a policy was too dangerous: 'If there is any doubt as to the attitude of Japan and the United States of America, we cannot, with our present strength, afford to risk the loss of these ships ... we should have insufficient ships to send to the Far East even if we abandoned the Eastern Mediterranean.'[24]

The government was completely hemmed in, unwilling to risk a strong policy in one area for fear that it would be unable to deal with a problem in the other. It was left, therefore, virtually impotent in both the Mediterranean and the Pacific. The sight of

the cabinet in 1939, powerless to move against either Japan or
Italy, even after five years of rearmament, illustrates dramatically
the problems experienced by British policy-makers stemming from
a failure to reconcile an over-extended Empire and multiple threats
with inadequate resources.

Although the British were keen to try and involve the United
States in controlling Japan, the overall relationship between the
two countries was ambivalent. Neither government had much
direct knowledge of the other and their leaders rarely, if ever, met.
What they did know hardly fostered better understanding. Although President Roosevelt was personally sympathetic towards
the British and French attempts to contain and come to a deal
with Germany, most Americans believed that both powers were
quite strong enough to look after themselves. Indeed the US
government regarded the British as far too dominant, particularly
after the failure of the international attempts in 1933 to agree a
programme for world recovery from the depression and the emerg-
ence of the sterling bloc and imperial trade preference. Both
developments were seen as a direct threat to American economic
interests. American public opinion did not see any need for US
involvement in Europe's quarrels and the possibility of direct
intervention did not arise. The British tended to see the Americans
as a junior power untrained in the realities of world diplomacy,
long on words but short on action and help. Rab Butler, junior
minister at the Foreign Office and pillar of the Tory establishment,
wrote in July 1939, 'In my political life I have always been
convinced that we can no more count on America than Brazil.'[25]
The British themselves were opposed to American interference in
European diplomacy, since they were worried that any such
intervention might involve a price, in terms of meeting US interests, that they did not want to pay.

But as the threat of war with Germany grew greater, the
possibility that US help might be necessary at some stage was
reluctantly recognized by the policy-makers in Whitehall. One
result of such thinking was the signature of a trade agreement
between the two countries, involving major British concessions,
in 1938. The next year, King George VI paid the first ever visit by
a monarch to the ex-colony. The British government, painfully
aware of the fact that US financial and industrial assistance had
been essential to victory in the First World War, had to face the

fact that there was no guarantee of a repeat performance. American legislators had introduced a number of obstacles in the intervening years. The Johnson Act of 1934 debarred countries that had defaulted on repaying debt from the First World War from raising any more funds. Since Britain had defaulted in 1931, this meant any future purchases would have to be paid for in cash. Worse still, the 1935–6 Neutrality Acts, which had been passed because of the widespread feeling that Allied war purchases had dragged a reluctant United States into the war, actually placed an embargo on arms sales to any belligerent. President Roosevelt's attempt to modify the legislation so that countries at war could buy arms on a cash basis and transport them in their own and not American ships was rejected by Congress in the summer of 1939. Although Britain could hope that the necessary amending action would be taken once war started, there was no guarantee of success. Yet the multiple threats facing Britain forced the government to admit in early 1939 that US help was likely, once again, to be crucial in the event of war. On this occasion the chiefs of staff advised that Britain should fight to preserve the independence of the Low Countries, but at the same time they acknowledged that ultimate success would depend on fighting a long war with Germany and that this would probably tempt Italy and Japan to join in as well. This would create, they advised, 'a position more serious than the Empire has ever faced before. The ultimate outcome ... might well depend upon the intervention of other Powers, in particular of the United States.'[26]

Britain's weak position – stemming from an over-extended Empire, multiple threats, only one ally and inadequate industrial resources – was now made worse by reliance on the United States even though there was no guarantee that help from them would be available. In the last months before the outbreak of war the last of the forces working to undermine British power – limited financial resources – became increasingly apparent.

British doubts about their ability to sustain a long war were growing rapidly in 1939, even though the military planners thought a long war not only likely but essential for victory. The balance of payments deficit was increasing and the gold and dollar reserves, which had reached a peak of £825 million in March 1938, had fallen by twenty-five per cent to just over £600 million a year later and to £500 million by June 1939. A month later the Treasury reported to the cabinet on the financial situation.[27] They pointed out that in addition to the reserves Britain had only just over £200 million worth of foreign securities that could be requisitioned and sold, giving total assets of £700 million for foreign purchases, mainly from the United States. Yet in the 1914–18 war, to buy raw materials and armaments, Britain had needed to sell gold and securities and in addition take out over £1 billion in loans from the Americans. Since such loans were now prohibited, Britain was left with the prospect of woefully inadequate resources to sustain the war effort. They concluded that the military assumption – that a war of three years would be needed – was 'very likely much too optimistic' and again stressed the key role of the Americans: 'Unless, when the time comes, the United States are prepared either to lend or to give us money as required, the prospects for a long war are exceedingly grim.'

The coded language of Whitehall disguised a terrifying prospect. Britain might run out of money to continue the war before military victory could be achieved. If the United States did not come to the rescue, either military defeat or a compromise peace would be the inevitable consequence.

From March until 2 September 1939 the British government made a last attempt to come to terms with Germany and avoid war. After the German occupation of Prague and the demolition of what remained of the Czech state after Munich, the next target was clearly Poland. Hitler wanted revision of the Versailles settlement, which had created the anomalous Polish corridor to the free city of Danzig, separating East Prussia from the rest of Germany. To many commentators the British decision to extend a guarantee to Poland on 31 March, widened in early April to include Rumania and Greece, marks the end of appeasement and the start of a policy of standing up to Hitler. That was not how the government saw the decision at the time. For them it was a last-ditch effort to avoid war. The guarantee to Poland was hurriedly put together and announced in the face of military advice not to go ahead. The cabinet hoped that the guarantee would place them in a position to put pressure on the Poles to reach a settlement. For this reason the guarantee covered only the independence and not the territorial integrity of Poland.

The Allies found that the Poles were expert negotiators who were not prepared to make any concessions. The guarantee created a problem of how Britain and France could help the Poles if they were attacked. One possible solution was to involve the pariah of European politics, the Soviet Union, in an anti-German alliance. The French were keen, but Chamberlain and most of the British government were not and they did their best to slow up the negotiations. Sir Alexander Cadogan, the head of the Foreign Office, reported in May: 'In his present mood, P.M. says he will resign rather than sign alliance with the Soviet [sic].'[28]

An insuperable obstacle was that the Poles did not want Soviet help. They knew that Soviet troops would have to move into Poland to attack the Germans and doubted whether they would leave afterwards. Polish–Soviet antagonism in the immediate past went back twenty years to the bitter fighting after the First World War, and Beck, the Polish Foreign Secretary, warned the British that '[they] could negotiate with Soviet Russia if they liked; they could even undertake obligations towards her. These obligations would in no way extend the obligations undertaken by Poland.'[29] Under French pressure the British eventually accepted the idea of a pact with the Soviet Union but resisted a binding alliance. Rather they preferred an arrangement whereby Soviet help would be available if required and the small states of eastern Europe would decide whether to call on Soviet assistance. Not surprisingly, the Soviet Union was not keen on this idea and the talks rapidly reached deadlock. To break the stalemate the Soviet Union suggested the start of military conversations on the mechanics of providing assistance. The British and French accepted but sent their delegates by the slowest possible route to Leningrad.

In parallel with these moves the British government made one more attempt at reaching a deal with Germany. During four days of talks in London in the middle of July the British offered a comprehensive agreement based on a massive loan from the UK to help the German economy during a transition to a peacetime state following a general European settlement. The prospect of an Anglo–German non-aggression and non-interference treaty was hinted at, linked to disarmament and co-operation in foreign trade. Hints were also given that Britain would be willing to ditch the Poles in the event of an agreement. But Britain was dealing with Hitler, not a politician with limited aims, and he preferred a military solution. On 3 April (three days after the British guarantee to Poland) he had already ordered the military to be ready to invade Poland at any time from 1 September onwards.

The decisive events took place in Moscow in the middle of August. On 14 August, when the Allied talks with the Soviet Union reopened, the Soviet negotiators asked the crucial question: would Poland and Rumania allow Soviet troops into their countries so that they could attack the Germans? The British and French, knowing that the answer was in the negative, tried to avoid the issue, but three days later the Soviets adjourned the talks. Already the Soviet government had received indications that the Germans could offer what the Allies could not: a divison of eastern Europe and an expansion of the Soviet Union westwards into the areas lost in the aftermath of war and revolution twenty years before. On 23 August the Nazi–Soviet non-aggression pact was announced, though not its secret clauses on the cynical carving up of the territory lying between the two countries.

With war now almost inevitable the guarantee to Poland was extended into a full-scale alliance. But in the last week of peace the British government put extensive pressure on the Poles to send someone to Berlin to negotiate or be browbeaten into surrender, as had happened with the Austrians and Czechs. Contacts, through a Swedish intermediary (Dahlerus), took place between Britain and Germany and on 29 August Hitler agreed to negotiate with the Poles. The next day the US Ambassador in London, Joseph Kennedy, reported that Chamberlain was 'more worried about getting the Poles to be reasonable than the Germans'.[30] On 31 August the German demands for the return of Danzig and a plebiscite in the Polish corridor to the sea were conveyed to the British. More pressure was put on the Poles, but they remained unyielding and on 1 September the German invasion began. For two days the British and French ignored their alliance with Poland while they tried to reach a deal with Germany. Then on 3 September they reluctantly declared war.

Although Britain was at war the worst fears of government were not realized. Mussolini had panicked at the last moment and refused to join Germany. Japan, which had been allied to Germany and Italy in an anti-Soviet pact, was so disgusted by the Nazi–Soviet deal that it too stood aside. Nevertheless, the situation facing Britain was far worse than in 1914: then Britain's only major enemy had been Germany and it had taken a terrible four-year war involving France, Russia and the United States to ensure victory. In 1939 Britain faced the same enemy, but was supported only by a weakened France, with the United States friendly but neutral and offering no prospect of any military assistance, and the Soviet Union neutral and unfriendly. Not only that, but two allies from 1914–18, Italy and Japan, looked likely to join in on the other side this time. The British had to plan on the assumption that Italy would probably enter the war at the first favourable opportunity and also face the possibility that the threat from Japan would grow if there were military reverses in Europe.

Britain therefore entered the Second World War in an extremely weak position. Successive governments had found no way of resolving the potentially fatal amalgam of pressures undermining Britain's ability to defend itself and the Empire. Britain was still responsible for the defence of territory and interests in every part of the world. It had to face one actual plus two likely enemies but only had the economic and industrial resources to provide an adequate defence against one of them. The major rearmament programme under way since 1934 was already straining the economy to breaking point but had not acted as an effective deterrent. Britain had been unable to find any way of reducing the number of enemies it faced. Its diplomacy had been constrained by public opinion, the need not to alienate the United States and the difficulty of finding any basis for agreement with expansionist and irrational dictators. Its only ally was France; the Soviet Union had been rejected for ideological reasons and the reluctance of other states to allow their army to move westwards. The role of the United States was recognized to be vital, but the extent of its help in the war effort remained unclear. Its resources were badly needed to compensate for British inadequacies by supplying essential raw materials, food, industrial goods and arms. Even if the Americans were to change their restrictive policy and allow Britain to buy these goods now that war was declared, it was unlikely that Britain would be able to do so for very long before its supplies of gold and dollars ran out. The British government had not begun to think about what might happen then, but there was no guarantee that the Americans would save them from potential bankruptcy.

British policy-makers in the 1930s were painfully aware of all these weaknesses. They were in the unenviable position of presiding over the undermining of British power and influence while being unable to arrest the process. Given Britain's overwhelming strategic weakness in the 1930s, there were few options available. The government chose a two-pronged approach. Rearmament as a deterrent was coupled with negotiations to see if any agreement could be reached with Germany, Italy and Japan to give them increased status and power while preserving as much of British influence and power as possible. It was probably the best option available, but it failed. It failed because the three powers were not content with the little that Britain was willing to offer. The alternative of major concessions was unthinkable if Britain were to retain its status as a world power and was never considered by the government. But the prospect of war in order to defend Britain's position was also potentially disastrous. One of the main reasons the government tried so hard to avoid war was the knowledge that a world war would almost certainly mean the end of British power. Either Britain would be defeated or, in the attempt to secure victory, the two most powerful nations in the world – the Soviet Union and the United States – would become involved. Once they were drawn in, the former might well end up dominating Europe and Britain would become economically and politically dependent on the latter. In 1940 the devastating combination of factors which had been working to undermine Britain's position came together. Their impact was to end Britain's long history as an independent power in the world.

The looming disaster facing Britain was made painfully clear to the war cabinet only a week after war was declared. They considered a paper from the Chancellor of the Exchequer on the financial position, an assessment so alarming that all copies had to be returned to the cabinet secretaries immediately after the meeting. It told them the stark facts that Britain's total resources for financing the war were about £700 million and that 'there is no real chance of any addition to this figure'. It reminded them that total resources were vastly inferior to those available in 1914 and 'extremely meagre for the financing of a long war'. The paper could only conclude that: 'It is obvious that we are in grave danger of our gold reserves being exhausted at a rate that will render us incapable of waging war if war is prolonged.'[31] With this grim warning ringing in their ears the government embarked on a war for national survival.

3

Failure

The war that began on 3 September 1939 was not a world war;
it was not even a full-scale European war. The only countries
involved were Germany, France, Britain and the Empire, and
Poland (defeated within a month). A number of nations that had
taken part in the First World War – Russia, the United States,
Japan, Italy, Turkey and Belgium – remained neutral. Only gradually were more countries dragged into the conflict: Denmark
and Norway in April 1940; Belgium, Holland and Luxemburg in
May; Italy in June; Greece in the autumn and then the Balkans
and the Soviet Union in the early summer of 1941. From a
European conflict it became a world war only in December 1941,
with the entry of Japan and the United States.

Until May 1940 the basis of Anglo–French strategy was to keep
the conflict as limited as possible and avoid a world war. Detailed
planning had begun in the spring of 1939 with an agreement to
re-create the structure that had been in existence at the end of the
First World War: a Supreme War Council composed of the prime
ministers and other senior ministers of each country; overall
French control of land strategy in western Europe, with the small
British army in France under French command; and a series of
committees to oversee military co-operation and joint purchases
of armaments. Allied planning was based on one fundamental
premise, which was also to dominate British strategy throughout
1940. Intelligence experts had assessed, from the mid-1930s, that
the German economy was being fully mobilized for total war and
in September 1939 their advice was that it was working at full
stretch and at a pace that was unsustainable for more than a
short period. They thought that the Germans could only survive
an Allied naval blockade (which had been very effective in the
First World War in preventing supplies reaching Germany) for at

most eighteen months before shortages of raw materials and food and the strain of armaments production so depressed domestic consumption that the Germans would collapse internally as they had done in the autumn of 1918. This belief turned out to be totally erroneous: in fact the German economy had plenty of surplus capacity and was far from being fully mobilized in the first half of the war.

On the basis of this false assessment the Allies decided that their best plan was simply to wait for Germany to collapse. The first stage was to survive any immediate German assault and demonstrate that a quick and easy victory was not possible. This would give time for the Allies to use their control of the sea and superior overseas resources, together with United States production, so that in the second year of the war they would be able to build armies capable of attacking and eventually defeating what was likely to be by then a severely weakened Germany, if it had not already collapsed. The so-called 'phoney war', in which the Allied and German armies faced each other in western Europe from September 1939 until the spring of 1940 without taking any offensive action, was not an aberration on the part of the Allies but reflected the belief that they were implementing their best strategy. Naval supremacy was quickly established and the blockade of Germany started. The Germans did not attempt a 'knock-out' blow from the air (the main fear of pre-war planners) and the French seemed well established on land in a strong defensive position. The first stage of their plan having been accomplished, the Allies began the long process of building armies capable of attacking Germany. Chamberlain was heavily criticized in April 1940 and afterwards for saying, just before the invasion of Scandinavia, that Hitler had 'missed the bus' by failing to attack in the first six months of the war. But his opinion reflected the strongly held Allied view that the longer the real war was postponed the better for Britain and France. Such optimistic opinions were in fact universal within the British government. As early as the end of October 1939, Anthony Eden said that 'already Herr Hitler has lost the initiative' and by the end of January 1940 Churchill was confident that 'Hitler has already lost his best chance'.

The minimalist strategy also reflected fears about Britain's ability to sustain an all-out war. Underlying the increasingly desperate pre-war moves to keep the peace was the belief that any war, even if Britain emerged victorious, would fatally undermine British power. After war broke out, the British government hoped that mainly economic pressure could destabilize the German economy and lead to the fall of the Nazi regime. It would then be possible, they hoped, to do a deal with a successor regime and obtain a new European settlement. This would avoid an all-out war and the consequences, both internal and external, that such a war entailed. They hoped to avoid the social and political risks they associated with moving to a full-scale war economy in Britain: the threat of financial collapse, dependence on the United States and the possible involvement of the Soviet Union in the war. As a strategy it was not heroic, but one suited to Britain's weakness, which was steadily becoming more apparent to the government. Shortly after the start of the war, the war cabinet agreed that the aim should be to create a fifty-five-division army. The Chancellor of the Exchequer, Simon, accepted that decision but told his colleagues that equipping an army on this scale would involve major imports of raw materials, machine tools and armaments. The United States had now lifted its embargo on arms exports but Britain would still have to pay in hard cash. Taken together with the major naval and air programmes already under way, the cost was probably more than Britain could afford and was bound to lead to 'very serious difficulties' of finance by the end of the second year of the war.[1] In February 1940 Simon circulated a paper to his colleagues on 'Our National Resources in Relation to Our War Effort'.[2] It gave a pessimistic assessment of the long-term prospects facing the country. The balance of payments deficit in the first year of the war was likely to be at least £400 million and would increase as armaments production grew. This deficit could be financed only by drawing on the reserves of gold, dollars and foreign investments and he warned the war cabinet that 'the extent to which recourse can properly be made to these, our last capital assets, must depend primarily upon the view taken as to the probable length of the war'. Even on the most optimistic assumptions, the Treasury prediction was that they would not last more than two to three years. Simon concluded that the plan for a fifty-five-division army could not be implemented in full and that the overall rearmament programme could not be afforded. He ended his assessment with sobering words: 'This is a dark and sombre picture, and one which shows all too

clearly the limitations which financial considerations alone necessarily impose on our war effort.'

When the war cabinet discussed the paper, the Prime Minister,
Neville Chamberlain, summed up by saying that 'we were already
encroaching upon our exchange resources beyond the margin of
safety'.[3] Within a couple of weeks Treasury officials had concluded that resources would not last for three years and that after
two years of war 'the prospect at the very best is that we should
have to contract our war effort to a vast extent'.[4]

Within its first six months, the war, even without the advent of
full-scale fighting, was developing into a race to see which economy
would collapse first. The Allies, convinced that the German economy was at breaking point and anxious to avoid fighting on the
western front, looked for ways of applying extra pressure in
peripheral areas. This led them to spend the winter of 1939–40
embroiled in Scandinavia in a series of increasingly dubious
schemes that resulted in the first outbreak of serious fighting
with the Germans in Norway in April 1940. In the autumn of 1939
the Allies rapidly convinced themselves that their best option was
to stop Germany importing iron ore from Sweden. They based
this conclusion on the idea that half Germany's imports came
from the mines in north Sweden around Gallivare. In fact these
Swedish imports were far less important than the Allies imagined,
since they accounted for only about a quarter of total German
consumption. Germany also had a large stockpile of ore and
access to other sources of production on the continent. In any
case, forty per cent of German steel output was still going to the
civilian sector, so there was plenty of scope for shifting this to
military production if necessary. Stopping imports from Sweden
was going to have only a long-term impact at best, and was
certainly not going to produce a quick end to the war. Nevertheless
the Allies began to look for ways of cutting off supplies. During
the summer months the iron ore was sent by sea from the port of
Lulea down the Gulf of Bothnia and across the Baltic to Germany.
Churchill, who had joined the government as First Lord of the
Admiralty on the outbreak of war, indulged in a considerable
amount of wishful thinking about sending the Royal Navy into
the Baltic to cut this supply route. But it was not a feasible
operation to send warships, without air cover, into an area dominated by the Germans. During the winter, however, the Baltic was

frozen up and the ore went by rail to the Norwegian port of Narvik and then down the North Sea to Germany. This route did provide an opportunity for Allied naval intervention to stop supplies. The problem was that the German ships carrying the ore normally kept within Norwegian territorial waters during their journey south and could therefore be attacked only by violating Norwegian neutrality. As early as mid-September, Churchill proposed laying mines inside Norway's territorial waters to force the ships out on to the high seas, where they could be attacked. The war cabinet rejected the proposal on two counts: because of its illegality and also for the simple reason that in the autumn no ships were using the route. They agreed to look at the subject later in the year.

The Soviet attack on Finland at the end of November 1939, and the stout Finnish resistance, opened up new possibilities for intervention in Scandinavia. Although the near-moribund League of Nations, in its last action of any consequence, expelled the Soviet Union, many in the British government wanted to go further. This desire reflected the widespread view, apparent long before the attack on Finland, that the real enemy was not Germany but the Soviet Union. 'Chips' Channon, the socialite Conservative MP who was Rab Butler's parliamentary private secretary, wrote on the day war was declared: 'I feel that our world, or all that remains of it, is committing suicide, whilst Stalin laughs and the Kremlin triumphs.'[5] Neville Chamberlain's private secretary went even further five weeks later: 'Communism is now the great danger, greater even than Nazi Germany ... we should play our hand very carefully with Russia, and not destroy the possibility of uniting, if necessary, with a new German government against the common danger.'[6] Senior members of the government saw the threat from the Soviet Union in the same way. As Lord Halifax told ministers from the dominions at the beginning of November:

One important result of the [Nazi–Soviet] Agreement was the danger of Bolshevism spreading to Western Europe ... It was a danger however we had to face, and we had to make up our minds whether we should tackle it by drawing apart from Russia or even declaring war upon her ... The alternative policy was to concentrate *first* on the German menace, and it was this policy which the United Kingdom Government had decided to adopt [my italics].[7]

The French view of the Soviet threat was similar. Daladier, the Prime Minister, told the Americans in 1938 he was worried that 'Germany would be defeated in the war ... but the only gainers would be the Bolsheviks as there would be social revolution in every country of Europe ... Cossacks will rule Europe'.[8]

The Soviet attack aroused widespread sympathy for the Finns, increased by their valiant resistance throughout the winter. The Nazi–Soviet agreement and the Soviet supply of raw materials to Germany only intensified hostility to the Soviet Union. To many the struggle put up by Finland created a great opportunity to go to their aid and attack the Soviet Union at the same time. Lord Cork and Orrery, the director of plans at the Admiralty responsible for Scandinavian policy, told Churchill, one of the most fervent proponents of Allied intervention against the Bolsheviks after the First World War, that British aid for Finland could provide 'a wonderful chance – and perhaps the last – of mobilizing the anti-Bolshevik forces of the world on our side'.[9] Although the government knew that their resources for fighting Germany were inadequate they nevertheless, during the winter of 1939–40, brought themselves to the brink of war with the Soviet Union. This reflected not only strong ideological dislike of the Soviet government but a disdain for Soviet military strength that seemed to be confirmed by their inept performance against Finland. The idea of attacking the Soviet Union was justified on the grounds that it was helping Germany economically, but there may well have been the hope in ministers' minds that Germany (under another government) would still see sense and unite against the common enemy. A number of hare-brained schemes were therefore considered for attacking the Soviet Union. As late as the end of March 1940, a fortnight after the Finno–Soviet peace treaty, the Supreme War Council, meeting in London, considered detailed plans drawn up for an air attack from the Middle East on the Soviet oilfields at Baku on the Caspian Sea. These, they believed, 'would have the double advantage of paralysing Russia's economic structure and effectively preventing her from carrying out military operations outside her own territory'.[10] On another occasion the French suggested sending warships into the Black Sea to stop Soviet supplies to Germany, a plan also put forward by Churchill in October 1939, but this idea had to be abandoned because of Turkish hostility to the passage of the ships through the Straits.

These wilder fantasies were put on one side, but throughout the winter of 1939–40 the Allies kept returning to the question of how to intervene in Scandinavia, where the desire to stop Swedish exports of iron ore to Germany, to aid Finland and attack the Soviet Union could be combined. The possibility of an Allied expedition to take control of the Norwegian port of Narvik and the Swedish iron ore mines under the guise of aiding Finland was raised by the French on 19 December. The problem was first whether the Finns would invite the Allies to assist them, and second whether Norway and Sweden, both neutral states, would allow Allied troops and supply lines into their countries. When the British government discussed the proposal the next day these objections did not worry Churchill, who favoured a more high-handed approach: 'We should make a friendly offer of assistance to the Scandinavian countries, as was proposed by the French, but we should make it quite clear that whether they accepted it or not we should come in and take possession of the minefields.'[11] The war cabinet did not support Churchill's suggestion, but agreed that the chiefs of staff should begin planning for inter-vention in Scandinavia.

In the first few days of 1940 the war cabinet considered two plans for landings in Scandinavia. The first of these was to go ashore at Narvik and advance across Norway to the Swedish mines, and the second involved the 'defence of southern Sweden', although against what threat was less clear. The latter idea got no further than a plan for section D of MI6 to blow up the port of Oxelösund, just south of Stockholm, which was agreed by senior ministers on 17 January but discovered and foiled by the Swedes. On 12 January the war cabinet agreed to leave the option of landing at Narvik (to stop the transit of ore along the railway from Sweden) on one side until the plans for large-scale inter-vention to aid the Finns were ready. At the beginning of February the Supreme War Council met in Paris to discuss future policy. The Finns had by this stage asked for supplies and 30,000 men to help their hard-pressed army. The Allies decided to prepare three or four divisions (a total of 30,000–40,000 troops) to go to their assistance. Finland was to be asked to make an appeal for help, at which point Britain and France would demand transit rights across Norway and Sweden. The plan was for the Finns to make their 'appeal' on 5 March and for the Allied troops to land at Narvik on 20 March. Preliminary discussions with the Norwegians and Swedes revealed, however, that co-operation would not be forthcoming and only a small number of 'volunteers' would be allowed passage. For the rest of the month intense pressure was put on the two neutral governments to allow Allied troops through to attack the Soviets, but without success. On 12 March the British government finally decided the objections of the neutrals should be ignored. The landing at Narvik would go ahead, the troops would move along the railway line to Sweden, secure the orefields and then aid the Finns. Only 'serious fighting' would halt the operation; limited resistance by the Norwegians would be overcome. The British and French were saved from their own folly, from a likely war with the Soviet Union and the invasion and violation of Norwegian and Swedish neutrality, only by the Finnish decision to seek peace on 13 March. Churchill wanted to go ahead anyway and seize the orefields, but the war cabinet ordered the dispersal of the troops assembled for this ill-thought-out and potentially disastrous expedition.

Although preparations for land operations in Scandinavia were temporarily abandoned, the idea of mining Norwegian territorial waters to stop their use by ships carrying ore to Germany was not. The main proponent of the operation was Churchill, but considerable opposition from many different quarters led to continual postponement. On 6 January the Norwegians were told of the Allied intentions, but the strength of their opposition, and that of the Swedes and some dominion governments, was such that the plan was cancelled six days later. After the Royal Navy had rescued captured merchant sailors from the German freighter *Altmark* in a Norwegian fjord on 16 February, Churchill and the Admiralty revived the plans for minelaying. When the leaders of the Liberal and Labour Parties, Sinclair and Attlee, were consulted, only the former was in favour of the operation. On 29 February the war cabinet, worried by neutral opinion – particularly that of the United States – decided once again not to proceed. Churchill had more luck a month later when the Supreme War Council endorsed the idea and linked it to a plan to float mines down the Rhine to disrupt German river traffic. Within

2

3 three days the French abandoned the Rhine plan because of worries that the Germans might use it as an excuse to start an all-out bombing campaign. Churchill, still lobbying strongly for the plan, went over to Paris to try and change their minds, but finished up changing his own and accepting the French objections. Meanwhile the British war cabinet had decided, in Churchill's absence, to go ahead with the Norwegian minelaying anyway. The operation began on 8 April. The fact that it was the British who first violated Norwegian neutrality was to cause major problems for the Allied prosecutors at the Nuremburg war crimes trials after the war, when they accused the Germans of planning aggressive action in violation of international treaties in their attack on Norway.

Allied interest in Scandinavia had attracted the attention of the Germans from the end of 1939. After the *Altmark* incident and the interception of messages between the Allies and Finland, Hitler, worried about possible Allied intervention, on 21 February authorized planning to start for an invasion of Denmark and Norway. The operation was carried out, with great rapidity, on 9 April. Denmark was overrun within a few hours and German troops captured Oslo in the morning and began landings along the Norwegian coast, including Trondheim and Narvik in the north. This move should have played into the hands of the British by enabling them to use their naval superiority, together with the plans for intervention already developed, to respond quickly and counter the German invasion. In practice the British response, though handicapped by German air superiority, demonstrated confused strategic thinking, shifting objectives and poor command on the ground. The result of all these weaknesses, combined with brilliant and imaginative German tactics, was a decisive British defeat and an ignominious withdrawal, followed by growing political pressure on the Chamberlain government and demands for more effective control of the war. The beneficiary of these criticisms was Churchill who, ironically, was mainly responsible for the poor decisions taken in the early stages of the campaign.

Despite nearly six months of deep interest in Norway and Scandinavia, the British were caught unawares by the German invasion. The earliest warning of German intentions came from agents inside Germany a month before the attack, and over the following weeks it was backed up by various reports of advance

military and naval preparations. These reports were discounted
by the military and intelligence staffs in London because of the
conviction that the Germans would not try an invasion in the
face of British naval supremacy. It was this overconfidence that
was at the heart of the first blunder committed by Churchill.
As reports of German ships moving from the Baltic into the
southern North Sea reached London, he decided that it was a
purely naval move designed to break out into the Atlantic. He
therefore ordered the removal of British troops from the ships
supporting the minelaying in Norway, troops which could have
either pre-empted or dealt rapidly with the German landings
along the coast. From the start the British were, therefore, left
in a position of having to respond to German moves. Intelligence
remained a major handicap throughout the operation. The lack
of British preparation was painfully clear when the RAF had
to use a 1912 Baedeker guide to Norway to find their bombing
targets. Some Luftwaffe signals were being intercepted, but the
highly efficient system for disseminating such crucial intelligence to field commanders which was developed later in the
war was not available, and the information had no impact on
the campaign. The Germans, however, were reading about a
third of British naval signals and had advance information
about the British landings along the coast.

The other fundamental British problem was an over-complicated
decision-taking system that failed to produce decisive leadership.
The first level was the chiefs of staff committee, which provided
military advice to ministers. Immediately above them was the
Military Co-ordination Committee, composed of the ministers in
charge of the three services, which made recommendations on
possible action to the war cabinet, on which the same three
ministers also sat with their more senior colleagues. This elaborate
committee structure made it almost impossible to take swift
decisions and also failed to provide a clear way of giving political
directions to the military. In this inadequate system the dominating personality of Churchill caused more problems. Although only
First Lord of the Admiralty, he believed that he should have a
dominant say in the overall direction of the war. He chaired the
co-ordination committee, and often gave instructions without
formally consulting the chiefs of staff or his political colleagues;
moreover his tendency to make erratic and swiftly changing

decisions compounded the problems. Churchill was also determined to try and lay the ghost of his perceived failure in planning
and controlling the naval operations and subsequent landings at
the Dardanelles and Gallipoli in the First World War, which had
led to his resignation from the Liberal government and a reputation for poor leadership and over-impulsive decision-taking. The
fact that Britain was at war did not mean that political ambition
was forgotten, and Churchill, in his sixties and with his career
until 1939 a comparative failure, still harboured an intense desire
to be Prime Minister. Driven by a combination of these two
motivating forces, he saw a successful campaign in Norway as a
way of enhancing his reputation and possibly leading on to
higher things.

As news of the German invasion reached London the war cabinet
met at 8.30 a.m. on 9 April. The mood was confident, with Churchill
remarking, 'We have the Germans where we want them.' The Royal
Navy was ordered to clear Bergen and Trondheim and troops were
readied to recapture these two ports from the Germans and also to
take Narvik. Within hours the gravity of the situation became clear.
By midday the war cabinet knew that the Royal Navy ships off
Narvik had failed to stop 4,000 German troops capturing the port.
The attack on Bergen was called off because the Germans were
judged to be too strongly entrenched. That evening, ministers agreed
a chiefs of staff recommendation to concentrate on Narvik and
recapture the port (with the idea of going on to the Swedish orefields
still in the background). The next day German forces beat off a naval
attack on Narvik and Churchill was forced to admit privately to
Admiral Pound, the First Sea Lord, that 'we have been completely
outwitted'.[12] On 11 April he gave a very poor performance in
the House of Commons in an attempt to explain the position.
One of his strongest supporters, Harold Nicolson, described the
occasion:

> He starts off by giving an imitation of himself making a speech,
> and he indulges in vague oratory coupled with tired jibes. I
> have seldom seen him to less advantage ... He hesitates, gets
> his notes in the wrong order, puts on the wrong pair of
> spectacles, fumbles for the right pair, keeps on saying 'Sweden'
> when he means 'Denmark', and one way and another makes a
> lamentable performance.[13]

Nevertheless the British expedition, with the army now embarked, was under way to recapture Narvik. That evening (11 April) Churchill, in a condition described by a member of the naval staff as 'half tight', began thinking about diverting it to Namsos, 300 miles south of Narvik, in an attempt to capture Trondheim another eighty miles to the south. This was the first sign of the continually shifting objectives in British strategy that were to mar the whole campaign.

On 13 April a naval attack on Narvik was brilliantly successful and seven German destroyers were sunk, but there were no troops available immediately to follow up and capture the port. At the war cabinet, ministers, thinking that Narvik was already virtually in their hands, were keen to divert troops to Trondheim though Churchill was now opposed. However, early the next morning he pressurized the Chief of the Imperial General Staff, General Ironside, into diverting the rear part of the troop convoy heading for Narvik to the port of Namsos as the first step in a Trondheim operation. A day later the landings at Narvik took place, but some way from the town. No attempt was made to capture the port. The troops were not equipped for an assault and crucial anti-aircraft equipment had been diverted to Namsos, where no landing took place. In London the chiefs of staff, with Churchill strongly dissenting, decided to call off any attempt to secure Trondheim for a week.

By 16 April the confusion and lack of firm plans in the British operation had produced chaos. The Germans had been allowed to establish themselves in all the key ports along the Norwegian coast and no effective riposte had been made. The only British troops ashore were near Narvik and there the commander, General Mackesy, refused to advance on the town and decided to wait until at least the end of the month, when he hoped the snow would melt, before making any attempt to capture the port. Desperate urgings from the chiefs of staff and the war cabinet did not change his mind. Whitehall was in revolt over Churchill's erratic and idiosyncratic methods of conducting the war. The chiefs of staff felt they had no opportunity to give their advice properly and other ministers on the co-ordination committee and in the war cabinet felt ignored and bypassed. That morning Churchill was forced to ask Chamberlain to take over the chairmanship of the co-ordination committee in order to defuse a full-scale row over his conduct of the campaign.

It still proved impossible, however, to give any coherence to the operations in Norway. On 17 April the chiefs of staff decided to attack Trondheim direct on 22 April, only to call off the operation two days later. On 18 April the landings at Namsos and Andalsnes went ahead with the idea of mounting a pincer attack on Trondheim. Within three days, further landings at Namsos had to be called off because of heavy German air attacks and because troops at Andalsnes were making no progress towards Trondheim. On 22 April, with the landings in the south on the point of failure, Churchill argued that they should go back and concentrate on Narvik (where ten days earlier he had reduced the forces by moving them south), although he still wanted a direct attack on Trondheim by the Royal Navy without troops. On 26 April the war cabinet finally decided to throw in their hand in central Norway and evacuate all the troops, a decision opposed by Churchill, who now wanted to fight on around Trondheim in order to avoid the stigma of withdrawal. By the end of the month evacuation was under way. At Narvik General Mackesy still refused to attack, and although the war cabinet were tempted to order him to attack anyway they drew back because they did not want to be blamed in the event of failure. Mackesy was eventually relieved of his command on 13 May but still no attack was made until the end of the month. Ministers then decided that the port should be captured (which cost the lives of 150 soldiers) even though they had decided to withdraw immediately it fell. It was a futile but fitting end to a disastrous campaign.

The dimensions of the military fiasco in Norway were clear, both to ministers and to the public, by the end of April, following the decision to withdraw from central Norway and with the lack of action at Narvik. Explanations were clearly required. At the meeting which decided to pull out from around Trondheim ministers were already trying to work out how to defend themselves. The reputation of the government and of individual ministers was at stake as they manoeuvred to gain advantage and allocate blame. As General Ironside commented: 'They all, including the P.M., began making up stories they could tell the public and make out that our stroke against Trondheim was to put the Germans off Narvik.'[14]

Churchill may have been relieved, earlier in the month, to give up chairing the military co-ordination committee and reduce his own responsibility just as the operation ran into real difficulties. He was also keen to use the fiasco to improve the system for directing the war and at the same time enhance his own power and standing. On 24 April he drafted a letter to Chamberlain saying that he was glad not to be chairing the co-ordination committee any longer and that he would not take it back until he was given real decision-taking powers. The letter was not sent, but the two men met that evening to discuss the situation. Chamberlain knew that he could not afford to let Churchill resign over the conduct of the war because it might well bring down the government. On the other hand he could not give him effective power to direct the war on his own without irretrievably diminishing his own position as Prime Minister. During the next few days a compromise was worked out. Churchill was to chair the co-ordination committee, which would give guidance to the chiefs of staff and be able to summon them at any time, and he would be able to preside over chiefs of staff meetings. He was also given a small military staff of his own headed by General Ismay, who as a member of the chiefs of staff committee would be able to see that Churchill's instructions were carried out. While retaining the title of First Lord of the Admiralty, Churchill was in effect made a quasi-minister of defence, more equal than his two colleagues in charge of the army and air force, though still subject to the overall control of the war cabinet. Not surprisingly, the other two service ministers, Hoare (Air Ministry) and Stanley (War Office), objected strongly to their new position under Churchill. It was only when Chamberlain threatened to resign and let Churchill become Prime Minister that they agreed to go along with the new arrangements. This new structure, which would not have resolved the problem of Churchill claiming too much power without responsibility, was given no time to work.

The Norwegian campaign, indeed the whole Scandinavian episode, was, in terms of the overall history of the Second World War, no more than a sideshow of little long-term strategic significance. It is important, however, not just as an illustration of British military incompetence (which was also to be illustrated later in 1940), but as the precursor of the political crisis that was to bring Churchill, despite his major role in the Norwegian failure, to power in early May. By late April the government's future was clearly at stake as the political row over Norway developed. Many in the government were trying to lay the blame for the Norwegian fiasco on Churchill personally, since he had after all taken a number of the key decisions. 'Chips' Channon reported on 25 April that Chamberlain's parliamentary private secretary, Lord Dunglass (later Sir Alec Douglas-Home), was wondering whether 'Winston should be deflated' and at the end of the month Harold Nicolson noted: 'The Whips are putting it about that it is all the fault of Winston who has made another forlorn failure.'[15] Aware of this threat, Churchill was manoeuvring for his own future and kept in close touch with senior members of the opposition parties: Attlee and Alexander (Labour) and Sinclair (Liberal). These contacts did not go unnoticed, as Channon wrote in his diary on 25 April; 'Winston, it seems, has had secret conversations and meetings with Archie Sinclair, A. V. Alexander and Mr Attlee and they are drawing up an alternative Government.'[16] And six days later: 'Tonight Churchill sat joking and drinking in the smoking room, surrounded by A. V. Alexander and Archie Sinclair, the new Shadow Cabinet.'[17]

Many of his political colleagues and senior figures in Whitehall had doubts as to whether Churchill ought to be Prime Minister. In the autumn of 1939 Anthony Eden's former private secretary wrote that 'AE is beginning to doubt whether Churchill could ever be P.M. so bad is his judgement.'[18] Sir Alexander Cadogan, the head of the Foreign Office, thought that Churchill was 'useless'.[19] Lord Hankey, former secretary to the cabinet and now a member of the war cabinet, who had watched Churchill's performance in the First World War from close quarters, echoed the doubts about his leadership qualities when he described Churchill as 'a dictator whose past achievements, though inspired by a certain amount of imagination, have never achieved success'.[20] The search for alternative candidates became increasingly desperate. In the House of Commons the rumours at the beginning of May centred on the formidable leader from the First World War, as Nicolson noted: 'People are so distressed by the whole thing that they are talking of Lloyd George as a possible P.M. Eden is out of it. Churchill is undermined by the Conservative caucus. Halifax is believed (and with justice) to be a tired man.'[21]

The political crisis, stemming from the failure in Norway and what was widely perceived to be inadequate direction of the war, arrived in the first week of May with a two-day debate in the Commons. When the crisis began, its outcome was unclear, there being no consensus about whether the Chamberlain government could, or should, be brought to an end, or about what to put in its place. When the crisis was resolved the consequences were profound. A new regime was put in power that lasted for the rest of the war and shaped the future of British politics for decades after 1945.

4

The New Regime

The outbreak of war ended neither political manoeuvring nor the personal ambitions of individual politicians. Indeed in many respects the war intensified these struggles and produced new issues for politicians to exploit as they sought to gain advantage. The political crisis brought on by the government's inept handling of the Norwegian campaign had to be resolved within a pre-war political structure reflecting the long Conservative dominance after the collapse of the wartime coalition government in 1922. In the following eighteen years there were only two short-lived, minority Labour governments and the second of those had collapsed in 1931 when it failed to agree on the cuts in social spending demanded by the international financial community in return for supporting the pound. From 1931, Britain was ruled by a coalition government, led at first by the ex-Labour Prime Minister Ramsay MacDonald, but in practice under Conservative control. MacDonald had been replaced by the Conservative leader Stanley Baldwin in 1935, then, on Baldwin's retirement in 1937, by Neville Chamberlain. Both the Labour and Liberal Parties were badly split in 1931, with small 'national' Labour and Liberal representatives in the coalition government but the majority staying in opposition. The national government had been overwhelmingly re-elected in 1935, winning 432 seats, and although the Labour Party recovered from its near annihilation in 1931, it had only 154 MPs and the independent Liberals fewer than twenty. The government remained highly popular and, if war had not intervened, there seemed no reason why Neville Chamberlain and the national government would not have been easily re-elected again in the election due in 1940.

On the outbreak of war Labour made it clear that while they would support the war effort they were not prepared to enter a government run by Chamberlain, partly because of his poorly disguised contempt for the opposition. The Liberals rejected the offer of a post of cabinet rank but outside the war cabinet. Five days after war was declared the parties agreed to allow the sitting party an uncontested run at any by-elections, but there was no general political truce. This overall situation suited Chamberlain, given his twin determination to avoid an all-out war if at all possible and instead topple Hitler mainly by economic pressure. If these tactics were successful in a relatively short time, as the intelligence experts predicted, then a restructuring of British politics could be avoided and Conservative dominance, and Chamberlain's own future, would be assured. The main risk from Chamberlain's point of view was that a quick and relatively painless victory would prove impossible and full-scale mobilization of the nation's industry and manpower would be necessary. In view of the complexity of that task and the need for widespread consent in order to implement it effectively, a national coalition embracing all political groups would probably be required and Chamberlain might not survive such fundamental political changes. The political problems brought on by total war had had a similar effect on the Liberal government in the First World War when, after six months, it had been obliged in March 1915 to bring the opposition Conservatives into the government.

During the six months after September 1939, in the absence of any similar crisis of political confidence, there was little that the opposition parties could do but await developments. The Liberals were largely irrelevant as a political force but would have to be included if a truly national coalition were to be constructed. The Labour Party agreed to contacts between ministers and their opposition spokesmen, but reserved their right to offer constructive criticism on the conduct of the war. They had been in contact with the small group of Conservatives who dissented from the government's foreign policy, particularly after Munich, but without large-scale dissatisfaction on the Conservative backbenches there was no way that Labour could bring down the government. One of the major problems facing the Labour Party was that its leadership seemed weak and ineffective. The parliamentary party had selected Clement Attlee as leader before the 1935 election but he was widely regarded as a stop-gap, the only choice available from the fifty or so MPs who survived the 1931 election disaster.

With a majority of over 200 and a weak opposition, Chamberlain could be brought down only by a revolt within his own party, and at the start of the war his domination of that party was almost total. He had been the undisputed successor to Baldwin in 1937 and the party had, with the exception of only a few insignificant backbenchers, enthusiastically supported his policy for the next two and a half years. By 1939 he had no obvious rivals. Anthony Eden had lost his chance of an early succession with his resignation in 1938; Sir Thomas Inskip had been a failure as the minister co-ordinating the defence effort; and Sir Samuel Hoare did not recover from his failure as Foreign Secretary. The only other possibility was Lord Halifax, but he seemed to be excluded by virtue of his peerage. Chamberlain himself had a strong sense of mission and of his fitness for the job. In March 1939 he wrote to his sister Ida: 'Like Chatham I know that I can save this country and I do not believe that anyone else can ... Barring accidents ... I ought to be good for at least one more Parliament after this.'[1]

The outbreak of war changed this calculation in one important respect: the weight of public expectation forced him to find a place in the war cabinet for Churchill, whose opposition to the government's foreign policy and advocacy of rearmament appeared to be vindicated by events. Until 1939 Churchill's long political career had been dogged by persistent failures. His rapid rise through the Liberal government before the First World War had ended in resignation following the fiasco at the Dardanelles and Gallipoli. Although rescued from the backbenches by his old friend Lloyd George, he had been only a relatively minor figure in the coalition government until 1922. As Chancellor of the Exchequer under Baldwin from 1924–29 his decision to restore sterling to the gold standard at its pre-1914 rate had been largely responsible for the disastrous state of the British economy. Since 1929 he had been out of office. He was widely regarded as being on the far right of the Conservative Party with his anti-Bolshevik, pro-Mussolini views and his total opposition to the government's decision to introduce a form of limited self-rule in India. His judgement was thought to be erratic and impulsive, a view stemming from his poor direction of the operations against Turkey, reinforced by his support for Edward VIII in the abdication crisis. He was also distrusted for being the only politician successfully to have changed political parties twice (he had been elected as a Conservative, joined the Liberals over free trade, deserted them when they collapsed after 1918 and returned to the Conservative fold). Baldwin, when Prime Minister in the 1930s, described him as 'a military adventurer who would sell his sword to anyone'.[2]

Churchill's exclusion from office in the 1930s was largely self-inflicted, although whenever a vacancy in the defence area occurred – First Lord of the Admiralty in 1935, then Minister for Defence Co-ordination and finally Minister of Supply in 1939 – he hoped for a recall. The Conservative establishment, however, saw no reason to saddle themselves with such a disruptive and difficult influence when there was no particular necessity to do so. Isolated within his own party, Churchill had few supporters among the backbenchers or the opposition. In 1936 he sought to make common cause with elements from the Labour and Liberal Parties who also dissented from the government's foreign policy, but Chamberlain's success in avoiding war at Munich left him, as one of the few opponents of the deal, politically isolated. Attlee kept his distance, as did Eden, and Churchill was left with the support of only a few maverick backbench MPs such as Harold Macmillan and Bob Boothby plus the imperialist hardliners Leo Amery and Lord Lloyd, together with his old cronies such as Brendan Bracken. His opposition to Munich brought major problems with his constituency party and for much of 1939 he took little part in politics, preferring to finish his *History of the English-speaking Peoples*. Nevertheless, like Eden and other dissidents such as Duff Cooper, he made it clear to Chamberlain that he was keen to join the government.

Churchill's return to office as First Lord of the Admiralty in September 1939 was clearly his last chance to salvage his political career and he was determined to use the opportunity to get to the top. Two things worked in his favour. First, the vacuum at the top around Chamberlain meant that Churchill was rapidly established as an alternative Prime Minister, although he remained widely distrusted within Whitehall and the political establishment. Nevertheless, Churchill still had a long way to go to oust Chamberlain, who remained highly popular with the public. An opinion poll at the end of 1939 showed that over fifty per cent wanted Chamberlain as Prime Minister compared with less than a third for

Churchill, and in April 1940 nearly sixty per cent still approved Chamberlain's performance as Prime Minister. Second, Churchill was fortunate in being put in political charge of the Royal Navy. With no action on the western front and the air force reduced to dropping leaflets over Germany, he was the one minister able to report action, including such spectacular battles as the attack on the *Graf Spee* in the south Atlantic. Churchill had a flair for publicity and always insisted that he should personally announce any good news. He was also prepared to go further and give out inflated claims to improve his own standing. For example, on 20 January 1940 he declared that half of the German U-boat fleet had already been destroyed, whereas official Admiralty figures put this at a maximum of nine out of sixty-six. A month later he was claiming forty-five submarines, or over two-thirds of the force, destroyed.

The Norwegian campaign provided an opportunity for Churchill to advance his drive to the premiership, but it was one that needed to be handled carefully. Many Conservative loyalists were trying to lay the blame on him, with some justification, and he needed to ensure that he was not made the scapegoat. His contacts with the opposition parties, which were well developed by the end of April, had to be discreet to avoid accusations of disloyalty to his own government and Prime Minister. Churchill navigated this minefield with skill, aided throughout by the growing discontent among parliamentarians about the conduct of the war and by their increasing desire for a more determined leadership. Earlier in the war a 'watching committee' of peers and MPs, under the chairmanship of a pillar of the Conservative establishment – Lord Salisbury – had been set up and Churchill was in touch with Salisbury during the last ten days of April. He was also discussing the construction of a possible national coalition with his old friend Archie Sinclair, the leader of the Liberals, and with prominent Labour leaders.

Discontent with the government came to a head in a two-day Commons debate on Norway on 7–8 May. The Labour Party did not expect to bring down the government, and although there was discontent on the Conservative backbenches it was still inchoate and undecided about its objectives. There was a growing feeling that some changes in the direction of the war were required but no overwhelming desire either to make Churchill Prime Minister or to bring Labour into a national coalition. At the start Chamberlain believed he could remain as Prime Minister. As he left to open the debate he told one of the staff at No. 10, 'I am quite confident we shall get away with it.'[3] He expected his majority to fall, but his parliamentary private secretary, Lord Dunglass, told Rab Butler that Chamberlain would carry on as long as the majority was above sixty. The debate on the first day included poor speeches from Chamberlain and Attlee, but was enlivened by a contribution from Admiral Keyes – an old friend of Churchill who appeared in full dress uniform to criticize the Trondheim operation – and a powerful speech from Leo Amery, who quoted Cromwell's words to the Rump Parliament: 'You have sat too long for any good you have been doing. Depart, I say, and let us have done with you. In the name of God, go!'

By the morning of the second day of the debate the mood of optimism at No. 10 had changed to despondency. The political crisis dominated everything: as one of the private secretaries wrote, 'Everybody is concentrating their energies on an internal crisis instead of taking thought for the morrow about Hitler's next move.'[4] Witnessing the rising Conservative discontent with Chamberlain, the Labour Party had to decide whether to risk turning the debate into a vote of no confidence in the government. A senior member of the party, Hugh Dalton, told Butler, who passed the message to Halifax, that Labour would not join a government that included Chamberlain, Hoare and Simon, whom they regarded as the arch-appeasers. The 'watching committee' met that morning but was reluctant to suggest a vote against the government. At the start of the second day's debate Morrison announced the decision to force a vote of confidence. Chamberlain made the tactical mistake of saying that he 'still had friends in this House', thereby turning it into a personal vote of confidence. In a determined effort to buy off the Conservative rebels he offered concessions and used the threat of Labour participation in a coalition to stop them voting against the government. Chamberlain told Leo Amery that he could have any job he liked in the government (apart from Prime Minister) if the rebels backed down. Lord Dunglass told rebel Conservative MPs that Chamberlain was also willing to abandon his friends and sack Hoare and Simon if they would support the government. After a final speech from Churchill defending the government's handling of the Nor-

wegian campaign, the vote was taken. The government won by
281 votes to 200. Over three-quarters of Conservative MPs had
loyally supported Chamberlain. Forty-one had voted against and
about fifty had abstained, reducing the government's majority,
normally over 200, to eighty-one.

Chamberlain rapidly accepted that he could not continue, but it
took two days to resolve the question of who would replace him,
and not until the evening of 10 May did Churchill become Prime
Minister. He achieved his ambition, according to A. J. P. Taylor,
'by calling in the people against the men at the top'.[5] In fact the
people had nothing to do with the decision. It was the result of
manoeuvring and high politics that would not have been out of
place in a mid-nineteenth-century cabinet. The only alternatives
to Chamberlain were Halifax and Churchill. Halifax's peerage
was no longer an obstacle, since it was accepted by the political
establishment that because of the war he would be allowed to sit
in the Commons. Halifax was favoured by the overwhelming
majority of those at the top of political life, including King George
VI, Chamberlain, Margesson (the Conservative chief whip who
reflected the views of the party in the Commons), most of the
cabinet and, on the Labour side, Dalton, Attlee and Morrison.
Apart from Churchill, about the only person who did not want
Halifax as Prime Minister was Halifax. In the end it was only his
refusal to serve that allowed Churchill to become Prime Minister.

On the morning of Thursday 9 May, the day after the House of
Commons vote, Sir Alexander Cadogan noted that Halifax was
'very gloomy – thinks P.M. will go and fears he (H.) may be asked
to take over'.[6] Chamberlain spent the morning trying unsuccess-
fully to persuade Halifax to become Prime Minister. Churchill
lunched with Eden and Kingsley Wood. The latter had been a
Chamberlain loyalist since his early career as a junior minister
under him at the Ministry of Health in the 1920s. Now he changed
sides and offered Churchill advice on how to play his hand. He
told him Chamberlain wanted Halifax as his successor and that
he intended to ask Churchill to serve under Halifax. If Churchill
agreed, then the pressure on Halifax to accept office would be
overwhelming. Wood therefore advised Churchill not to answer
Chamberlain's question about serving under Halifax and let the
latter's reluctance be the determining factor. The crucial meeting
between Chamberlain, Halifax, Churchill and Margesson took

place at No. 10 at 4.30 p.m. The Prime Minister said he would try and get Labour to serve in a national coalition under him, and if they refused, as he expected, he would then resign. The vital question of who should try to form a national government if Chamberlain failed then had to be answered. In his war memoirs Churchill gives a dramatic account of how he remained silent for a couple of minutes and won the succession. But that version was written six years after the event and Halifax's contemporary account is more reliable. According to Halifax, Chamberlain suggested he should try but Halifax was worried about not being in effective control of military operations (no doubt convinced that Churchill would insist on a dominant role), saying: 'I should speedily become a more or less honorary Prime Minister.'[7] Churchill did not demur from this judgement and Halifax went on to argue that he did not want the job and anyway was the wrong man. His diary concluded: 'The P.M. reluctantly, and Winston evidently with much less reluctance, finished by accepting my view.'[8]

At 6.30 p.m. the leader of the Labour Party, Clement Attlee, and his deputy Arthur Greenwood, were called to No. 10 to see Chamberlain, Halifax and Churchill. Chamberlain first asked them whether they would join a national government under him. Attlee, who earlier in the day had to be persuaded by Greenwood and the Liberal MP Clement Davies not to agree to serve under Chamberlain if Hoare and Simon were sacked, refused. Chamberlain then asked whether they would join under a different Prime Minister. Attlee said he thought the answer was yes but that it would be necessary to consult the National Executive Committee of the party at Bournemouth the next day (where they were meeting for the Labour Party conference over the Whitsun weekend). At no time were the Labour leaders given any say in the choice between Churchill and Halifax. That evening over dinner with Sinclair, Eden and his two closest advisers – Brendan Bracken and Professor Lindemann – Churchill began to allocate jobs in the government he expected shortly to be forming.

Early on the morning of Friday 10 May the Germans attacked Belgium, the Netherlands, Luxemburg and France. Chamberlain's first reaction was that he was now saved. He wrote to Lord Beaverbrook: 'We cannot consider changes in the government while we are in the throes of battle.'[9] His closest supporters,

Hoare and Hankey, took the same view and even an opponent, Sinclair, issued a press statement agreeing that changes should not be made. It was Chamberlain's lapsed protégé, Kingsley Wood, who argued that the military crisis only made it more imperative for him to resign immediately. For most of the day nothing was resolved. Lord Dunglass tried to persuade Butler to use his influence to get Halifax to reconsider, but without result. There were two meetings of the cabinet and two of the co-ordination committee to direct operations. It was late in the afternoon that a message was received at No. 10 from a phone box in Bournemouth that Labour would not serve under Chamberlain but would be willing to serve under someone else. Chamberlain immediately went to the Palace to tender his resignation and to convince the reluctant King that there was no alternative but to send for Churchill.

Early in the evening, on his return from the Palace, Churchill wrote to Chamberlain offering him the posts of Lord President of the Council and Leader of the House of Commons. Halifax was also asked to stay on at the Foreign Office. Churchill later met Attlee and Greenwood on their return from Bournemouth and offered them posts in the war cabinet alongside Chamberlain and Halifax. However, they strongly objected to Chamberlain as leader of the Commons, arguing he was unacceptable to Labour back-benchers. Churchill was forced to back down and withdrew his earlier offer. That same evening Churchill was also able to tell the King the names of the new ministers for the service departments. The three departments were carefully divided between the parties, with Alexander (Labour) at the Admiralty, Eden (Conservative) at the War Office and Sinclair (Liberal) at the Air Ministry. These jobs were no longer to be in the war cabinet. Earlier in the year Churchill had argued that it was essential that they should be members, a judgement that may have been influenced by the fact that he held one of the posts at that time.

For the next three days – as the Germans advanced across Holland and Belgium – the attention of the politicians and bureau-crats in Whitehall was concentrated almost entirely on the com-position of the new government. One former member of the war cabinet, Lord Hankey, found this neglect of the worsening military situation deplorable. He wrote to Hoare on 12 May: 'I found complete chaos this morning. No one was gripping the war in its crisis. The Dictator, instead of dictating, was engaged in a sordid wrangle with the politicians of the left about the secondary offices. NC [Chamberlain] was in a state of despair about it all.'[10]

The first step that Churchill took in constructing the government was to resolve the long-standing problem over the political direction of military operations by making himself Minister of Defence. His powers were carefully undefined, but he chaired a new defence committee and informal meetings with the chiefs of staff and issued instructions through General Ismay, who was also a member of the chiefs of staff committee. Increasingly the war cabinet delegated their authority to Churchill and left him in undisputed political control of operations. In addition Chamberlain, Halifax and other members of the old government stayed in office. Simon was moved from the Treasury to Lord Chancellor. The new Chancellor of the Exchequer, Kingsley Wood, was duly rewarded for changing sides and supporting Churchill. Of the three former non-politicians, Sir John Anderson stayed as Home Secretary, Lord Hankey left the war cabinet but stayed on as Chancellor of the Duchy of Lancaster to oversee co-ordination of the secret services, and Lord Chatfield was sacked. Lord Reith, the former Director-general of the BBC whom Churchill hated for keeping him off the radio in the 1930s, was moved from Information to Transport. Sir Samuel Hoare was sacked (and sent to the embassy in Madrid), while Oliver Stanley resigned rather than move to the Dominions Office.

Churchill was able to give jobs to most of his old supporters in the Conservative Party, but none, apart from Eden who had rejoined the government in 1939, had posts of any consequence. Leo Amery was made Secretary of State for India, Lord Lloyd was put in charge of the Colonial Office and Duff Cooper was sent to Information. The others – Bob Boothby, Harold Macmillan and Harold Nicolson – became junior ministers. Lord Beaverbrook was given the task of setting up the new Ministry of Aircraft Production, which was separated from the Air Ministry. Attlee and Greenwood were given non-departmental posts in the war cabinet, but otherwise the Labour Party obtained only four jobs of any consequence: Alexander went to the Admiralty; Ernie Bevin, the leader of the Transport and General Workers Union, became Minister of Labour to direct the mobilization of the workforce; Hugh Dalton was made Minister for Economic Warfare and Herbert Morrison, after a great deal of hesitation, became Minister of Supply. Morrison decided against leading the opposition to the government in the Commons, a task that fell by default to Manny Shinwell, who refused the offer of Minister of Food.

Like other Prime Ministers, Churchill rapidly moved his personal staff into No. 10. Sir Horace Wilson, Chamberlain's éminence grise, was given a couple of hours to move out, although he remained head of the Treasury and the civil service. In his place came Professor Lindemann, Churchill's confidant for many years, and Brendan Bracken, his parliamentary private secretary who became his adviser on patronage and honours. Desmond Morton, head of the industrial intelligence centre which produced the misleading assessments of the state of the German economy and the source of leaks of top-secret information to Churchill in the 1930s, was made intelligence adviser. Churchill was also able to look after his family. His son-in-law, Duncan Sandys MP, was brought into the Ministry of Defence to take charge of home defence, his brother Jack often accompanied him on official visits and his troublesome son Randolph, who had stood as an anti-Conservative candidate in the 1930s, was finally found a seat, in October, as Conservative MP for Preston.

Perhaps the most remarkable feature of the new Churchill government was the small amount of change introduced. Apart from the Ministry of Defence and the new Ministry of Aircraft Production, the structure of Whitehall and the machinery of government remained unchanged. The civil service carried on as before, as did the military chiefs. The net result was no more than a reshuffle of the pack of politicians and the arrival of a few new faces. Overall the government remained intensely Conservative, reflecting the balance in the old House of Commons rather than a coalition of national forces. Apart from two seats in the war cabinet, the Labour Party had achieved little and the Liberals accepted what they had rejected when it was offered by Chamberlain in 1939: a job outside the war cabinet. In the new government the Conservatives held fifty-two posts, Labour sixteen and the Liberals three. The Labour Party also failed to secure its main objective: the removal of the men who had previously directed British policy. Chamberlain, Halifax and Simon stayed in office, and the first two remained crucial influences within the new government.

The new government was greeted with something less than enthusiasm. Subsequent mythology has disguised the fact that Churchill was not chosen as Prime Minister in order to save the country. The choice was made before the German attack began, and nobody expected that within three weeks the British army would retreat, defeated, from the continent and that within six weeks the French would be out of the war. Churchill became Prime Minister because of discontent over the Norwegian campaign and because Halifax refused to take the job. Many in the Conservative Party were immediately hostile to the new regime. Chips Channon described 10 May as 'perhaps the darkest day in English history',[11] and that evening joined the stalwarts of the old Chamberlain regime, Lord Dunglass, Rab Butler and Jock Colville (Chamberlain's private secretary), at the Foreign Office to drink, in champagne, the toast of 'the king over the water'. On that occasion Butler, a scion of the Conservative establishment who had earlier described Churchill's war speeches as 'beyond words vulgar',[12] furiously denounced Churchill, declaring that 'the good clean tradition of English politics ... had been sold to the greatest adventurer in modern political history ... a half-breed American'.[13] Halifax too was unhappy about Churchill and his entourage, as Butler recorded in a conversation with him on 14 May: ' "It's all a great pity, isn't it?" I replied, "That is because you did not take the Premiership yourself." He said, "You know my reasons, it's no use discussing that – but the gangsters will shortly be in complete control." '[14] Opinion abroad was not generally favourable either. President Roosevelt was unimpressed; he had disliked Churchill because of his rudeness on the only occasion they had met, just after the First World War. He remarked to his cabinet, 'Apparently Churchill is very unreliable when under the influence of drink. I suppose that he is too old.'[15]

Conservative backbenchers soon repented of their hasty decision to revolt against Chamberlain, as Hely-Hutchinson, the chairman of the backbench 1922 Committee, told Butler on 13 May: 'You must not underestimate the great reaction which has been caused among Conservative members, among whom you will find over three-quarters who are ready to put Chamberlain back.'[16] When Churchill made his first appearance in the House of Commons as Prime Minister on 13 May (the occasion of his 'blood, toil, tears and sweat' speech) Channon described the scene:

He [Churchill] went into the Chamber and was greeted with some cheers but when, a moment later, Neville entered with his usual shy retiring little manner, MPs lost their heads; they shouted; they cheered; they waved their Order Papers, and his reception was a regular ovation. The new PM spoke well, even dramatically . . . but he was not well received.[17]

Churchill's cold reception continued at every appearance in the Commons, including his famous speech on 4 June ('we shall fight on the beaches') until he had been in office for nearly two months. Then, after journalists in the lobby complained to Chamberlain that the hostility shown to Churchill was having a bad effect abroad, the chief whip, Margesson, forced backbench MPs to their feet to cheer Churchill on 4 July when he announced the British attack on the French fleet at Oran. But the private views of many Conservative MPs remained unchanged. As late as the end of September, after the fiasco at Dakar, Channon reported that 'feeling at the Carlton Club is running high against him [Churchill]'.[18]

Churchill's political position remained weak until the autumn of 1940, particularly in the period before July 1940, when it was still not finally decided whether Britain would fight on alone. Within the war cabinet he could not rely on the automatic support of Chamberlain and Halifax and instead depended on Attlee and Greenwood and, on one crucial occasion, on Sinclair, the Liberal leader who was not in the war cabinet. The primary cause of this weakness was the fact that Chamberlain remained leader of the Conservative Party and many regarded Churchill as no more than a temporary expedient who could be disposed of after the war in the same way as Lloyd George had been in 1922. The day after Churchill's appointment as Prime Minister, Lord Davidson, a former stalwart of the party, wrote to Stanley Baldwin to tell him that 'the Tories don't trust Winston . . . After the first clash of war is over it may well be that a sounder government may emerge.'[19] Although he had been displaced, Chamberlain did not give up hope of becoming Prime Minister again until after his operation for cancer in August. He then wrote in his diary of the need 'to adjust myself to the new life of a partially crippled man, which is what I am. Any ideas of another Premiership after the war have gone. I know that is out of the question.'[20] It was not until Chamberlain's death in October that Churchill became leader of the party. This, together with his popularity in the country, ensured his political future.

From the start Churchill realized that he did not have substantial endorsement within the Conservative Party and that he depended on the support of the backbenchers, most of whom had been strongly behind Chamberlain for years, if he was to continue in office. Churchill remained grateful to Chamberlain for the ex-Prime Minister's magnanimous attitude in agreeing to serve under him, in stark contrast to Asquith in 1916 when he was replaced by Lloyd George. Chamberlain, until his illness, played a crucial part in the government as one of Churchill's most trusted advisers and he, rather than Attlee, was the real Deputy Prime Minister. It was this need to appease the broad mass of the Conservative Party that led Churchill to keep Halifax at the Foreign Office, give Simon a job in the government and retain the large number of ministers inherited from Chamberlain. When, after Dunkirk, the press turned on the supposedly 'guilty men' responsible for the British defeat and demanded the sacking of the old ministers, particularly Chamberlain, Churchill told the press that he would not agree and that they must call off the campaign. Similarly, when he was considering whether or not to include Lloyd George in the government, he consulted Chamberlain first (the two were mortal enemies from the First World War, when Lloyd George had sacked Chamberlain for failing as director of conscription) and, when Chamberlain offered to go to allow Lloyd George in, Churchill preferred to stick with his trusted colleague. It was not until late in 1940 that the new Prime Minister felt strong enough to begin the reshaping of his government.

The first move came in August with the inclusion of Churchill's trusted adviser, Beaverbrook, in the war cabinet. Chamberlain's resignation at the end of September, when he knew that his cancer was fatal, seemed to be a suitable moment to start making changes in key posts. Churchill wanted Eden to go the Foreign Office and asked Halifax to move to Chamberlain's job as Lord President of the Council. The reluctant Halifax enlisted Chamberlain's help and the latter told Churchill that 'the change at the Foreign Office would be taken to mean a change of policy and a condemnation of my policy'.[21] Churchill did not feel strong enough to override the former Prime Minister's veto and Halifax stayed in the post. Instead, Sir John Anderson took over Chamberlain's old job and the responsibility for co-ordinating policy on the home front. His move from the Home Office was essential following the chaotic and inadequate civil defence planning for the Blitz on London and Londoners' evident lack of confidence in those direct-ing the emergency response. He was replaced by Herbert Morrison, who did have the confidence of the capital's population. The only other changes were the promotion of Kingsley Wood to the war cabinet (as further recognition of his crucial help to Churchill on 9–10 May) and, by way of political balance for that appointment, the inclusion of Ernie Bevin.

The chance for further changes came with the unexpected death of Lord Lothian, the ambassador in Washington, on 12 December. British survival depended on American help and the new ambassador could have a vital role to play in securing that assistance. Churchill, however, was mainly concerned to seize the opportunity to remove one of his main rivals from the political scene. His first choice for the Washington job was Lloyd George. Although out of office for almost twenty years, Lloyd George had not lost his political ambition and in 1940 would have been the almost certain choice as Prime Minister if Churchill had failed and peace with Germany became inevitable. As the acclaimed leader from the First World War, he could have played the role of Marshal Pétain in Britain and tried to rally the nation in defeat. He had been pessimistic from the start about the possibility of victory. Early in 1940 he talked to Cecil King of the *Daily Mirror* about 'this damn crazy war',[22] in which he did not expect either side to achieve victory after a long-drawn-out conflict. He prefer-red to keep his freedom of action rather than join Churchill's government. King reported, after a conversation with him on 15 May, that '[he] expects that Churchill will get into a mess and that he, the victor of the last war, will be called in too late and will have no alternative but to sue for peace'.[23] Lloyd George was convinced that his strategy of waiting in the wings would be successful in the long term. After the fall of France he wrote a private memorandum on the situation facing Britain, drawing comparisons with the First World War. Then it had taken four years, a war on two fronts and massive casualties to defeat Germany. Now France was out of the war, there was no western front and the Soviet Union was neutral. This time round, he did not expect any substantial American help and did not see how Britain could, on its own, reinvade the continent and defeat Germany. He therefore advocated a compromise peace in the near future, before Britain was crippled by the war effort.[24] He saw that his best chance lay in doing nothing until he was called in to save the country. As he told his secretary at the beginning of October, 'I shall wait until Winston is bust.'[25]

Churchill was aware of this lurking threat to his position. At the end of May Chamberlain recorded him as saying that he 'did not trust Lloyd George and did not know whether he might not be a defeatist'.[26] Early in June, with France about to go out of the war, Chamberlain withdrew his veto on Lloyd George's participation in the government, but the latter then asked for time to think about whether or not he wanted to join. By 18 June, the day after the French request for an armistice, and with no reply from Lloyd George, Chamberlain remarked to Churchill, 'Perhaps he is waiting to be the Marshal Pétain of Britain' and received the reply: 'Yes, he might, but there won't be any opportunity.'[27] With Lloyd George still waiting for his opportunity, the death of Lothian provided an ideal excuse for Churchill to remove him as a threat. Churchill asked Roosevelt if the choice was acceptable, but on the day the President concurred Lloyd George turned down the offer, ostensibly on the advice of his doctor. A more likely explanation, with Britain's future prospects still grim and no hope of final victory visible, was that Lloyd George felt that his hour might still come.

Following Lloyd George's refusal, Churchill had to consider other possibilities. Within a couple of days he decided to carry out the plan he had failed to implement in the autumn. This time Halifax did not have Chamberlain to protect him and Churchill was keen to remove another critic of his policy of continuing to fight. He tried to dress up the move as a new start, arguing, as he told his private secretary, that Halifax

would never live down his reputation for appeasement which he and the Foreign Office had won themselves here. He had no future in this country. On the other hand he had a glorious opportunity in America, for, unless the United States came into the war, we could not win, or at least we could not win a really satisfactory peace.[28]

When Halifax and his wife saw Churchill in an abortive attempt to talk him out of the move, they recognized the Prime Minister's real motives. As Cadogan wrote: 'They had found it useless ... had realized P.M.'s object really was to get rid of H.' And three days later he found Halifax 'resigned ... and rather resentful'.[29] With Halifax out of the way, Churchill was at last able to move Eden back to his old job at the Foreign Office. According to Eden, he was told that 'the succession must be his' and that the Prime Minister would 'not make Lloyd George's mistake of carrying on after the war'.[30] Others were much less impressed by Eden's potential and more suspicious about the reasons Churchill wanted him at the Foreign Office rather than the more independently minded Halifax. Harry Hopkins, Roosevelt's personal envoy to Britain at the beginning of 1941, wrote disparagingly of the Foreign Secretary: 'I am sure the man has no deeply rooted moral stamina ... I fancy Churchill gives him high office because he neither thinks, acts – much less say[s] – anything of import-ance.'[31]

Not until the end of 1940 was Churchill's political future made secure. By then his main opponents, Chamberlain and Halifax, were out of the government and his position as national leader was firmly established. Appointed as the second best candidate in May, he had the role of national saviour thrust upon him later in the year. To many, particularly in the Conservative Party, he was, for much of 1940, no more than a disagreeable expedient to be dumped after the war. During the first two months of his govern-ment it was an open question as to whether Britain would make peace with Germany, and on at least two occasions the option was considered. Not until July was Churchill able to impose the policy of fighting on in the expectation that the United States would save Britain. If peace had had to be made in 1940, either as France fell, or as a result of an American failure to rescue the British from military and financial collapse, then Churchill would have gone down in history as no more than a short-term gallant failure. The margin of success was very narrow.

Although the actual changes to the government made in May 1940 were small, the repercussions of the formation of the new regime were to have profound consequences for British politics for decades to come in terms both of policy and of the fortunes of individual politicians. It meant the integration of the Labour

Party into the British political system. May 1940 marked the point when the political establishment finally accepted that the Labour Party played a vital part in the state and that their participation in government was essential for national survival. Until then they had been in office only for two short periods, both without an overall majority, and their split and collapse in 1931 seemed likely to rule them out of office for a generation to come. A Conservative victory in the election, which would have been held in 1940 if war had not intervened, seemed a foregone conclusion. However, the need to mobilize the country's resources, both material and human, and ensure the whole-hearted consent of the population meant that a full-scale war effort could not be made without Labour's participation in government. After all, nearly forty per cent of the country had voted for them in 1935. The creation of the coalition in May 1940 made this co-operation possible; its most powerful symbol was the appointment of Ernie Bevin, a leading member of the trade union movement, as Minister of Labour in charge of mobilizing the workforce for the national effort.

The fact that Labour shared power for five years after 1940 had important consequences for the government's policy. With Churchill immersed in the direction of the war and military strategy, Labour ministers were given considerable freedom on the home front to implement some of their ideas. This freedom, combined with the unprecedented levels of government intervention in the economic and social fields required by the war effort and the need to build a consensus within society about the positive results that would come in peace as a result of the wartime sacrifices, produced policies radically different from those of the pre-war Conservative government. The first signs of this were apparent very quickly in 1940. In June free milk for mothers and children under five was introduced, followed in July by free school meals. Bevin was also able to use his position to improve workplace conditions for employees. Later in the war, fundamentally new policies were being worked out: the commitment to full employment, the Beveridge proposals for social security and the idea of a National Health Service. These were to form the basis for the work of the post-war Labour government (although the first two ideas were both devised by Liberals). The sharing of power also had important consequences for the Labour Party itself, particularly in the fields of defence and foreign affairs. The assumptions of the wartime coalition – acceptance of the almost total dependence on the United States, the belief that Britain was still a great power and a strong ally of the Americans with a world-wide role to play – were to form the basis for the post-war bi-partisan foreign and defence policy. The 1945–51 Labour government made Britain a nuclear power, maintained military bases and alliances around the globe, helped create NATO and involve the US in the defence of Europe and agreed to the stationing of American forces in the UK in peacetime. All these policies were the direct result of their participation in the wartime coalition and as central to the post-war consensus as the agreement over important aspects of social and economic policy.

The coalition created in May 1940 was also crucial for the subsequent careers of both Labour and Conservative politicians. It secured Attlee's leadership of the Labour Party. In 1940 he still seemed the inadequate man chosen in 1935 only because better men were not in parliament. Had Labour lost the 1940 election, as seemed likely, Attlee probably would have lost the job. Instead he served as Deputy Prime Minister from 1940 to 1945 and was the only man, apart from Churchill, to sit in the war cabinet for the whole of that period. By 1945 he had emerged as a national figure and led the party for another ten years. Within the Conservative Party the events of 1940 revived Eden's career and started Macmillan's rise to the premiership. More important, without the war Churchill would not have been brought back into government and, without the Norwegian failure and Halifax's refusal, he would not have become Prime Minister. His wartime leadership gave him an unassailable position and despite his overwhelming rejection in the 1945 election he remained party leader. He regained power in 1951 and stayed as Prime Minister until his resignation in 1955. His fifteen years as leader and two periods as Prime Minister would have been unimaginable in 1939, when he was an erratic backbencher shunned by nearly all his colleagues.

5

Collapse

The German attack on the west which began on 10 May was the most brilliant and successful campaign in modern military history. Within five days the Allied front was smashed beyond repair. After another five days the Allied armies were split in two when the German army reached the Channel coast, and at the end of May the British army ignominiously withdrew from the continent. The Germans then turned on the remnants of the French army, and by the middle of June the campaign was over when the French asked for an armistice. This stunning victory inside six weeks cost the Germans 27,000 dead, fewer than those killed on some days in the First World War.

The military professionals, politicians and press, who had been expecting a long battle of attrition as in the First World War, popularized the idea of a revolutionary new form of warfare – *blitzkrieg* – to explain the Allied defeat and complete humiliation. This new concept, they argued, was based on a highly mobile, mechanized German army. Large concentrations of modern tanks were used to break through defences, followed by swift advances to exploit the resulting gaps and disrupt any attempt to mount counter-attacks. The German army, they believed, not only outnumbered the Allies but must have been equipped and organized to implement this new doctrine. In fact, the term *blitzkrieg* was not a German invention and the Germans did not believe they had developed a new type of military operation. The term (literally 'lightning war') was first used by a journalist on *Time* to describe the German campaign in Poland in September 1939. The rapid Polish defeat was the result not of some new form of warfare but of the immense problems facing Poland. The Polish army, with only 200 obsolescent tanks and equipment of First World War vintage, was deployed along the 3,000-mile German border (which had no defensible barriers) and also had to keep some troops in reserve to meet the expected stab in the back from the Soviet Union (which came in the middle of September). The Polish decision to use a thin linear defence all along the border then ensured their rapid defeat without the Germans needing to produce anything more than a competent campaign.

None of the Allied beliefs about the German army was in fact true. The army which achieved such an unexpected triumph in the early summer of 1940 was a badly equipped, ramshackle force and as reluctant as any other army to adopt new ideas. Under the Versailles treaty the German army was restricted to no more than 100,000 men. The rapid rearmament after 1935 brought it up to a mobilized strength of 103 divisions and three million men in 1939. Not surprisingly, this rate of expansion brought with it enormous problems in training and equipping the new army. It suffered from a lack of trained officers and NCOs. Its organization was highly conventional. Although in the inter-war years the German army contained its advocates of highly mobile armoured warfare such as Guderian, they were a minority like their opposite numbers in Britain (Fuller and Liddell-Hart) and the French army (de Gaulle). The Germans had, by 1939 – like the British and French – created small armoured contingents, but this did not involve a revolution in either tactics or strategy.

The German army which faced the Allies in 1940 was in a poor state. Only five per cent of its strength was in armoured Panzer divisions and ninety per cent of the tanks in those divisions were obsolete training models dating from the early 1930s or taken over from the Czech army in 1939. Only the modern Panzer Mark III and Mark IV matched Allied models and Germany produced just forty-five Mark IVs in the whole of 1939. Within the Panzer divisions only a fifth of the vehicles were tracked and therefore capable of keeping up with the tanks. And only four infantry divisions were motorized so that they could operate with the Panzer divisions. Truck production for the army was insufficient to replace normal peacetime wear and tear. Half the German army depended for transport on requisitioned civilian vehicles and the rest relied on 500,000 horses for mobility. (During the war the German army used 2.7 million horses – twice as many as in the First World War.) The standard rifle was based on an 1898 design, half the divisons had no machine pistols, light or heavy mortars and there were huge shortages of munitions: stocks in 1939 were seventy per cent below requirements and enough to last for about a month's fighting. The German army was also outnumbered. In May 1940 it had 135 divisions with 2.7 million men deployed against an Allied (French, Belgian, Dutch and British) force of 130 divisions and 3.7 million men. German tank numbers were inferior to the Allies' – 2,500 against 3,600 – as were the artillery – 7,700 against 11,500. The one area where the Germans were superior was in the air, where the Luftwaffe had greater numbers and the right aircraft and philosophy to operate in close support of the army.

The Germans were able to turn this dismal situation into a decisive victory largely through luck and some superb leadership on the battlefield. They were also fortunate in having being prevented by bad weather in the autumn and winter of 1939–40 from implementing an uninspired plan. At the end of September 1939, Hitler ordered planning for an attack in the west with the intention of carrying it out in November. The generals were strongly opposed to the timing, arguing that the army had not recovered from the Polish campaign. At the beginning of October there was only enough ammunition to supply a third of the army for fourteen days. Hitler was unimpressed by these arguments and it was only the bad weather throughout the autumn and winter that caused twenty-nine postponements until the Scandinavian operation put off the attack until May. The German operational plan for an attack in the autumn or winter would almost certainly not have produced a decisive outcome. It was an unimaginative, scaled-down version of the Schlieffen plan from the First World War: it envisaged an attack through Holland and Belgium to push the Allies out of the Low Countries and northern France. This, the Germans argued, would enable them to gain valuable airfields, but they had no expectations that the plan would lead to the immediate defeat of France. This was indeed exactly the attack the Allies expected and they were optimistic that they would be able to retreat, keeping their line intact, to re-establish a defensive position somewhere near the old First World War battlefields.

The endless delays, however, enabled the Germans to develop a brilliant plan that put their greatest strength at the point of greatest Allied weakness. On 10 January 1940 a German plane went off course in bad weather and landed near Mechelen in Belgium. The passenger, a German staff officer, tried to destroy the documents he was carrying but was stopped by the Belgian police. The documents turned out to be the German plan for the attack on the west. The neutral Belgians passed them discreetly to the British and French. Even though Hitler suspected that the plans were compromised, he stuck with the existing strategy for another week. It was only after yet another postponement due to bad weather that a rethink took place. Hitler had for some time contemplated the idea of moving the main German thrust through the hilly and wooded country of the Ardennes to attack the centre of the French defence at Sedan on the River Meuse, the scene of the decisive Prussian victory over the French in 1870. The German Army Group 'A', which was responsible for this sector of the front, had devised such a plan but had had problems in getting the planners in the army high command to take it seriously. By chance Hitler heard about the Army Group 'A' plan in the middle of February and decided to adopt the new approach. By the end of the month the radically different strategy had been adopted. Under the new plan about thirty German divisions would move through Belgium and Holland, hold the Allied armies and stop them disengaging. The main force of forty-five divisions, including seven Panzer divisions, would attack in the centre, focused on Sedan, and move across northern France to the Channel, cutting the Allied armies in two. The remaining units would be deployed opposite the Maginot Line from the Ardennes to the Swiss border to hold the French troops in their positions. This was a daring and imaginative plan, although the Germans did not expect it to produce quite such devastating results. Indeed the main German problem in May was how to keep their nerve and exploit the opportunities opened up as the Allies disintegrated.

The problem for Britain and France was how to devise an effective response to the German attack, which they expected to be launched through Holland and Belgium, when those two countries remained neutral but expected Allied help if they were attacked. The Belgians refused staff conversations so as not to antagonize the Germans but also because they did not expect any great help from the Allies. The British and French believed they had solved the problem, and met the French desire to fight as far away from northern France as possible by agreeing to advance into Belgium when the Germans attacked and fight as far forward as practicable. The problem was that there were no obvious defensive positions in Belgium where they could engage the advancing Germans. After considerable argument in the autumn of 1939, a plan was adopted for an advance to the River Dyle in the middle of Belgium. This strategy would have been an effective counter to the original German strategy, but with the revised attack on the centre of the Allied line it was a disaster. It aided the Germans by drawing Allied strength away from the crucial central sector and made it easier for them to surround the armies that advanced into Belgium. Even after the original German plans were discovered in January, the Allies did not change their strategy even though they must have guessed the Germans would be likely to make revisions. Throughout March and April there were increasing indications from air reconnaissance and from intelligence through Swiss sources that the weight of the German attack was shifting to the centre and away from the north, but the Allies stuck rigidly to their original ideas. The result was that only nine divisions, including three third-rate French divisions at the vital Sedan crossing, were left at the hinge of the Allied armies on the Meuse between the static Maginot Line defences and the armies that would advance into Belgium. These nine divisions were to face the full force of the German attack.

When the German attack began on 10 May, Holland was quickly overrun and the key Belgian defences were captured by glider-borne troops. The Allied armies advanced steadily and reached the River Dyle. But the crucial events were taking place behind them in the Ardennes, where the German Panzer columns were advancing to the Meuse. By 13 May the first German infantry units were across the river and then, backed up by massive air attacks, the tanks crossed the Meuse. Under this intense attack the poor-quality French defences disintegrated. On the evening of 15 May, the Germans were forty miles beyond Sedan and moving rapidly westwards as the French collapsed over a fifty-mile-wide front. The next morning the full scale of the disaster was apparent to the French government. The Prime Minister, Paul Reynaud, telephoned Churchill and told him: 'We have lost the battle.' A flabbergasted Churchill flew to Paris that afternoon to find that the French, expecting the Germans to advance directly on Paris, were already burning the secret papers of the Quai d'Orsay. He also found the French high command in a state of confusion that was to last for the next ten days and make it impossible to mount any effective counter-attack on the advancing Germans.

The Allied command system, based on that used in the later stages of the First World War, was slow and cumbersome, with divided responsibilities and too many levels. French military communications generally were poor: the overall command centre at Vincennes had no radios and relied on motor-cycle despatch riders who were soon overwhelmed by the vast tide of refugees on the roads. The system was suitable for dealing with slow-moving trench warfare but collapsed under the pressure of the fast-moving German attack. Other command problems stemmed from rivalries between the generals and their political supporters. General Gamelin, the overall commander, was supported by the War Minister Daladier but not by Reynaud, who had tried to sack him the day before the German attack began. Reynaud preferred Gamelin's deputy, Georges, but did not have the power to promote him. The military problem was that Gamelin had deployed most of the French army in the front line and had few reserves available to counter the German breakthrough. Not until 20 May was Gamelin sacked and replaced by Weygand (Foch's right-hand man in the crucial battles of 1918), who was now seventy-three and stationed in the Levant. Despite the crisis caused by the loss of fifteen divisions, with another forty-five almost surrounded in Belgium and a 100-mile gap opening up between the two forces, Weygand abandoned the plans Gamelin was formulating for a counter-attack and spent 20 May asleep after his flight from the Middle East. Then, on 21 May, he flew north to assess the situation but in the chaos produced by the retreating armies failed to meet the commanders on the spot. On 22 May Gamelin was back in Paris drawing up plans for a joint attack by the armies in the north and the south to try and isolate the German armour advancing across northern France. This plan was agreed by Reynaud and Churchill on 23 May but by then it was too late: the situation had deteriorated beyond the point at which Allied recovery was feasible and it proved impossible to co-ordinate the Allied armies to take joint action. Vital time had been lost and, with it, the battle.

If the Allies had been able to take rapid counter-measures the effects would have been devastating because of the exposed

German position. As it was, once the Panzers had broken through the French positions on the Meuse they had no opposition of any consequence in front of them as they advanced to the Channel. On some days they were able to move forward forty miles. The problem for the Germans was a lack of highly mobile infantry to consolidate the advance made by the tanks. They were therefore constantly worried that the Panzers would get too far ahead and be easily cut off by counter-thrusts from north and south of the gap between the Allied armies. Far from revelling in the 'new-style' warfare, Hitler and his generals remained deeply suspicious of the Panzer commanders on the ground for trying to move too quickly. On 17 May Hitler and the German high command ordered the first of a series of halts in order to consolidate. The advance was resumed on 18 May, when it reached Cambrai. Two days later, Amiens fell and the Allied armies in the north were cut off when the leading German tanks, travelling sixty miles in a day, reached the Channel coast at Abbeville. The next day, 21 May, showed what might have happened if the Allies had been able to co-ordinate their response. A scratch British force of two territorial battalions, seventy-four tanks and a motor-cycle battalion attacked the German advanced units near Arras. The Germans, believing they faced a massive Allied counter-attack of five divisions, panicked, and it took decisive action from Rommel to stabilize the situation. The Germans recovered quickly and on 22 May advanced another sixty miles in a day to reach the outskirts of Calais and Boulogne. Once again Hitler and the high command were worried by their success and the over-extended and highly vulnerable position it had created. On 24 May the Panzer divisions were again halted fifteen miles short of Dunkirk to allow the supporting troops to consolidate the position. The advance was not resumed until 26 May and then at a much slower pace while the weight of the German attack was shifted to the forces advancing on the surrounded Allied troops from the north.

The pre-war relationship between Britain and France had been far from happy and, although the cracks had been papered over, the stunning German success brought out all the latent hostility between the two countries. Until 1939 Britain had adopted a quasi-isolationist policy and concentrated on home defence and air rearmament. Only in the last week of the Czechoslovakian crisis in September 1938 had they reassured the French that they would fight alongside them in the event of a German attack. Only in the spring of 1939, under intense French pressure, had the British introduced conscription and begun slowly to build a full-scale army. Many French politicians distrusted and disliked the British. In February 1939 the Prime Minister, Daladier, told the US ambassador in Paris, William Bullitt, his real opinion of his allies:

> He considered Chamberlain a desiccated stick; the King a moron; and the Queen an excessively ambitious woman who would be ready to sacrifice every other country in the world in order that she might remain Queen Elizabeth of England ... he considered Eden a young idiot ... He felt England had become so feeble and senile that the British would give away every possession of their friends rather than stand up to Germany and Italy.[1]

By May 1940 the British contribution to the Allied forces was minuscule – just seven per cent of the total. The British Expeditionary Force (BEF) in northern France totalled nine divisions (less than the Dutch army and only forty per cent of the size of the Belgian) compared with the French army of eighty-eight divisions, raised from a population smaller than Britain's. The discrepancy confirmed long-standing French suspicions that Britain expected its allies to bear the brunt of the fighting and made for strained relations even before the events of May 1940. Under the pressure of war and the sudden prospect of defeat, conflicting national interests came rapidly to the fore. The French, quite naturally, regarded the battle in northern France as the decisive moment of the war and took the view that every effort should be made first to contain and then defeat the Germans. For the British this was not the crucial battle and they believed it was more important to preserve their forces so that they could continue the war on their own. During the last three weeks of May the inter-Allied conflicts centred on two key issues: the involvement of the RAF in the defence of France and the British evacuation of their forces from Dunkirk at the end of the month.

Air support in the land battle was crucial to its outcome. The Luftwaffe had established supremacy over the battlefield very quickly; the Dutch and Belgian air forces were wiped out on 10 May and after three days the RAF and the French air force had suffered fifty per cent losses, mainly caused by trying to use obsolete aircraft against modern fighters. Yet if the Allied ground operations were to have any chance of success in stopping the German tanks crossing the plains of northern France it was vital to wrest air supremacy from the Luftwaffe. The overwhelming majority of the RAF's modern fighters were based in Britain and the question was whether the government would commit enough of them to the battle over France to have some chance of defeating the Luftwaffe, or whether it would retain them to defend Britain. Their deliberations were complicated by the fact that the RAF constantly changed its advice about how many aircraft were needed to defend Britain, how many it actually had available and therefore how many it was safe to send to France. Even if this problem had been clarified the war cabinet showed that it was unable to adopt a consistent policy and instead shifted uneasily from one expedient to the next under conflicting pressure from the French and the RAF.

At the beginning of the battle on 10 May, the war cabinet decided to reduce the number of fighter aircraft moving to France. They agreed that only two RAF squadrons should go instead of the four earlier authorized to move on the outbreak of full-scale fighting. As the situation deteriorated, they tried to decide on their priorities. At a meeting of the war cabinet on 13 May the RAF argued that they had only thirty-nine squadrons available for home defence whereas they believed they needed sixty squadrons for defence against German air attacks launched from Germany. If the Germans flew from airfields in the Low Countries or France, the RAF argued, they would need even more squadrons. Churchill agreed that the available fighters must be retained for home defence and that 'it must not be thought that in any circumstances it would be possible to send large numbers of fighters to France'.[2] The next day Reynaud reported the German attack at Sedan and asked for ten more squadrons of fighters, but Churchill again told his colleagues that 'we should hesitate before we denuded still further the heart of the Empire'.[3] On 15 May, at a chiefs of staff meeting, Dowding argued that the existing thirty-nine squadrons would be adequate for home defence (a very different view from that expressed two days earlier) but if more were sent over the Channel 'they would not achieve decisive results in France, and he would be left too weak to carry on over here'.[4] Half an hour later the war cabinet met and agreed that 'no further fighter squadrons should for the present be sent to France'.[5]

The next day, 16 May, following Reynaud's dramatic early-morning telephone call to Churchill forecasting imminent Allied collapse and asking, once again, for ten extra fighter squadrons to try and save the battle, the war cabinet decided to change their earlier decision. Churchill wanted to send six squadrons but it was finally agreed to send four with preparations to send two more (though the French were not told of the latter possibility). When Churchill arrived in Paris that afternoon the different national interests were painfully apparent after less than a week of real war. Reynaud argued that this was the decisive battle into which every available resource had to be thrown: 'Britain's fate is being sealed in this salient ... Britain can't send over one more division to France ... because their men are not trained ... so let Britain at least send airplanes. London has to be defended right here.' For his part Churchill made it clear that in the last resort the British could manage without the French: 'As long as the British could hold command of the air over England and could control the seas of the world, they were confident of the ultimate results, and it would always be possible to carry on.'[6] The French, facing immediate conquest, were, not surprisingly, unmoved by Churchill's argument and rhetoric. In order to placate the rising French anger Churchill felt that he should consult his colleagues about changing the decision made that morning. He telephoned London and asked for another six squadrons (which would, with the squadrons sent that morning, meet the original French request for ten), adding that 'it would not be good historically if their requests were denied'. The war cabinet met at 11 p.m. but were not prepared to agree to Churchill's request or send even the two extra squadrons provisionally allocated that morning. They could agree only that all six asked for by Churchill should be 'available for operations in France' while still based in England.[7] Given the limited range of the Spitfires and Hurricanes, this meant they would not be effective over the crucial areas of north-east France.

This was as far as the British were prepared to go, despite the still worsening situation in France. On 18 May the chiefs of staff circulated a paper to the war cabinet arguing that they needed a minimum of fifty-two squadrons to defend Britain (not the sixty-plus or thirty-nine stated earlier), but had only thirty-seven available (although on the calculations made on 16 May it should by now have been thirty-five). The paper concluded that 'we have already reached the absolute limit of the air assistance we can afford to France'.[8] The war cabinet discussed the paper two days later and agreed that no more aircraft should be sent. Ministers took a very different view when the evacuation of the BEF from Dunkirk was at stake, authorizing full RAF fighter support, a fact that did not pass unnoticed by the French. Immediately after Dunkirk the French made two further appeals for support, both of which were rejected. Once the BEF was safely back from the continent the British no longer had much direct involvement in the battle, as Churchill told the cabinet defence committee on 8 June: 'We should recognize that whereas the present land battle was of great importance, it would not be decisive one way or the other for Great Britain ... If this country were defeated, the war would be lost for France no less than for ourselves.'[9]

The meagre nature of the air assistance given to France and the lack of any political will to do more can be judged not just by the failure to send fighters during the crucial days in May but by the situation at the beginning of June. Then Britain had three fighter squadrons operating in France (six and a half per cent of the total British strength), less than had been available on 10 May at the start of the battle. This was despite the fact that production was greater than the number lost in combat and, as a consequence, the number of squadrons available for home defence had risen to forty-five.

The other issue that embittered relations between Britain and France during these weeks was the role of the BEF and its evacuation from Dunkirk. The BEF was only a small part of the Allied forces and, like the Belgian forces, was placed under overall French command. On 10 May it began the planned advance to the River Dyle although its first action was, unfortunately, to attack the retreating 10th Belgian division. The retreat from the Dyle to Dunkirk began on 16 May, when the British moved without informing the Belgians on their flank. The next day Lord Gort, the British commander, refused to accept French orders to fight on the River Senne and continued to withdraw. This left the Belgians with the choice of keeping the Allied line intact or giving up more of their country to the Germans. They supported their Allies and retreated alongside the British. On 19 May Gort rejected a French request to fight alongside the 1st French army and the BEF retreat continued. The British did not have to fight their way back to the coast (they sustained only 500 casualties in the first eleven days of the campaign), leaving the bulk of the fighting to the Belgians and French. On 20 May the war cabinet ordered Gort to attack southwards to disrupt the Germans moving towards the coast and link up with the French armies on the other side of the German salient. This led to the limited British attack around Arras on 21 May (the only BEF offensive action of the campaign), but when this failed Gort placed all the emphasis on evacuation through the Channel ports. The withdrawal from around Arras was made without consulting the French and it convinced them that the British were interested only in saving themselves. This view was reinforced by events at Boulogne. The British occupied the port on 22 May but were evacuated by sea within twenty-four hours (when armed sailors had to stop drunken troops rushing the ships) and left the French to defend the port against the Germans for another thirty hours. The British, on leaving, sank a ship in the harbour, which stopped the French evacuating any of their troops before the port finally fell. On 24 May there were similar scenes at Calais. British stevedores refused to work under sporadic German shelling and had to be dragged out of hiding by armed troops. But with the British about to abandon the port after holding it for forty-eight hours, the French formally protested. The British commander was ordered not to surrender 'for the sake of Allied solidarity' and received a message full of Churchillian rhetoric and designed primarily for publication. In private Churchill was scathing about the performance of the British army and telegraphed to Gort: 'Of course if one side fights and the other does not, the war is apt to become somewhat unequal.' Churchill omitted this sentence when he published the text of the message in his war memoirs.

British interest in withdrawing the BEF from the continent began very early in the campaign. On return from his 16 May visit to Paris Churchill asked Chamberlain to start planning for evacuation and the military were also instructed to begin preparations. Gort had his first plans ready by 19 May and a week later, before the start of the Dunkirk evacuation, the British had already brought 28,000 troops back to the UK. As the surrounded Allied armies retreated into a pocket around the port of Dunkirk, the British relied on their Allies to hold the Germans without offering to evacuate their partners. The Belgians were encouraged to keep fighting and on three occasions held positions to enable the British to retreat, though from 24–26 May the British rejected five appeals from the Belgians to counter-attack. The British showed little respect for Belgian military prowess and still less interest in their fate. General Pownall, Gort's chief of staff, described them in his diary as 'rotten to the core and in the end we shall have to look after ourselves'. When asked about the possible evacuation of the Belgians, Pownall replied, 'We don't care a bugger what happens to the Belgians.'[10] Early on the evening of 25 May Gort told Eden, Secretary of State for War, that he was moving the BEF back to the coast for evacuation. Eden replied, 'It is obvious that you should not discuss the possibility of the move with the French or the Belgians.' The next day Gort ignored a French order to attack southwards and break out of the pocket, relying instead on the strong resistance put up by the 1st French army around Lille, which lasted until 1 June, to hold off the encircling Germans. On the evening of 26 May Gort asked for the Canadian division in Britain to be sent to France to hold the bridgehead while the British were evacuated. This move was rejected after strong Canadian pressure against the sacrifice of their only trained troops.

The large-scale evacuation of troops from Dunkirk began on 27 May. The British were given only a small part of the bridgehead to hold because the French did not expect them to fight. When the Belgians surrendered late that evening the French took over their part of the front. The senior Royal Navy officer at Dunkirk, Captain Tennant, commented on 29 May: 'The French staff at Dunkirk feel strongly that they are defending Dunkirk for us to evacuate, which is largely true.' On that day French troops were manhandled off British ships and soldiers from the two armies came close to shooting each other. By 29 May 73,000 troops had been evacuated but only 655 were French. One of the reasons for this was that the French had not been informed about the evacuation. Churchill had not told Reynaud of the decision when he visited London on 26 May and did not do so until 29 May. On the next two days another 83,000 British troops left Dunkirk but only 23,000 French. At the Supreme War Council meeting in Paris on

31 May, Churchill, after French protests about the situation, offered them half the future evacuation places. Since at that stage there were only 50,000 British troops left compared with 200,000 French, this was a less generous offer than it appeared. Only in the last few days, when virtually all the British troops had been evacuated, did the French numbers exceed the British. At the 31 May meeting in Paris Churchill had insisted that the British should act as the rearguard for as long as possible. However, at Dunkirk the British commander, General Alexander (who had taken over after Gort left), though nominally under French command, agreed with Eden that evening that the British should not be left behind and would pull out within twenty-four hours. The French held the bridgehead for another two days after the final British withdrawal, until they surrendered on 4 June.

One of the myths of Dunkirk is that the troops were evacuated from the beaches by an armada of small boats manned by volunteers from all over England. In fact two-thirds of those evacuated were lifted directly on to Royal Navy ships from the east mole of Dunkirk harbour. No public information about the evacuation was given until the evening of 30 May when nearly three-quarters of the BEF had already been rescued. Only then could volunteers come forward and play a part in the operation. Over the last four days of the operation the small boats helped lift 26,000 troops from the beaches, about eight per cent of the total evacuated from Dunkirk.

As part of the myth surrounding the operation it also came to be represented as an heroic episode in British military history. Like that of other armies in retreat, the morale and cohesion of the BEF was poor as it moved through France and Belgium towards the coast. The problems began on 10 May when the German attack caught the BEF by surprise and with many key personnel on leave. This confusion was compounded by Gort's decision to move his headquarters near to Lille while leaving his operational and intelligence staffs at Arras. This confusion was made worse by the almost total collapse of communications during the retreat: the wireless system broke down and the telephones did not work. Within ten days there were only three days' rations left (although plenty of ammunition because of the lack of fighting) and the troops looted what they required from the locals. In the panic about 'fifth columnists' there were a large number of shootings of 'suspicious' characters, many of whom had done nothing worse than possess fair hair. British troops were also using dumdum bullets, banned under the Geneva convention, and had orders not to take prisoners except for interrogation. The Germans replied with two massacres by the SS of a total of 170 British prisoners. When the first troops arrived at Dunkirk discipline nearly broke down altogether and for the first two days of the evacuation order had to be kept by armed naval personnel until more disciplined regiments arrived on 29 May. Even then men were rushing the boats in their anxiety to get away and General Alexander was shocked by the behaviour of the soldiers. Later in the year, during a secret session of the House of Commons, several MPs told how a large number of officers had run away and deserted their troops so as to get on to the earliest boat. Privately, the War Office was alarmed at the state of the army. As the Director of Statistics later told one newspaper editor: 'The Dunkirk episode was far worse than was ever realized in Fleet Street. The men on getting back to England were so demoralized they threw their rifles and equipment out of railway-carriage windows. Some sent for their wives with their civilian clothes, changed into these, and walked home.'[11] In private, Churchill told his junior ministers that Dunkirk was 'the greatest British military defeat for many centuries'.[12]

None of this, the government and military decided, could be told to the public. They were able to enforce this decision because no journalists were present at Dunkirk. Once it was clear that the BEF was being evacuated, General Mason-Macfarlane, the head of military intelligence, summoned journalists on 28 May and told them: 'I'm afraid there is going to be a considerable shock for the British public. It is your duty to act as shock-absorbers, so I have prepared ...a statement that can be published, subject to censorship.'[13] The journalists were also told to blame the French for not fighting and to say that the BEF was undefeated; both statements were travesties of the truth. No news of the events at Dunkirk was released to the public until the 6 p.m. BBC news on 30 May, five days after the evacuation had started and when nearly three-quarters of the BEF were already back in Britain. The public were then told, in a statement approved by the Ministry of Information, that 'men of the undefeated British Expeditionary Force have been coming home from France. They have not come back in triumph, they have come back in glory.'

When the Dunkirk evacuation was completed on 3 June the Allies had lost a total of sixty-one divisions and three-quarters of their modern equipment. There were only fifty-one divisions, 200 tanks and 175 fighters left to face 104 enemy divisions. The German army quickly regrouped and began to attack southwards across the Somme on 5 June. The French put up strong resistance for a while but, heavily outnumbered, they were overrun. On 10 June the government evacuated Paris, which was declared an open city. Mussolini decided that the time had come to enter the war and, he hoped, pick up for himself some of the spoils of victory won by others. On 11 June Churchill flew to Briare for a conference with the French at which the different national perceptions of the situation were starkly apparent. Once again he rejected French pleas that this was the decisive battle and argued that the German assault on Britain would be crucial: if Britain survived for three or four months they would be able to continue the war and then 'we will win it back for you'. These rhetorical gestures failed to impress a French government facing total defeat. When Churchill spoke of sending one more division to add to the two divisions still on the continent, but offered no more before 1941 and recalled the grim days of March and April 1918, Marshal Pétain, who had been recalled to the French cabinet, retorted, 'In 1918, I gave you forty divisions to save the British army. Where are the forty British divisions that would be needed to save ourselves today?'[14] In fact, the British were about to stop any more troops going to France and start evacuating those that remained. The French pressed for more fighter squadrons, but on his return Churchill told Reynaud that the fighters would stay in Britain and operate at the limits of their range. This meant nothing, because the fighting in France was now beyond the range of fighters operating from southern England.

Back in London on 12 June, Churchill told the war cabinet that 'it was clear that France was near the end of organized resistance'.[15] The last week before the French request for an armistice was one of confusion and poor communication between the two governments as the German army swept on to occupy three-quarters of France. At first it was hoped that President Roosevelt might step in to save the Allies. On 10 June Reynaud asked for American assistance. Roosevelt's reply on 13 June – saying that everything possible was being done to supply the Allies and urging the French to carry on fighting – was taken as very encouraging. That evening in London ministers were euphoric. Beaverbrook argued that 'it was inevitable that the United States would declare war' and Churchill agreed that the message 'came as near as possible to a declaration of war' and that he expected the Americans to be in the war within a fortnight.[16] This optimism collapsed when the Allies asked Roosevelt's permission to publish his message. He refused, adding that his earlier response 'was in no sense intended to commit and did not commit the government to military participation in support of Allied governments'.[17]

On 13 June Churchill made a last flight to France to see Reynaud at Tours. Reynaud asked to be released from the Anglo–French agreement not to seek a separate peace, noting acidly that 'it is quite natural for Britain to continue, given that until today she has not suffered much'. The British delegation refused to discuss the French request and left for England. Reynaud had omitted to tell Churchill that the French cabinet were waiting to see him and the latter's failure to appear only reinforced their view that Britain was no longer interested in the fate of France and strengthened the hand of those arguing for a separate armistice. On the morning of 16 June the British offered to release the French from the agreement provided the French fleet sailed to British harbours immediately. Early in the afternoon details of a projected Anglo–French union were sent to France. When the French cabinet met at 5 p.m., the British idea of union was read out but not the demands about the fleet. The overwhelming opinion in the French government was that they were on their own and had to seek the best deal they could for France, regardless of British views. The possibility of fighting on from north Africa was rejected in favour of asking the Germans for armistice terms. Reynaud resigned and was replaced by Marshal Pétain. The next day, 17 June, the French asked for an armistice. The German terms, which left the French in control of an unoccupied zone, the fleet and the overseas empire, were generous enough to ensure their acceptance. Some in Britain were glad that the French had collapsed. 'Chips' Channon wrote in his diary, when Pétain set up the Vichy government in July: 'The third French Republic has ceased to exist and I don't care; it was graft-ridden, incompetent, Communistic and corrupt and had out-lived its day.'[18]

After six weeks of fighting the alliance had collapsed amid

recrimination and bitterness. The British convinced themselves that they had been let down by the Belgians and the French and from as early as the first week of the campaign were planning on a French collapse. The French felt betrayed by the limited British help and Britain's consistent placing of national self-interest before the needs of the alliance. The French complaints had much substance. British casualties in three weeks of fighting were 3,500 killed, almost the same as the Dutch lost in a few days. This compared with French losses of 120,000 killed, 250,000 wounded and 1.5 million prisoners; a scale equivalent to some of the worst phases of the Verdun slaughter in the First World War. The British sent pitifully small forces to the continent and paid the price for their decisions in the 1930s not to provide an army to support France by seeing their ally overwhelmed. At the crucial moment they refused to send their fighter squadrons across the Channel to try to win air supremacy over the battlefield. In the long run that decision preserved the RAF for the air battle over England; but that was little consolation at the time for the French, who were facing a catastrophic defeat. The British actions at Dunkirk reinforced the French view that their ally was mainly interested in self-preservation.

The British, thrown back on their own painfully limited resources, now faced some agonizing decisions. Could they continue the war with a reasonable prospect of surviving, let alone continuing until victory? Should they make their own peace with Germany before their prospects deteriorated any further? The British government had already begun to discuss these questions in the last week of May as they faced the humiliation of Dunkirk. The French request for an armistice brought them to the top of the agenda. On several occasions, both at the end of May and in the middle of June, the war cabinet discussed the possibility of peace with Germany.

6

Peace?

The British government entered the war in September 1939 with a distinct lack of enthusiasm. For two days after the German invasion of Poland they tried to avoid declaring war. They hoped that if the Germans would agree to withdraw, then a four-power European conference sponsored by Mussolini would be able to devise a settlement at the expense of the Poles. But Hitler remained obdurate and the British government, under immense pressure from the House of Commons, finally declared war seventy-two hours after the German attack on their ally. Until the summer of 1940 they continued to explore numerous different approaches to see whether peace with Germany was possible. The main advocates of this policy after the outbreak of war were the Foreign Office, in particular its two ministers – Lord Halifax and Rab Butler – together with Neville Chamberlain. But the replacement of Chamberlain by Churchill had little effect on this aspect of British policy and the collapse of France forced the government into its most serious and detailed consideration of a possible peace. Even Churchill was prepared to cede part of the Empire to Germany if a reasonable peace was on offer from Hitler. Not until July 1940 did an alternative policy – carrying on the war in the hope that the Americans would rescue Britain – become firmly established.

British peace efforts in the period 1939–40 remain a highly sensitive subject for British governments, even though all the participants are now dead. Persistent diplomatic efforts to reach peace with Germany are not part of the mythology of 1940 and have been eclipsed by the belligerent rhetoric of the period. Any dent in the belief that Britain displayed an uncompromising 'bulldog spirit' throughout 1940 and never considered any possibility other than fighting on to total victory is still regarded as severely damaging to Britain's self-image and the myth of 'Their Finest Hour'. The political memoirs of the participants either carefully avoid the subject or are deliberately misleading. Normally, government papers are available for research after thirty years but some of the most sensitive British files about these peace feelers, including key war cabinet decisions, remain closed until well into the twenty-first century. It is possible, however, to piece together what really happened from a variety of different sources and reveal the reality behind the myth.

The rapid defeat of Poland in September 1939 left the British in a quandary. They wanted to avoid a full-scale war because of their weak strategic and financial position, but a deal with Hitler seemed unlikely, as their experience before the war had demonstrated. They believed that economic pressure on Germany, together with what they hoped was the fragile state of the Germany economy, might lead to Hitler's being replaced by a more moderate leader with whom a deal would be possible. Chamberlain spoke privately of having a 'hunch' that the war would be over by the spring because the Germans would simply cave in. Outside the government, too, there was a widespread feeling that the war would soon be over. At that stage only twenty per cent of the public thought it would go on as long as three years. At the beginning of October Joseph Kennedy, the American Ambassador in London, reported to Washington that Churchill was talking about accepting an armistice with Germany if offered reasonable terms.[1] What sort of deal did the government have in mind? In other words, what were Britain's war aims in the autumn of 1939? The British government never did manage to define clearly what it would want to achieve in a peace conference. Restoration of Poland, as the ostensible cause of the war, was, in some form, essential although the status of Danzig and the corridor might be altered. But how could Poland be restored with the Soviet Union occupying the eastern part of the country? And what about Czechoslovakia? Were the Munich settlement and the German take-over of March 1939 to be reversed? Provided these issues could be resolved satisfactorily, the British government felt it had few quarrels with Germany and would be quite willing, as long as the Germans renounced future aggression, to concede effective German domination of central and south-eastern Europe.

After the defeat of Poland at the end of September 1939, Hitler publicly offered peace to Britain and France, although on carefully undefined terms. The British reply, equally vague, was partly drafted by Churchill and, as he told Chamberlain, it 'does not close the door upon any genuine offer' from Germany.[2] When Chamberlain replied to Hitler on 12 October, using Churchill's suggestions, all that he said in the House of Commons was that: 'The peace which we are determined to secure, however, must be a real and settled peace, not an uneasy truce interrupted by constant alarms and repeated threats. What stands in the way of such a peace? It was the German government and the German government alone.'[3] British policy in 1939, and throughout 1940, was not to insist on the unconditional surrender of Germany. Only in 1943, at the Casablanca conference, and at American insistence, did it become Allied policy to force the unconditional surrender of Germany and to continue the war until Germany collapsed and there was no government left to negotiate an armistice. Previous wars had ended, as did the First World War in 1918, by one side seeking an armistice and then negotiating peace. In 1939 and 1940 that was how the British assumed the war with Germany would end. Indeed the British had at that juncture no interest in bringing about the collapse of Germany, which it wanted to retain as a bulwark against communism.

In the autumn of 1939 the British government tried at least five different officially approved approaches to Germany to explore possible peace terms. The most long-lasting of these various attempts were the contacts established in the last days of August via a Swedish businessman, Dahlerus. He was acting as an intermediary to Goering, on whom the British placed great reliance as a possible 'moderate' replacement for Hitler. Dahlerus's efforts to avoid war in August, including visits to Britain on Goering's behalf, had failed, but Chamberlain and Halifax saw him again at the end of September and made it clear that Britain wanted a new regime of some sort in Germany followed by the re-creation of an 'independent' Poland and Czechoslovakia, though their borders were left undefined. Dahlerus's mission continued, without success, until a final meeting on 19 October and was called off, at German, and not British, insistence, only on 11 November. The most disastrous contacts between Germany and Britain occurred in late October. British MI6 agents in the Netherlands made contact with German army officers who they believed were conspirators against Hitler and prepared to replace him subject to guarantees about British policy towards a successor government. Chamberlain and Halifax, without consulting the cabinet until it was too late to draw back, spent a considerable amount of time drafting various assurances and hoping that they would soon be able to deal with the sort of safe conservative German government they had long wanted. The episode ended ignominiously when the 'conspirators' turned out to be German intelligence agents, who trapped the British agents into crossing the border to Germany, where they were arrested and the MI6 network in the Netherlands was broken up.

The main contacts in the autumn of 1939 were, as in 1940, made through the various neutral countries, which were still able to act as intermediaries between Britain and Germany. Early in October contacts were established with the German ambassador in Ankara, von Papen, but these came to nothing. A more substantial approach was made via the Irish. On 3 October the Irish Foreign Office told the German embassy in Dublin that Chamberlain and those around him wanted peace, provided that British prestige was preserved. This approach was not an Irish initiative but represented a British attempt to explore a possible basis for peace with Germany. The subject is still regarded as highly sensitive and all British files remain closed until 2016. Some evidence of the sort of terms the British may have had in mind is provided by Rab Butler's conversation with the Italian ambassador in London on 13 November. Butler, obviously intending that the message should be passed on to Germany, said that the Germans would not have to withdraw from Poland before negotiations to end the war began. He also made it clear that Churchill, with his more bellicose public utterances, spoke only for himself and did not represent the views of the British government.

The possibility of peace was also high on the agenda in the spring of 1940 before the German attack on Scandinavia. Influential individuals within the British establishment thought peace should be made. When the foremost independent military expert in the country, Sir Basil Liddell-Hart, was asked in early March what he thought Britain should do, he replied: 'Come to the best possible terms as soon as possible ... we have no chance of avoiding defeat.'[4] Lord Beaverbrook, proprietor of Express Newspapers, was even prepared to back 'peace' candidates run by the

Independent Labour Party at by-elections. He offered £500 per candidate and newspaper backing, but the scheme never got off the ground. Within the government there were similar yearnings for peace. On 24 January Halifax and his permanent secretary, Sir Alexander Cadogan, had a long conversation about possible peace terms. Cadogan reported that Halifax was 'in a pacifist mood these days. So am I, in that I should like to make peace before war starts.' The two men believed that peace was not possible with Hitler on any terms that he would find acceptable and were worried that either the Pope or President Roosevelt might intervene with their own proposals. If they did, then Allied terms would have to be put forward, but neither Halifax nor Cadogan could think what they should be. Cadogan concluded: 'We left each other completely puzzled.'[5] The British were also under pressure from the dominions to make peace. This was urged by both New Zealand and Australia. The Australian Prime Minister, Robert Menzies, wrote to his High Commissioner in London, Bruce, that Churchill was a menace and a publicity seeker and that Britain, France, Germany and Italy should make peace before real war made the terms too stiff and then combine together against the real enemy: Bolshevism.

The British put out one or two feelers for peace in the spring. The Swedish minister in London, Bjorn Prytz, reported to Stockholm in January that opinion was growing within the Foreign Office that Sweden should mediate. On 27 January formal contacts between the British and German ministers in The Hague were authorized by London. These contacts came to nothing but in February the British did have to cope with a development they had both expected and feared. President Roosevelt, facing an election in November at which he had still not decided whether or not to stand for an unprecedented third term, sent the Assistant Secretary of State, Sumner Welles, to Europe to explore the possibilities for peace. If his European diplomacy were successful, Roosevelt would either leave office in glory or have a strong base from which to be re-elected. Even if Welles failed, Roosevelt would be able to claim the credit for trying. Much as the British wanted peace if the right terms could be found, they did not want it as a result of Roosevelt's efforts, and they certainly did not want him participating in any peace conference and influencing the final terms. The British idea was, therefore, according to

Halifax, to 'state the conditions which while not such as to invite rejection by considerable elements in Germany, are such as Hitler would find it impossible to accept'.[6] This was the old policy of trying to tempt the conservative elements in Germany to overthrow Hitler and make peace.

When Welles came to Europe at the end of February and early March, he visited Rome, Berlin, Paris and London, but achieved nothing. Nevertheless a conversation one of his team, Moffat, had with Rab Butler is illuminating about the views of the Foreign Office and how far Britain might have been prepared to go to get peace. Butler said that only 'some aspects' of Nazism would have to go in any peace treaty and that there were 'more realistic' elements in Whitehall than Churchill and Eden. If Hitler did go, then there would be no repeat of the Versailles treaty and the terms would be very generous. Butler expected a German peace offensive soon, but reflected sadly that 'he was reaching the conviction that Germany would be sincere but that no one in England or France at present would believe it'.[7] Later that afternoon (13 March) Butler spoke to Halifax and recorded in his diary: 'I said I would not exclude a truce if Mussolini, the Pope and Roosevelt would come in, to which Halifax replied: "You are very bold, what a challenging statement, but I agree with you."'[8] The Welles peace mission petered out, but that did not discourage Butler. Even after the German conquest of Norway and Denmark he put out more feelers at the end of April through the British minister in Bern, Sir David Kelly, to dissident German elements led by Prince von Hohenlohe in the hope that they might be encouraged to lead to a coup against Hitler and enable peace to be made with a new conservative regime.

All of these tentative contacts illustrate a persistent desire for peace within the British government and reveal the difficulty of finding the right formula. The staggering events in France in May and June completely changed the situation. As its ally collapsed the British government had to decide whether it could continue the war or whether it should seek peace, not as a compromise to avoid a real war, but as a necessity following military defeat.

The collapse of France was a devastating blow to the British because it undermined a central pillar of their defence strategy. Throughout the 1930s they assumed that the French army would be the bastion defending the west against any German attack, leaving the British to concentrate on naval and air defence while providing token support for the French army. Even in 1939, after the British decision to begin equipping a large army for continental warfare, the French still provided the overwhelming majority of land forces: about ninety divisions compared with the UK's nine. All Britain's experience from the First World War suggested that this was a reasonable policy to adopt. Then the French army had withstood every crisis: the Marne in 1914, Verdun, the mutinies of 1917 and the last great German offensive in the spring of 1918. In May 1940 the British suddenly had to adjust to the fact that within a week the French army had been routed and that the complete collapse of France was the most likely outcome of the battle. Within a fortnight of the opening of the campaign, the British had to face the loss of the Channel ports, something that had never happened in the First World War, and the fact that most of the British army on the continent would be lucky to escape back across the Channel. This was a catastrophe of such proportions that it left the British government stunned.

In December 1939 Halifax had told the war cabinet that if the French government ever wanted peace then 'we should not be able to carry on the war by ourselves'.[9] On 14 May, following Reynaud's message to Churchill about the collapse at Sedan, ministers tried to adjust to the fact that France might be out of the war within weeks. That night Joseph Kennedy told Washington that Churchill, Eden, Sinclair and Alexander were in a bad state: 'They were very low tonight although they are tough and mean to fight.' Kennedy added to their gloom by telling them that Italy looked ready to declare war and reported that Churchill 'considers the chances of the Allies is slight with the entrance of Italy [sic]'.[10] Chamberlain gave a direct indication of some of the views within the war cabinet as the crisis deepened when he wrote in his diary next day that if France collapsed Britain would only be 'fighting for better terms, not for victory' and that 'our only chance of escaping destruction would be if Roosevelt made an appeal for an armistice', although he doubted whether Hitler would accept such an appeal.[11] On 15 May, in his first message as Prime Minister, Churchill warned Roosevelt that: 'You may have a completely subjugated Nazified Europe established with astonishing swiftness, and the weight may be more than we can bear.'[12]

The events of the following fortnight were to create a state of panic in Whitehall. As the Germans swept to the Channel, captured Boulogne and Calais and surrounded the British and French armies, the government expected them to turn on Britain next before finishing off the French. Neither ministers nor the military expected to rescue more than 40,000–50,000 men of the BEF (compared with the 330,000 Allied troops actually saved). On 22 May draconian powers for the government to control and direct all property, businesses and individuals were rushed through parliament. In a state of wild uncertainty about a 'fifth column' virtually all aliens were interned, a special Security Executive was established, powers were taken to close down newspapers and tap anyone's telephone and open their mail. On 26 May the Chancellor of the Exchequer, Kingsley Wood, forced through emergency arrangements to ship all of the Bank of England's holdings of gold and securities to Canada. On 27 May the Canadian government were warned to expect the arrival of the royal family in the near future.

It was in this fervid atmosphere that the war cabinet formally considered whether Britain should seek a compromise peace. None of this was made public, although the American government was aware very quickly of what was happening inside the war cabinet. In public Churchill had declared, in his first speech as Prime Minister, that the government's policy was 'victory at all costs, victory in spite of all terror, however long and hard the road may be, for without victory there is no survival'.[13] After the war Churchill was determined to maintain the heroic myths that by then already surrounded the dramatic days of the early summer of 1940. He wrote in his war memoirs: 'Future generations may deem it noteworthy that the supreme question of whether we should fight on alone never found a place upon the War Cabinet agenda ... we were much too busy to waste time upon such unreal, academic issues.'[14] The first part of that statement is just about technically correct in that most of the discussions in the war cabinet about whether to sue for peace were under the heading of 'Italy: Suggested Direct Approach to Signor Mussolini', but it is an example of Churchill being extremely economical with the truth. The second part of the statement is untrue and designed to conceal the five meetings held by senior ministers during the three days 26–28 May at which the questions of peace and whether Britain should fight on alone were debated at length.

As the situation in France disintegrated, both the British and French governments became increasingly worried that Italy would take advantage of the German victory to enter the war and secure some of the benefits. On 23 May the French suggested that Roosevelt should be asked to approach Mussolini and find out what Italy wanted from the Allies. This idea fitted in with Halifax's own views about the role the Americans might play. He told Kennedy on 23 May that he was 'definitely of the opinion that if anybody is able to save a débâcle on the part of the Allies if it arrives at that point it is the President'.[5] The war cabinet met on 24 May and agreed that Roosevelt should be asked to intervene, though he should make it look as though he were doing so on his own initiative. The idea was for him to tell Mussolini that Britain and France were prepared to consider reasonable Italian claims at the end of the war and that Italy could be present at the peace conference.[16] This was unlikely to achieve very much because Mussolini would not be naïve enough to believe that if the Allies won the war they would be prepared to give him some of their territory. But it was a first attempt to open up negotiations with the Italians.

On the evening of 25 May Halifax saw the Italian ambassador, who dropped some fairly clear hints that the Italians would be prepared to initiate a general European conference to agree on peace. This was a continuation of the role that Italy had played in setting up the Munich conference in 1938 and the failed attempt to hold a similar conference over Poland and avoid war in August 1939. But if Britain and France were now to agree to a conference they would, assuming Hitler was co-operative enough to agree to talks, have to make a number of concessions in view of the military disaster developing in northern France. No doubt Mussolini thought he might get his share without having to go to the trouble of declaring war. Halifax cautiously told the ambassador that the UK would consider any proposals for peace 'provided our liberty and independence were assured', a formula which certainly did not rule out territorial concessions.

On the morning of 26 May, Reynaud flew to London to see Churchill. The situation had taken a major turn for the worse. The attempted Allied counter-attack on the German forces that had broken through to the Channel had failed. The British decision to retreat from around Arras and move towards Dunkirk was regarded by the French, according to Reynaud's notes for his meeting with Churchill, as the 'last straw'. At a meeting of the French war cabinet the previous evening the question of an armistice with Germany had been openly discussed. The British war cabinet was hastily summoned to a meeting at 9 a.m. before Reynaud arrived in London. Churchill announced that he expected Reynaud to say that the French were giving up the fight and he had therefore asked the chiefs of staff to draw up an assessment of the situation. Specifically, they were asked for their views about whether or not Britain could fight on against Germany and Italy, and to say if they could hold out 'reasonable hopes of preventing serious invasion', bearing in mind, not the chances of victory, but that 'a prolongation of British resistance might be very dangerous for Germany engaged in holding down the greater part of Europe'. Halifax reported on his discussion the previous evening with the Italian ambassador about a peace conference initiated by Mussolini and added that the situation was so grim that 'we had to face the fact that it was not so much now a question of imposing a complete defeat upon Germany but of safeguarding the independence of our own Empire and if possible that of France'.[17] The discussion then tailed off into the question of what sort of armistice terms the Germans might impose upon France.

The war cabinet met again briefly at 2 p.m. after Churchill had seen Reynaud. The French Prime Minister, Churchill reported, was extremely pessimistic. The Allies were heavily outnumbered on land, no new forces were expected from the UK until 1941, the blockade of Germany would not work now that, following their conquests, the Germans had access to new raw material sources and no practical help was likely from the Americans. Reynaud thought that France might not be able to continue the war, but that it might be possible to buy off the Italians to stop them coming in and making the situation even worse. He believed that the Italians might be satisfied by being given effective control of the Mediterranean through the neutralization of Gibraltar, Suez and Malta and the limiting of Allied naval forces in the area. There was time for only a very short discussion of whether or not to approach Mussolini with this idea, which Halifax favoured, before Churchill had to end the meeting in order to see Reynaud again.[18]

The five members of the war cabinet – Churchill, Chamberlain, Halifax, Attlee and Greenwood – reconvened later that afternoon for what was to be a momentous discussion about Britain's future.[19] There was little debate about trying to bribe Mussolini to stay out of the war; Chamberlain merely said he did not like the French idea and preferred to play on Italian fears of a dominant Germany and hope they wanted a general European settlement. Instead, the debate focused on a much more fundamental issue raised by Reynaud. He had asked for British views by the next day on whether or not the Italians should be asked to approach the Germans to find out what their peace terms would be as part of a general European settlement. The French were pressing Britain, who had the most to offer Italy in the Mediterranean, to make the bulk of the Allied concessions and had been told that Britain would be willing to do so as part of a general settlement. The Labour members contributed little to the debate: Attlee merely said that he thought Hitler was aiming to finish the war by the end of the year (reflecting Britain's long-held illusion that the German economy could not withstand a long war) and implied that the UK might be able to hang on until then. Greenwood was worried that Mussolini might demand Malta, Gibraltar and Suez but 'he saw no objection to this line of approach being tried'. Churchill, who had been Prime Minister only for a fortnight and whose political position was still extremely weak, did not dominate the debate. He did not argue that Britain should fight on to total victory. His position was that 'the only thing to do was to show him [Hitler] that he could not conquer this country' and that no approach for peace terms should be made at this stage: 'We must not get entangled in a position of that kind before we had been involved in any serious fighting.' The debate was in fact dominated by Halifax, who was keen to explore the possibility of obtaining a reasonable peace. He favoured 'allowing France to try out the possibilities of a European equilibrium' and argued that by negotiating now 'it might be possible to save France from the wreck'. He was quite clear that Mussolini would have to be told that 'if there was any suggestion of terms which affected our independence we should not look at them for a moment' but 'we might consider Italian claims'. Halifax summed up his views by saying: 'If we got to the point of discussing the terms of a general settlement and found that we could obtain terms which did not postulate the destruction of our independence we should be foolish if we did not accept them.' Chamberlain said little, but generally supported Halifax.

The meeting also considered what Britain might have to give up in order to obtain a settlement. There was general agreement that Mussolini would want Gibraltar, Malta and Suez and Chamberlain thought he might well add Somaliland, Kenya and Uganda to the list. It was more difficult to see what might have to be conceded to Hitler. The war cabinet were united in agreeing that Britain could not accept any form of disarmament in a peace settlement but that the return of the former German colonies taken away in the Versailles settlement was acceptable. At one point Halifax asked Churchill directly 'whether, if he was satisfied that matters vital to the independence of this country were unaffected, he would be prepared to discuss terms'.[20] Churchill's reply shows none of the signs of the determined attitude he displayed in public and the image cultivated after the war. It reveals little difference between his views and those of Halifax, and shows he was prepared to give up parts of the Empire if a peace settlement were possible. He replied to Halifax's query by saying that 'he would be thankful to get out of our present difficulties on such terms, provided we retained the essentials and the elements of our vital strength, even at the cost of some cession of territory'. Neville Chamberlain's diary records the response in more specific terms than the civil service minutes. He quotes Churchill as saying that 'if we could get out of this jam by giving up Malta and Gibraltar and some African colonies he would jump at it'.[21]

As the debate, which lasted for four hours, proceeded, Churchill was beginning to lose the argument over whether or not to ask Mussolini to mediate. He tried to put off a decision by saying that 'it was best to decide nothing until we saw how much of the Army we could re-embark from Europe'. The war cabinet finally agreed to take up the discussion again the next day, when Sinclair would be present. He was invited to attend not because of his position as Secretary of State for Air but as leader of the Liberal Party. In view of the gravity of the issues being discussed, the members of the war cabinet clearly wanted all the political parties represented in the coalition to be present. Churchill may also have wanted his support to help outweigh the arguments of Halifax and Chamberlain. The war cabinet also agreed that

Halifax should circulate the text of a possible approach to Italy, which he did later that evening.[22] He suggested that the Allies should tell Mussolini that, in return for help in obtaining a general settlement, 'We understand that he desires the solution of certain Mediterranean questions; and if he will state in secrecy what these are, France and Great Britain will at once do their best to meet his wishes.' Halifax was realistic enough to point out to his colleagues that this attempted bribery 'holds out only a very slender chance of success'.

When the war cabinet (with Sinclair also present) met on the afternoon of 27 May, the situation had changed significantly. First the French had suggested, in the euphemistic words of the civil service minutes, that there should be greater 'geographical precision' to the Allied approach to Italy. In plain language this meant that the Allies would actually offer Mussolini territory at the start of the process. All those present, including Halifax, rejected the French suggestion. The second factor was that President Roosevelt had now made the approach to Mussolini which the war cabinet had agreed on 24 May he should be asked to initiate. Churchill and his three supporters – Attlee, Greenwood and Sinclair – were opposed to any approach by the Allies to try to buy off Italy and displayed some of the attitudes already evident on the continent as the British forces attempted to save themselves from the débâcle. They argued that the French were beaten anyway, that keeping Italy out of the war would make no difference, and they implied that Britain should simply look after its own interests. No one, however, wanted further to demoralize the French and so increase the chances of them going out of the war immediately (Britain needed as much time as possible to complete defensive preparations) by an outright refusal to talk to Mussolini. For this reason, the war cabinet accepted Chamberlain's suggestion that the French should be asked to wait until the results of Roosevelt's initiative were known.

The question of whether Britain should go further and ask Italy to mediate and find out German peace terms had not been resolved on 26 May. Now, during the debate on 27 May, Halifax was effectively isolated in advocating this possibility. Churchill argued in favour, not of continuing the war until victory, but of trying to get through the next two or three months before making a decision on whether or not to ask for peace. He was quite prepared for concessions to achieve peace: 'If Herr Hitler was prepared to make peace on the terms of the restoration of German colonies and the overlordship of central Europe, that was one thing.'[23] But as Churchill pointed out, acceptance of such a limited restoration of German strength after their stunning military victory was 'most unlikely'. Nevertheless, he revealed that though he was not prepared to ask Hitler for peace terms, he would discuss any offer that was made. Halifax thought that the situation was now so bad that it was best to try and see if a reasonable offer would be made by Germany before the Allied position collapsed irretrievably. He was annoyed by Churchill's long monologues and emotional arguments. At the end of the meeting he threatened to resign and afterwards told Cadogan, 'I can't work with Winston any longer.'[24] But after a long talk with the Prime Minister in the garden of No. 10 Halifax agreed to continue as Foreign Secretary.

The war cabinet, together with Sinclair, met again at 4 p.m. on 28 May in Churchill's room at the House of Commons.[25] The compromise agreed the previous day had been overtaken by the failure of Roosevelt's approach to Mussolini. The latter was clearly not interested in Allied bribes to stay out of the war. However, direct contacts between Vansittart, Chief Diplomatic Adviser to the government, and the Italian ambassador had revealed that Mussolini wanted 'a clear indication' as to whether the Allies would like to see mediation by Italy. The French had also asked for a direct Allied approach to Italy. Once more Halifax argued that there was no harm in trying, and that if Mussolini could negotiate a general settlement now, the terms would be better than after France had collapsed and Britain had been bombed. The other ministers did not agree. Greenwood and Sinclair were worried that once talks started they would broaden very rapidly into real peace negotiations and it would then be very difficult to draw back. The discussion was dominated not by Churchill but by Chamberlain. He argued that Britain was in 'a tight corner' and that fighting on was a great gamble, but so was the attempt to seek mediation. He agreed with Halifax that if terms 'which, though grievous, would not threaten our independence' were offered then they would have to be considered. But now was not the right time to approach Mussolini, although it might be within a week. He wanted to keep 'the concessions which it was contemplated we might have to make, e.g. in regard to Malta and Gibraltar' in hand for a general settlement with Germany rather than use them up on Mussolini. Chamberlain argued for sending the French what was a fairly bleak message, with the clear implication that Britain was looking after its own interests and would continue the war for a while in order to secure better peace terms. He suggested saying that 'we in this country felt that we had resources left to us of which we could make good use. If, as we believed, we could hold out, we should be able to obtain terms which would not affect our independence.' Churchill contributed little, except to support Chamberlain's suggestion of fighting on for a limited period. He told his colleagues: 'A time might come when we felt we had to put an end to the struggle, but the terms would not then be more mortal than those offered to us now.'

The meeting was adjourned while Chamberlain and Halifax drafted a message to the French. In the interval Churchill saw junior government ministers not in the cabinet. He did not tell them about the arguments in the war cabinet, but merely spoke about continuing the struggle. That meeting has often been described as crucial in backing Churchill against his colleagues in the war cabinet. In fact it was largely irrelevant. There was little difference in approach between senior ministers by 28 May and the war cabinet had already agreed on how to respond to the French. That reply was sent later in the evening, unamended from the Chamberlain and Halifax draft.

There are two significant points about these long debates, held over three days, about whether Britain should ask for peace terms. The first is that Churchill did not advocate a policy of absolute resistance and fighting on to the end. He favoured fighting on for a few months, a course of action which would, with luck, demonstrate to Hitler that he could not conquer Britain. He accepted that then it might well be necessary to make peace, but felt Britain ought to be able to obtain better terms at that stage than when France was collapsing. And in order to obtain that peace Churchill was quite prepared to trade British territory to Germany and Italy. Churchill's limited aims emerge in the minute he circulated to all ministers on 29 May asking them to keep up morale and continue the fight 'till we have broken the will of the enemy to bring all Europe under his domination'.[26] That was very far short of British victory over Germany. Churchill's doubts at the end of May were about whether Hitler wanted a general settlement, which is what Halifax thought possible, or whether it was more likely that he would demand a peace reflecting German military conquests. The second point that comes out from these extended discussions is that the rescue of the BEF from Dunkirk had no influence over the decision to continue the war. By 28 May, the day the war cabinet agreed to reject any approach to Mussolini (and by implication not to pursue peace), only 17,000 British troops had been evacuated back to the UK. Although the return of over 180,000 soldiers of the BEF by early June raised morale, it did not solve the military problems that the defeat in France caused. The BEF had to abandon all its major equipment on the continent and during the summer of 1940 it was shortage of equipment, not men, that was the crucial aspect of British military weakness.

After 28 May the question of peace did not reappear on the war cabinet agenda for three weeks. There were, however, still significant elements of opinion that wanted peace. At the end of the month the Australian Prime Minister, Menzies, suggested that Roosevelt should be asked to set up a conference to formulate a peace settlement. Churchill rejected the request. Within parliament there was also a group favouring a negotiated end to the war. It consisted of about thirty MPs and ten peers from all parties, organized by the Labour MP Richard Stokes. They looked to Lloyd George as a possible Prime Minister and argued that once any threat of invasion had been repelled Britain should then seek peace, since the only beneficiaries of continuing the war would be the United States and the Soviet Union. The continued deterioration of the military situation on the continent, however, brought the question of peace back to the top of the agenda. As the German army swept southwards across France, it was obvious that Britain would soon be left alone to face Germany, Italy and a hostile Europe. The Americans were clearly not going to enter the war immediately and Roosevelt had even refused to allow a vaguely supportive message to be published. On 14 June the Conservative MP 'Chips' Channon ruminated about Roosevelt and the dreadful prospects facing Britain: 'If he refuses to come in, it would seem that the war must come to an end, and this great Empire will have been defeated and humiliated.'[27]

The events of the three days 17–19 June, following the French request for an armistice, remain highly sensitive. Some key British documents covering this period remain closed, unlike those on the discussions at the end of May. Presumably this is because, in contrast to the earlier occasion, this time Britain made it clear that it was ready to enter peace negotiations. The situation facing Britain on 17 June was perhaps the worst in its history. Its only ally was about to go out of the war and the fate of the French fleet was still unclear; if it came under German control then British naval superiority would be difficult to maintain. The only possible hope lay with the Americans, but they appeared to have written off both Britain and France and to be concentrating on defending themselves. The key question was whether or not Britain should join France in asking for peace while it was still undefeated and had some military assets (the fleet and the RAF) and before further military setbacks, including a possible invasion, undermined Britain's bargaining position. Churchill recognized that this was the crucial period for deciding the way ahead. On the afternoon of 17 June he saw the US ambassador, Kennedy, who reported to Washington: 'I believe that there are a number of decisions being made here [about] their course of action' and added that Churchill wanted to know what he could count on from the Americans.[28]

Elsewhere in Whitehall even more significant events were taking place. Rab Butler, Halifax's deputy, asked the Swedish minister in London, Bjorn Prytz, to come to the Foreign Office. Not surprisingly, there is no British record of their conversation, and in 1946 and again in 1964 the UK intervened to stop publication of the Swedish version. In 1965, Prytz eventually published his telegram to Stockholm about the meeting. In it he recorded that: 'Mr Butler's official attitude will for the present be that the war should continue, but he must be certain that no opportunity should be missed of compromise if reasonable conditions could be agreed, and no diehards would be allowed to stand in the way.' The standard British interpretation of this talk is that perhaps Butler spoke slightly unwisely and Prytz may have read more into his words than Butler intended. That interpretation cannot be sustained. The views recorded by Prytz are consistent both with Butler's strong advocacy of a compromise peace from the autumn of 1939 and with his distrust of Churchill, Eden and others as 'diehards'. Reference to his 'official' attitude being that the war should continue 'for the present' suggests that his private attitude, which he may well have hinted at in his talk with Prytz, was different and favoured peace. And why should Butler take the initiative, at a key moment in the war, to talk about peace to the Swedes who, as neutrals, were the most obvious way of approaching Germany, if he did not expect some action would be taken?

The interpretation that this feeler to the Swedes was not merely some slightly unfortunate remarks by a junior minister is confirmed by other evidence. Towards the end of his talk with Prytz, Butler was summoned to see Halifax. They obviously discussed the Swede's visit because on his return Butler gave Prytz a message from Halifax that 'common sense and not bravado would dictate the British Government's policy'. Halifax thought that this indication of British policy would be welcome to the Swedes although they should not take it to mean 'peace at any price'. Armed with this information from a member of the war cabinet about Britain's willingness to consider peace, Prytz duly returned to his embassy to inform Stockholm about this new development. The Foreign Office did not, however, leave the initiative entirely in the hands of Prytz. Late on the evening of 17 June, a telegram was despatched to the British ambassador in Stockholm, Sir Victor Mallet. The text of the telegram is still not available for public inspection. Nevertheless, it is possible to deduce its contents.

When the war cabinet met at 12.30 p.m. on 18 June, Churchill was not in the chair. He was busy writing a speech to be delivered in the House of Commons that afternoon, a speech that included the memorable phrase 'Their Finest Hour'. In his absence the war cabinet was chaired by Neville Chamberlain. The official minutes for one unidentified item on their agenda that day remain closed.[29] Sir Alexander Cadogan, the head of the Foreign Office, was present, however, and recorded in his diary the following passage about the meeting, which cannot refer to any of the other items discussed: 'Winston not there – writing his speech. No reply from Germans.'[30] The only possible explanation for this cryptic note is that the Foreign Office were awaiting a reply from the Germans to the initiatives, sent via Prytz and the British embassy in Stockholm, about possible peace terms. The closed minute presumably refers to these initiatives. That this is the correct interpretation is made clear by what happened in Stockholm that day. Sir Victor Mallet saw the Swedish Foreign Minister, Gunter, to pass on the message he had received from London the previous evening. The General Secretary of the ministry (the senior civil servant), Bohemann, then asked the Italian ambassador, Francesco Fransoni, to call. In turn Fransoni reported the sequence of events and the British move to the Italian Foreign Minister, Count Ciano, in Rome:

> The British representative [Mallet] requested an interview with the Swedish foreign minister and notified him that the British government is inclined to enter into peace negotiations with Germany and Italy. The Secretary General of the foreign ministry here immediately informed me and in reply to my enquiry confirmed specifically that this declaration by the British representative is of official character.[31]

This Italian telegram makes it clear that Mallet was acting on instructions from London, which were separate from the Prytz conversation, and that the first step in the opening of peace negotiations had been taken. The Swedes, quite correctly, informed the Italians about such an important development. Italy, however, was only the junior partner in the alliance and any negotiations would be primarily with Germany. The most important Swedish move on 18 June was to summon their ambassador in Berlin, Richert, back to Stockholm for a full briefing. He returned to Berlin on 19 June to inform an incredulous von Weizacker, the senior official in the German Foreign Ministry, of the British initiative. The reason for von Weizacker's incredulity was that the initiative seemed totally at odds with Churchill's bellicose speech in the Commons on 18 June.

The explanation for this dichotomy lies in what happened in Whitehall. It seems clear that the initiative Halifax and Butler took with the Swedes had not been agreed by the government as a whole. They may have hoped that by opening a channel of communication via Stockholm they would bypass Churchill and obtain a definite offer of terms from the Germans to present as a *fait accompli* to the war cabinet and thus force a discussion on whether or not the terms should be accepted. Although not present at the war cabinet meeting on 18 June, Churchill would have learnt what was going on from the minutes or from his political allies who were there. Once he was aware of what was happening he appears to have intervened promptly to stop the Foreign Office initiative. He no doubt took the opportunity of the war cabinet meeting on 19 June formally to veto the initiative. Again one item in the minutes remains closed, presumably because it refers to Churchill's action and the previous day's discussion.[32]

This sudden abandonment of the British peace initiative left a diplomatic mess to clear up. On 19 June Gunter, the Swedish Foreign Minister, saw Mallet again to report progress in opening up communications with the Germans. At this meeting Mallet was shown the Prytz telegram for the first time, a further confirmation that he was acting on instructions from London in raising the question of peace the previous day. Gunter asked specifically whether or not the British now wanted the Germans to make a formal offer of peace terms. Mallet, who was now aware of what was happening in London (which suggests Churchill acted rapidly on 18 June to stop the Foreign Office committing Britain too far), replied that Britain did not want any more action for the moment. When Churchill saw Mallet's telegram of 19 June, which reported his talk with Gunter and forwarded the text of Prytz's telegram of 17 June about his talk with Butler, he wrote to Halifax complaining about Butler's 'strong impression of defeatism'. This was also an implicit criticism of Halifax for his involvement. The two Foreign Office ministers decided to stick together in the face of Churchill's wrath. Butler wrote a note of explanation to Halifax and admitted that he had told Prytz that 'if we were to negotiate, we must do so from strength'. Butler made an offer to resign but Halifax was careful not to pass this on to Churchill, fearing that it might be accepted.[33] Churchill, though, did not forget the incident. In December 1940 Halifax was sent to Washington and in 1941 Butler was moved to take charge of education policy, a nominal promotion but well away from the centre of wartime policy-making. He remained there for the rest of the war.

Action taken by Britain on 19 June was also designed to lessen any Swedish enthusiasm to be helpful over peace negotiations. The war cabinet agreed to seize four Swedish destroyers at the Faroes while they were sailing home. The pretext for the operation was that they might fall into German hands, although as Churchill explained it was better to seize the ships first and then 'we could consider later what explanations we should offer'.[34] When the

British took control of the ships the Swedes protested that they took 'the gravest possible view' of the incident because they had arranged for the safe passage of the ships with the Germans. The Foreign Office were now worried that the Germans would use the incident to demand control over Sweden. At this stage (23 July) the war cabinet were not prepared to hand back the ships. After further Swedish protests, however, they agreed to do so the next day. It was decided this should be done 'on the pretext' of new information from Sweden and accompanied by the mendacious public line that Britain had only been 'holding the ships pending investigations'.[35] A footnote to the story is that the Germans were clearly hopeful about what was happening in Britain after the British request for peace negotiations was transmitted to Berlin by the Swedes. Goebbels wrote in his diary on 22 June: 'This week is going to see a big turn-round in England. Naturally Churchill can't hold on. A compromise government will be formed.'[36] The Germans were unaware of how quickly Churchill had been able to reassert his control.

Although Churchill was now dominating the war cabinet and a consensus had finally emerged that Britain should continue the war — a resolution tangibly demonstrated by the attack on the French fleet at the beginning of July — there were still many influential individuals who wanted peace. In July the Australians kept up their pressure for compromise. Menzies wanted Britain to set out its war aims (which remained as undefined under Churchill as they had been under Chamberlain) as the starting point for a peace conference. Bruce, the High Commissioner in London, lost no opportunity to put forward these views when he met British ministers. At the Madrid embassy Sir Samuel Hoare was a keen advocate of peace. On 4 July he was reported as 'forcefully arguing for compromise', and a week later told the Spanish Foreign Minister, in reply to his offer to mediate, that 'it is possible it will come to it'.[37] In the middle of July the British minister in Bern, Sir David Kelly, revived his contacts with Prince Max von Hohenlohe. At a secret meeting he told the German that Churchill was unreasonable and under the influence of alcohol, but that Halifax and Butler were much more realistic. Nothing further came of these contacts. Halifax also remained wedded to the idea of compromise. Cadogan noted in his diary on 2 July that 'the Pope is making tentative half-baked suggestions for agreement. Silly old H[alifax] evidently hankering after them.'[38]

The last attempt of any consequence to obtain peace terms revolved around Hitler's speech in the Reichstag on 19 July. Billed beforehand as a major peace speech, in the event it contained nothing of substance. The contacts on this occasion were via the ambassador in Washington, Lord Lothian, who throughout the 1930s had been a strong advocate of appeasement. On 18 April 1940, he was reported as openly speaking in favour of a compromise peace in front of German diplomats. On 19 July a Quaker intermediary, Malcolm Lovell, passed a message to Lothian from the German *chargé d'affaires* saying that German peace terms were available if Britain wished to know them. When Lothian reported this to London, Churchill ordered Halifax to tell the ambassador not to reply to the German message. Halifax did not pass on this instruction and seems to have sent a very different message. When Lothian saw Lovell again he told him that 'dissidents' in the war cabinet had asked him to find out what Germany would offer 'a proud and unconquered nation'. This approach was passed on to Berlin, although the German papers on the subject went missing when they were in Allied hands after the war. However, the senior civil servant at the Foreign Ministry, von Weizacker, wrote in his diary on 23 July: 'A strange peace feeler turns up, from the British ambassador in Washington ... Lothian has made advances for which he must have obtained authorization if he were a normal British ambassador.'[39] In London, Churchill made sure that Halifax gave the official reply to Hitler's Reichstag speech, rejecting peace. Although Lothian tried to get Halifax not to slam the door shut completely, the initiative petered out. Other members of the government, though, were aware of what was happening in Washington and of how far Lothian had gone with the Germans. Harold Nicolson noted on 22 July that 'Lothian claims that he knows the German peace terms and that they are most satisfactory'.[40]

It is clear from the widespread evidence of war cabinet discussions and approaches via the Swedes and the Americans that in May and June 1940 not only did Britain seriously consider making peace with Germany, but that some members of the government went as far as to ask what terms the Germans would offer. Within the war cabinet there was a spectrum of views: from Halifax, who favoured trying to make peace before the military situation became even worse; to Churchill, who wanted to fight on for a few months. It is also clear from the war cabinet discussions that in May and June 1940 their policy was not an absolute commitment to fight on to victory. Instead they adopted a more short-term aim of preparing to resist any German invasion in the hope that Germany might collapse quickly or, if it did not, that Britain would at any rate be able to obtain better peace terms later on in the year, once any invasion had been repulsed, than in the immediate aftermath of the collapse of France. Churchill's position was very different from the heroic image he liked to project in public at the time and after the war. In private he did not argue for victory at all costs but instead agreed with his colleagues on a policy of seeing if Britain could keep going for a few months. If negotiations with Germany were necessary then he was quite prepared to give away British territory in order to obtain peace. No one went so far as to establish Britain's bottom line for negotiations, but instead used coded language about continued independence to gloss over the fact that they were prepared to concede a major transfer of British territory to Germany and Italy. At the time, great secrecy naturally surrounded these discussions, but it is hard to see the justification for the later attempt to pretend that they never happened at all.

Churchill's views in 1940, rather than the subsequent mythology about them, are well illustrated by his response to an initiative by the King of Sweden at the beginning of August 1940 to set up a conference to examine the possibility of peace. Churchill altered the draft Foreign Office response to make it much more general and commented: 'A firm reply of the kind I have outlined is the only chance of extorting from Germany any offers which are not fantastic.'[41] But if Churchill had been determined to fight on to the end, as he forcefully argued in public, why would he have shown any interest in even trying to obtain offers from Germany? Any proposals made by Germany at that stage were bound to be based on their dominant position in Europe and require British acceptance of much of what had been achieved by military conquest.

By the end of July 1940 a possible peace was no longer on the agenda. Britain had decided to continue the war for the immediate future in the hope that something might turn up (the collapse of Germany or perhaps help from the United States), or failing that, in the hope of establishing a better position from which to negotiate peace. Survival was now the absolute priority. The next few weeks would show whether the 'peace now' advocates, or the 'war now, peace later' advocates were right. If Britain could not repel any attempt at invasion, then the view that it would be better for an undefeated Britain to seek peace before Germany attempted an invasion would be proved right and the country would face the horrors of total defeat and German occupation. The preparations which Britain had made in the 1930s were now to be put to the test, but the crucial factor would be how the Germans conducted the battle. Did they have the right forces available to defeat Britain, and were they prepared for a full-scale invasion?

7

Survival

The collapse of France in mid-June 1940 left Britain in a simple but appalling situation. Any thoughts of eventual victory seemed merely fanciful and every effort had to be concentrated on the immediate task of survival. British expectations that Germany would turn on them after Dunkirk and before the final defeat of France had not been fulfilled; Hitler never considered any option other than victory over Germany's old enemy. The great triumph for the man who had been a private soldier, gassed in the trenches in the First World War, came when he forced the French to sign the armistice in the same railway coach at Compiègne where Marshal Foch had humiliated the Germans in November 1918. (The film of Hitler doing a 'jig' in front of the coach before the signing is a fake, part of a Canadian propaganda film.) Following the armistice, Germany was the most powerful nation Europe had seen since the days of Napoleon. It occupied Norway, Denmark, Belgium, Luxemburg, Austria and most of France, Poland and Czechoslovakia. It was allied with Italy (a dubious privilege); neutral countries such as Spain and the Soviet Union were friendly and others such as Sweden and Switzerland were rapidly adjusting to overwhelming German power. Hitler was also about to redraw the map of south-eastern Europe in favour of his friends – Hungary and Bulgaria – at the expense of Rumania. On the side of the Allies in the First World War, the Rumanians had benefited from the post-war settlement, but now had to pay the price of a fundamental shift in the balance of power. Few people in Germany, the rest of Europe, the United States or Japan thought it would be long before Britain was either occupied or forced to come to terms with a victorious Germany.

Britain's time alone against a seemingly all-powerful Germany started badly, with the first loss for centuries of part of the

British Isles to an invader. The Channel Islands had been a possession of the Crown since the twelfth century and, although they were not part of the United Kingdom, Britain was responsible for their defence. It was a responsibility that was to be botched in June 1940. As the Germans swept across France, the question of the Channel Islands, normally subject to benign neglect in White-hall, erupted on to the war cabinet agenda. On the morning of 12 June, shortly after the fall of Paris, ministers agreed to send army battalions to both Jersey and Guernsey to defend them against invasion and also agreed to start consultations with the island authorities about the possible evacuation of civilians. Five hours later, after Churchill had returned from France convinced that the French would hold out only for a few more days, Anthony Eden, Secretary of State for War, stopped the despatch of troops and told the war cabinet that he wanted to reconsider the question of defending the islands. The next day the chiefs of staff agreed that no British troops should be sent, that remaining forces should be withdrawn once British troops had been evacuated from France and that the islands should then be demilitarized. Having in effect conceded German occupation of the islands, the chiefs of staff then decided that the evacuation of civilians was 'un-necessary and undesirable'. The British government did not tell the island authorities about the decision not to defend them for another six days. That delay made any planned evacuation of the population almost impossible.

British troops and RAF personnel began withdrawing immedi-ately after 13 June but it was not until 19 June that formal authority was sought by the chiefs of staff for the abandonment of the islands.[1] At the war cabinet meeting Churchill spoke in romantic terms about the islands as long-standing possessions of the British Crown and wanted to use sea power to stop any invasion. The Vice Chief of the Naval Staff told him bluntly that 'the material necessary for the defence of the islands was not available' and with the Germans occupying all the adjacent French coastline, Britain had to recognize an unpleasant reality. Churchill conceded defeat and the discussion turned to the possibility of evacuation. The war cabinet generously agreed that Britain could not refuse to accept evacuees from the islands but insisted that all arrangements for evacuation should be made, and paid for, by the island authorities and not the British government. The scope for organizing orderly evacuation was made more difficult by the withdrawal of the last troops and the Lieutenant-Governors on 20 June. The islands were left to try to carry out a last-minute exodus from their own resources. The result, not surprisingly, was chaos. Alderney was totally evacuated but the population of Sark remained. Elsewhere, men of military age, women and children were supposed to be the priorities for evacuation but in the end luck decided who found places on the ships. Animals were shot, there was a run on the banks and a general lack of leadership from the island governments. Eventually about 23,000 people, a quarter of the population, were evacuated to the mainland.

The British, having decided on demilitarization, refused to tell the Germans of the decision on the ludicrous grounds that it might encourage them to occupy the islands. The result was that the islanders suffered the worst of both worlds: no defence and no announced demilitarization. The Germans, thinking the islands were still defended, started bombing and killed thirty-three civilians. Only then, on 30 June, did the British announce the demilitarization they had carried out ten days earlier. News of this fiasco was suppressed by Whitehall. The German occupation of the islands took place on 30 June and 1 July.

The Channel Islands remained occupied territory until the end of the war and the final German surrender. What happened during that period shows that a British population came to terms with German occupation in the same way as the rest of Europe: there was little or no resistance on the islands and a great deal of collaboration. Many Germans found the islanders far more co-operative than the French and the internal government of the islands continued normally under generally light supervision. Government members broadcast over German radio and even paid for the publication of a guide book for the occupying forces. Anti-Semitic laws were passed voluntarily by the local parliaments on both Jersey and Guernsey and the small number of Jews on the islands were sent to the death camps of eastern Europe. Little attention was paid to the islands during the war by Britain; there were for example no special programmes from the BBC to keep residents in touch with their families who had been evacuated to Britain. Churchill refused to allow in food ships for the civilian population in 1944, even though the Germans offered safe passage, in a fruitless attempt to starve out the garrison. After the war there was no elimination of the effects of occupation. Nearly all the wartime laws were confirmed as valid, people who had traded with the Germans were allowed to keep between twenty and forty per cent of the profits they had made and no prosecutions were brought for collaborating with the enemy. The example of the Channel Islands shows what might have happened if the Germans had mounted a successful invasion of Britain.

The question of whether Germany could crush Britain militarily hung in the balance during July, August and September 1940. Although the Germans appeared invincible they faced difficult strategic and tactical decisions in the summer of 1940. Neither Hitler nor his generals had expected such a stunning success against France and no plans had been made for an invasion of Britain because it had seemed such a remote possibility, even at the beginning of May. Hitler was also unsure about whether he wanted to eliminate Britain or turn on his ideological enemy the Soviet Union. This ambivalence was combined in Hitler's mind with a sneaking admiration for the British Empire and a belief that the British government would see sense and adjust to the reality of a German-dominated Europe. This reluctance to embark on an all-out assault was reinforced by a shrewd assessment of the difficulties involved in such an undertaking.

The Germans faced major problems in getting an army on to British soil. The most fundamental obstacle was geographical. The waters of the English Channel presented a formidable barrier. The German army consisted of nearly 150 divisions (compared with a British army now reduced to a handful of effective divisions), but as the Germans had no way of bringing that strength to bear, it was in many ways irrelevant to the outcome. Prepared for continental war, the German forces had no amphibious capability and no experience of anything greater than a river crossing. Even if a makeshift invasion fleet to carry the troops, tanks and horses across the Channel could be thrown together, the Germans had little time before the onset of unsuitable autumn and winter weather to carry out the immensely complicated task of planning an invasion and solving all the logistical problems involved. The German military planners quickly decided that they were not keen on mounting such a difficult operation. The first memorandum on a possible invasion, written at the end of June, stated that: 'A landing in England, therefore, should not have as its objective the military defeat of England ... but rather to give the *coup de grâce* ... An invasion must none the less be prepared in all details as a last resort.'[2]

Whether or not the Germans decided to risk an invasion depended entirely on Hitler. With the defeat of France he achieved one of his major aims: revenge for the humiliation of Versailles. After the armistice he spent time relaxing with some old cronies from the trenches, visiting old battlefields and basking in the glory of a stunning military success. From 23 June until 11 July he held no military conferences and showed little concern about the invasion of Britain. He believed that he had no quarrel with the British and that they would soon see sense and come to terms with him. He seems to have envisaged a deal whereby Britain kept the Empire in return for conceding German domination of Europe. He was reluctant to defeat Britain and dismantle the Empire. As one of his generals recorded, after a discussion on 13 July:

> The Führer is most preoccupied with the question of why England does not want to step on the path to peace. Like us, he sees the answer to the question in the hopes which England puts upon Russia. He therefore reckons to have to force England to make peace. But he does not like it very much. Reason: if we smash England militarily, the British Empire will collapse. Germany will not benefit from this. With German blood we would obtain something whose beneficiaries would only be Japan, America and others.[3]

Already Hitler's mind was turning towards the possibility of invading and defeating his real enemy: the Soviet Union. The primary aim was to exterminate the Bolsheviks and conquer more territory and resources. A secondary objective was to remove a source of possible help to the British and force them to make peace. During the summer of 1940, Hitler was unable to reach a decision about his strategic priorities though the Soviet Union was increasingly seen as the real enemy. Until an attack eastwards was possible in the summer of 1941, he was content to see whether Britain could be defeated or brought to the peace table. But on one point Hitler was absolutely certain: there would be no

invasion unless the outcome could be guaranteed. He was determined that his aura of invincibility would not be damaged by an
unsuccessful operation.

On 16 July Hitler issued a directive to the armed forces on the
invasion of Britain, codenamed Operation Sealion. It was based
on work already started by the military at the end of June, but it
reflected Hitler's ambivalence about the operation: it instructed
the planners to 'prepare for, and if necessary to carry out, an
invasion'. Five days later Hitler admitted to his generals that any
invasion would be 'very hazardous' and other ways of trying to
bring Britain to ask for peace would have to be tried first. That
same day (21 July) Hitler showed more interest in attacking
eastwards and asked for the first plans to be drawn up for an
attack on the Soviet Union. Meanwhile, the German army and
naval staffs were engaged in a major row about how to invade
Britain. The army originally wanted a massive thirty-division
landing along over 200 miles of coast. The navy rejected that as
totally impractical because they would be unable to protect such
an operation. Hitler showed little personal interest in these plans,
in complete contrast to his behaviour over the preparations for
the attack on France, and not until the end of August did he force
a compromise upon the army and navy. The result satisfied
neither. The army was to land a force it thought far too small
(nine divisions) in an area the navy thought too big to protect. By
early September German preparations were still far from complete.
The army had no landing craft and so river barges towed by tugs
that were hardly powerful enough to get across the Channel had
to be used. The problem was that the accumulation of river
barges in the Channel ports paralysed German river traffic and
could not be maintained for long without badly affecting the
economy. Even by 11 September only sixty per cent of the invasion
craft and twenty-five per cent of the tugs required were available.

All of these problems only reinforced Hitler's doubts about the
feasibility of an invasion, unless it was little more than a
mopping-up operation with Britain on the point of collapse. Other
methods were needed if Britain were to be forced to make peace.
The German navy could not accomplish the task. It was small and
had suffered major losses during the Norwegian campaign. It had
operational in the summer of 1940 just one heavy cruiser, two
light cruisers, six destroyers and a few torpedo boats. This was

completely inadequate to challenge the Royal Navy. The submarine fleet, with only about thirty operational U-boats, was not capable of halting Britain's seaborne trade. Hitler therefore had no alternative but to rely on the Luftwaffe to try and secure victory over Britain. But it was doubtful whether that force would be adequate for such a task.

Like the German army, the Luftwaffe had been created at breakneck speed after 1933. From a force of 550 pilots and 250 aircraft of little military value it had expanded to 20,000 pilots and observers with 3,500 aircraft by 1939. It had developed as a private fiefdom under Goering, who was grossly inadequate as a commander and organizer. His immediate deputies were no better at these tasks, and the one strength of the force was its complement of superb pilots. The Luftwaffe was, from its inception, built to support the army and not to fight a separate air offensive. It was organized into units linked to army groups and not into separate forces like Bomber Command and Fighter Command in the RAF. The attack on Britain, however, required the Luftwaffe to carry out exactly the type of operation for which it had not been designed and organized. Although many theorists between the two world wars had argued that, through bombing, an air force would be able to break the will of an opponent to resist, nobody had ever tried such a strategy. Now the Luftwaffe was being asked to embark on the task with no idea exactly how air power should be used in terms of targets and tactics in order to achieve a highly ambitious aim.

In 1940 no air force in the world was equipped with the necessary technical aids – navigation and bomb sights – to enable accurate bombing of specific industrial and economic targets to be carried out at night. This meant daylight operations were essential. The problem was that these were too hazardous against any competent air defence system. For this reason the RAF had abandoned daylight raids within a few days of the start of the war and the US air force encountered the same problems in its attacks on Germany in 1942–3. Although a different command structure and new methods of operating could be improvised by the Luftwaffe, types of aircraft could not be changed. The aircraft that had been built by Germany in the 1930s were inadequate for the task of attacking Britain. In 1940 no air force in the world had heavy four-engined long-range bombers of the type available later in the war. The Luftwaffe had considered two such designs in 1936, but had abandoned them in favour of aircraft optimized for army support. In 1940, therefore, it was forced to operate with vulnerable dive-bombers, short-range fighters, and twin-engined medium bombers which had only a light bomb load. Its one strength was its main fighter – the Me 109 – which was in most respects superior to any British design. The Me 110, a twin-engined fighter-bomber, was a hopeless compromise, no good at either role, and quickly had to be pulled out of operations against the RAF. In mid-July, therefore, when the Luftwaffe had been redeployed to bases in northern France ready for the attack on Britain, the Germans faced enormous problems in carrying out the planned air assault. Not only were they embarking on a strategy that had never been tried before in war, but they were handicapped by unclear objectives and aircraft designed for a much more limited task.

The British too faced major problems in repelling the German attack. The most fundamental was that, since its creation in 1918, the RAF had been based on the primacy of the bomber. Only by emphasizing the importance and effectiveness of a strategic bombing offensive had the RAF been able to ensure its continued independence and avoid being broken up into separate forces under the control of the Royal Navy and army. Rearmament in the 1930s had been directed mainly towards increasing the bomber force rather than the defensive fighter force, in the hope that this would act as a deterrent to German aggression. As late as April 1938 the RAF was planning on a strength of 1,360 bombers and only 600 fighters. It was in the autumn of 1938, after Munich, that ministers finally overruled the RAF chiefs and insisted on efforts being concentrated on providing an effective fighter defence for Britain. On 11 November 1938, the cabinet agreed to create an 800-fighter force by April 1940, rejected the RAF's request for increased bomber production and only endorsed enough orders to keep the production lines open. The other key to the outcome of the battle was technical development. In the early 1930s Baldwin had told the House of Commons that 'the bomber will always get through'. At the time that was true, because no warning could be given of an approaching bomber force and keeping fighter patrols continuously in the air was too great a strain. The development of radar as an early-warning system completely changed the picture.

Its feasibility was demonstrated in 1935 and by 1939 a complete chain of radar warning stations had been built around Britain's east and south coasts. Once these had been integrated with operational control rooms to plot the movements of bombers and fighters and linked to radio direction of fighter squadrons an excellent defence system had been created.

The Luftwaffe was not ready to begin large-scale operations against Britain until the beginning of August. A superficial glance at the respective strengths of the two air forces would suggest that the Germans held an enormous advantage. The Luftwaffe had a total front-line strength of 4,500 aircraft, compared with the RAF's 2,900. After allowing for transport aircraft and other unsuitable types, the fighter aircraft left to defend Germany, the RAF's 500 bombers and the Luftwaffe's Stuka dive-bombers (which were too vulnerable to use), the RAF had a fighter force of about 700 to face 800 German fighters and 1,000 bombers. This disparity in numbers, however, was largely offset by the tactical constraints of the battle. The German fighters had a very limited range and could operate for only about twenty-five minutes over south-east England. The longer-range bombers, which could not be left undefended, were therefore similarly restricted in their operations. The Luftwaffe also faced the greater risk of attrition once the fighting started. Because the battle would be fought over Kent and Sussex, the British would be able to recover pilots who bailed out and repair damaged aircraft, whereas the Germans would lose both. Thus when all these factors were taken into account the odds were not stacked heavily against the RAF.

Factors other than the balance of opposing forces, however, were crucial in determining the outcome of the Battle of Britain. During the summer of 1940 the key tasks facing Britain were to build and repair enough aircraft to keep the RAF in the air, find enough pilots to fly the aircraft and devise effective tactics to counter the Luftwaffe. The seeds of Britain's ability to produce more fighter aircraft than the Germans lay in the cabinet's decision in November 1938 to increase fighter production, thus ensuring the creation of the necessary industrial capability. The immediate cause of success was the decision to break up the Air Ministry in May 1940 and create a new Ministry of Aircraft Production under Beaverbrook, outside the RAF's control. Beaverbrook was Churchill's unorthodox choice for the job and his lack of Whitehall experience was a positive benefit in ensuring effective action. He inherited a situation where British aircraft production had equalled German output in 1939 and was planned to surpass it in 1940. But performance was still sluggish: in February and March 1940 actual production was fifteen per cent below planned levels. The new ministry did not resemble a normal Whitehall department and that was one of the reasons for its success. For a long time its headquarters was Beaverbrook's home (Stornoway House). He revitalized administration by introducing personally recruited outsiders and using informal and unorthodox methods, characterized by personal intervention, crisis management, demands for action and sheer willpower, to improve industrial output. Few records were kept, the functions of most individuals were left undefined and business was conducted mainly over the telephone. Beaverbrook also fought ruthless battles with the Air Ministry to overcome its incompetent management. One of the first was over the control of the RAF's storage units, which received aircraft from the manufacturers and then issued them to squadrons. Within days of taking office, Beaverbrook discovered that since October 1939 they had taken in over 1,000 aircraft but issued only 650 to squadrons. On 18 May the war cabinet agreed that the units should be taken out of RAF control and handed over to Beaverbrook. He also took over all work to repair and return damaged aircraft to the front line. His methods were ideally suited to the immediate task: a rapid improvement in fighter output and their speedy issue to the front line.

The crucial impact that Beaverbrook and the new ministry made can be judged from statistics, particularly for the vital period from May to August 1940. In the first four months of 1940, 2,729 aircraft were produced, of which 638 were fighters. In the next four months the total rose to 4,576, of which 1,875 were fighters. These figures represented increases of sixty-seven per cent and nearly two hundred per cent respectively. Fighter production was already projected to rise in the summer of 1940 but Beaverbrook comfortably exceeded the plans. From May to August actual output was almost fifty per cent above planned levels. The vital comparison, though, was with German production rather than with previously expected British output. During the summer of 1940, British fighter production was two and a half times greater than the German level, which was deliberately cut back below the levels planned on the outbreak of war. Taken together with the nearly 1,900 aircraft the British were able to repair and return to the front line, the result was that RAF effective strength was maintained. The number of fighters available for operations rose from 644 at the beginning of July to 732 at the beginning of October. During the same period the equivalent German figure fell sharply from 725 to 275. As a result of Beaverbrook's herculean efforts and those of the workers on the production lines the RAF was never short of aircraft during the Battle of Britain and only for a short period did losses exceed production.

Britain rose to the first challenge of supplying enough aircraft, but the second – providing the pilots – brought the RAF to the verge of disaster. The damage was essentially self-inflicted. Although almost 300 aircraft a week were being produced, the RAF could turn out only 200 pilots a week. This was because its training organization was highly inefficient. In the year before the summer of 1940, it took 4,000 training aircraft to produce 2,500 pilots, whereas the Germans produced one pilot for every aircraft in their training organization and their pilots were equally, if not more, skilled. The RAF made the situation worse by allocating more pilots than aircraft to each squadron (twenty-six compared with twenty). But even allowing for these problems, there were still about 9,000 pilots for the approximately 5,000 aircraft operational in the summer of 1940. Yet throughout the crucial summer months of 1940 the RAF persistently complained of a chronic shortage of pilots, and towards the end of August the pressure on the operational squadrons was so intense that it was doubtful whether they could continue flying for much longer. The reason for this apparently anomalous situation was the way the RAF allocated its pilots: only thirty per cent of the total strength was actually in front-line squadrons. Twenty per cent were engaged in the vital task of instructing and another twenty per cent, though qualified, were still receiving further instruction. The rest were in staff positions. Even at the height of the Battle of Britain, thirty per cent of the RAF's qualified pilots were engaged in office jobs. The reason for this went back to the origins of the RAF, when its founders decided that pilots would be the elite of the new force. All staff jobs were filled by pilots. No engineer was, for example, allowed to decide engineering policy, this being done by pilots.

This monopoly ensured that pilots held every post at the top of the RAF, but it also meant that during the Battle of Britain as many qualified pilots were sitting behind desks as were available to both Bomber and Fighter Commands together. Despite the gravity of the situation facing Britain and Churchill's repeated pressure, the RAF refused to change their policy and only a token thirty pilots were removed from administrative jobs to join the front line. The near fatal shortage of pilots during the Battle of Britain was therefore a situation entirely of the RAF's making.

The RAF also adopted other policies that made an effective response to the German attacks more difficult. Fighter Command was divided into four regional Groups, of which No. 11 – covering the south-east of England – and No. 12 in the Midlands were the most important during the Battle of Britain. No. 11 Group bore the brunt of the assault but too often was left with little help from other areas, so that its pilots and aircraft came under enormous pressure. This pressure was increased by a maldistribution of resources. The most effective British fighter against the Me 109 was the Spitfire, but seventy per cent of 11 Group's fighters were Hurricanes while other Groups further away from the fighting were composed of equal numbers of the two aircraft. In total, less than a third of Britain's best fighters were operating in the key sector. In addition, airfields in the vital 11 and 12 Group areas still accommodated four or five squadrons of virtually useless Blenheim twin-engined night fighters in space that could have been used for twice that number of Spitfires and Hurricanes. Demarcation disputes also reduced the number of fighters available in the south-east of England. Coastal Command retained its airfields and aircraft there, as did the Fleet Air Arm, which was under Admiralty control, and none of these facilities was used to bring more fighters into the crucial area.

The RAF also reduced effectiveness by insisting on retaining all the features of the peacetime squadron system. During operations the squadron remained sacrosanct and keeping it together was more important than keeping up the number of operational aircraft. Thus, each time a squadron was redeployed, all ground crew, stores and spares went with the aircraft instead of staying on the airfield to support the new planes and pilots. That meant a gap of nearly a week before the squadron on the move could become operational again from its new base. If a plane or a pilot

landed away from the squadron airfield they had to return to
their base before they were allowed to resume operations, which
meant that they were out of action for unnecessarily long periods.
Later in the war, during the Allied air attacks on Germany, the
Luftwaffe adopted a much more flexible system. They made no
attempt to keep squadrons together and allowed fighters to land
at any available airfield and fly again from that base, giving much
greater availability and concentration of fighter aircraft.

The decisions made by the RAF on the use of pilots and
aircraft could have cost them victory in the closely fought battle.
The fact that they did not was due to the inability of the Luftwaffe
to devise an effective strategy for winning the campaign. From the
start the Germans were unclear about the aim of the attack. Was
it to try and force the British to surrender, or was it to reduce
the strength of the RAF so that the Luftwaffe could achieve air
supremacy over south-east England as a possible prelude to
invasion? With the strategic aim not settled, it is not surprising
that the Germans could not evolve a coherent tactical plan. There
were a number of possibilities open to the Luftwaffe. Aircraft
factories could be bombed to cut back production and reduce
front-line forces. Airfields could be attacked and put out of action,
or radar sites could be knocked out to stop early warning of
attacks. Alternatively, mass formations of bombers and fighters
could be used to tempt the RAF into combat in the expectation of
inflicting heavy losses. The Luftwaffe never made a clear choice
between these different approaches, adopting all of them at different times, but never for long enough to produce decisive results.
This continual shifting between tactical expedients was the main
reason for their ultimate failure.

Right from the start the Germans failed to devise a clear battle
plan. Goering held his first major conference on the forthcoming
campaign on 21 July but no overall plan was worked out. On 31
July Hitler ordered the attack to start on 5 August. He instructed
that there was to be no 'terror bombing' of civilian targets but
otherwise gave no direction to the campaign. Bad weather then
postponed the start. The first phase of the battle lasted for ten
days from 8 August. During this period the Germans made, on 12
August, their only concentrated attack on the vital radar stations.
Six were attacked but only one (Ventnor on the Isle of Wight) put
out of action. The next day large bomber forces were committed

for the first time, but they were not used against any specific targets and the RAF inflicted losses of over three to one. The heaviest fighting of the whole battle occurred on 15 August. At seventy-five aircraft, German losses were the highest they suffered, and the RAF lost thirty-four, their second greatest of the campaign. Luftflotte 5, based in Norway, was involved for the only time in the battle but a loss of fifteen per cent of its strength, mainly in the outclassed Me 110, was too high to sustain. Bad weather from 18 August until 24 August marked the end of the first phase. The pause in operations provided an opportunity to rethink strategy. Goering called off attacks on radar sites because he thought they had not been effective and decided instead to concentrate directly on the RAF, in particular its airfields in Kent and Sussex.

The second phase, from 24 August until 6 September, was the most crucial of the whole battle and it brought the RAF close to defeat. The German attacks on RAF airfields had an immediate impact. Manston was put out of action on 24 August and heavy attacks at the end of the month on Kenley and Biggin Hill caused squadrons to be withdrawn. Inadequate resources for repairing damaged runways and equipment meant that after an attack a station could be out of action for a considerable period. By the first week of September five stations were not fully operational. Intensive operations took their toll of both aircraft and pilots, with the RAF losing 290 aircraft and the Luftwaffe 380. But only half the German losses were fighters, whereas British losses were considerably higher in this key area and, for the only time in the battle, outstripped the rate of production. Equally important in this phase was the loss, in the last week of August, of almost a fifth of the RAF's fighter pilots either killed or wounded. With the RAF still refusing to release trained pilots from office jobs, recently trained and therefore inexperienced men had to be sent to the front-line squadrons, which reduced operational effectiveness. The result was rising losses against the more experienced German pilots.

At the beginning of September British defences were near to breaking point. Had the Germans continued their attacks on RAF bases for another week or two the situation would probably have deteriorated to the point where the fighter squadrons would have had to be withdrawn from Kent and Sussex to north of London.

This would have significantly tipped the scales in favour of the Luftwaffe and given it local air superiority over the area where any invasion would be mounted. At this key moment in the whole campaign, the Germans changed their tactics yet again and took the pressure off the RAF. On 31 August Goering held a conference with his Luftwaffe deputies. They knew that they had not yet established air supremacy but faulty intelligence suggested that the RAF was running out of planes. The Germans believed that Fighter Command had only 420 aircraft left (the true figure was about 750) and that reserves were down to 100 aircraft (in fact they were double the German estimate). Goering decided to shift the attacks from RAF bases to London itself. (Hitler had given permission for the docks to be attacked after the British bombed Berlin.) Goering confidently believed that this change of tactics would force the RAF to commit the remains of its strength in a last battle to defend the capital. In fact the Germans made a fundamental miscalculation and were committing themselves to the most hazardous of all possible operations – daylight mass bombing – against a still intact and well-organized defence.

The Luftwaffe began to implement the new tactics on 7 September, when they launched a massive raid on the London docks that marked the start of the third phase of the campaign. The RAF badly misjudged the situation and thought the attack was still aimed at RAF bases. In the confusion the fighters did not attack the bombers until they were returning from London after inflicting major damage. The Germans lost only slightly more aircraft than the British and when the raid was repeated on 11 September suffered fewer losses than the RAF. Superficially, the German change of tactics seemed to be working, but during this phase the RAF bases were able to recover from previous damage and remain operational in the vital area of south-east England. It was at this point that Hitler had to make the crucial decision about whether an invasion should go ahead.

Hitler's lack of enthusiasm for any invasion that would amount to more than a straightforward occupation of an already defeated Britain had not altered by early September. For the previous month he had been content to wait and see if the Luftwaffe could defeat the RAF, and had made no effort to direct operations in the way he had during the attack on France. He was making it quite clear that he was not personally involved in what he saw as a highly dubious undertaking. Meanwhile the ramshackle invasion forces were slowly gathering in the Channel ports, where they came under attack from RAF Bomber Command, but preparations were far from complete. The German military had decided that the last possible date for an invasion, taking into account weather and tides, was 27 September. They needed ten days' warning to launch the attack and so a final decision was required by 17 September. On 13 September Hitler was still hopeful that an invasion would not be needed and that the Luftwaffe would be able to force Britain to make peace, although how still remained unclear. On 14 September he put off a final decision on an invasion for three days, until the last possible moment. The next day the Luftwaffe launched its biggest, and what it hoped would be its decisive attack against London. It only demonstrated that daylight bombing was too difficult, even with fighter cover, against a competent defence. Waves of bombers, heavily escorted by fighters, were launched in the morning and afternoon against London. The Germans made the mistake of not undertaking diversionary raids, and so the RAF was able to concentrate all its resources (twenty-three squadrons in the morning and thirty in the afternoon) against the attack. The result was a heavy defeat for the Luftwaffe, which lost about sixty aircraft to the RAF's twenty-six.

On 17 September, with a final decision on invasion required that day, Hitler held a meeting with his military planners. The events of 15 September demonstrated all too clearly that the RAF was still a potent force, and Hitler, deciding that his own scepticism about invasion was well justified, postponed the plan indefinitely. He was now free to turn his attention to his ultimate aim: the destruction of the Soviet Union. Three days after the meeting the dispersal of shipping was ordered but desultory activity was maintained in an attempt to confuse the British (without success). The Luftwaffe kept up its attacks, but apart from a few isolated raids on aircraft factories it concentrated more and more on night raids on cities, especially London. By the end of September the British government knew that an invasion was only a remote possibility, that the daylight raids had not defeated the RAF and that it could now probably expect a long winter of continued night-time bombing. Britain had survived.

Both at the time and since, Britain's survival has been attributed solely to the efforts of 'The Few': the pilots of Fighter Command. There can be no doubt that their skill and courage, maintained over a long period of intense combat, was essential in ensuring the defeat of the Luftwaffe. But the Germans too had highly skilled and dedicated pilots and modern battles are decided by more than individual heroism. After Dunkirk and the defeat of France, Britain had not only to survive but also to create a myth that would sustain the nation for the long and difficult period after immediate defeat had been avoided. The myth-creation process was strongly at work in the summer of 1940. British success was greatly exaggerated at the time and many of the misleading statistics issued in 1940 have since become accepted facts. For example, on 15 September, the date still celebrated as Battle of Britain day, the British claimed 185 German aircraft destroyed. The true figure was sixty. During the crucial phase, from 16 August until 6 September, the British people were given an unjustifiably optimistic picture of progress. Figures broadcast by the BBC gave British losses as 292 aircraft compared with an actual figure of 343, an underestimate of fifteen per cent. More important, German losses for this period were reported as sixty-two per cent higher than the real figure (855 instead of 527). The reality of combat was also very different from the stirring picture painted at the time and subsequently. Only half of the Spitfires and Hurricanes scrambled to intercept attacks ever engaged the German bombers and fighters, and only fifteen per cent of pilots were credited with shooting down any Luftwaffe planes at all. Real 'aces' were extremely rare: only seventeen pilots in the RAF accounted for more than ten aircraft each. The most successful squadron (No. 303) was not British, but manned by Polish pilots, and the two most successful individual pilots were a Czech and a Pole.

The real reasons for British survival in the summer of 1940 are more deep-seated than the courage of individual pilots, important though that was. The most significant factor was geography. The German army might dominate the continent, but it lacked the capability to launch an invasion. Such an operation was highly risky and required meticulous planning, as the Allies demonstrated before the Normandy landings in 1944. Hitler was right to be extremely cautious about launching an attack across the Channel without the British being on the point of defeat. The

German navy was too small to control the sea in the area and therefore everything turned on whether the Luftwaffe could defeat the RAF and establish local air supremacy. If they had done so, an invasion might have been feasible. The Royal Navy would have found it very difficult to operate in the Channel under German air attack and if the German army had landed then the poorly equipped British army was probaby too weak to do more than delay its advance. As the chiefs of staff told the war cabinet in May: 'Should the enemy succeed in establishing a force, with its vehicles, firmly ashore, the army in the United Kingdom, which is very short of equipment, has not got the offensive power to drive it out.'[4] Resisting the Luftwaffe attack on the RAF was therefore the key to survival. The RAF came perilously near to losing the Battle of Britain through its stubborn adherence to tradition and hidebound procedures even at a time of supreme national emergency. Under a more flexible system 'The Few' could have been more numerous. Victory in the air was achieved through two factors which in the end gave Britain a vital advantage. The first was Britain's ability to produce more aircraft than Germany. Here the advantages of unorthodox and makeshift methods in response to a national crisis were apparent. The second was rooted in German failings: although superior in numbers the Luftwaffe was hopelessly ill-equipped for the task of defeating the RAF over Britain, and this weakness was compounded by the erratic direction of the campaign, whereas fortunately for Britain the pre-war policy-makers had taken the right decisions.

The fall of France, followed by the threat of invasion, the Battle of Britain and the Blitz on British cities in the autumn and winter of 1940, for the first time brought the war to bear directly on the civilian population. How much did the war alter the nature of pre-war British society and how well did the civilian population stand up to these new strains? Just as important, how did the government view the task of controlling the country?

8

Government and People

One of the central myths of 1940, cultivated at the time and embellished since, was that Britain was galvanized by crisis to change old ways of working, and became united as never before, with a strong bond of equality of sacrifice. Presiding over this new national spirit was a benevolent government that provided inspirational leadership. The reality was very different. Britain in the 1930s was a deeply divided and unequal society. War, the threat of invasion and the Blitz did not alter that situation; indeed the pressure of war in 1940 fell most heavily on the less privileged, leaving the rich and powerful to adapt with relative ease. A study of life in Britain in 1940 shows that the pattern inherited from the 1930s continued almost unchanged and that the government, in seeking to control and organize the country, was deeply conservative, instinctively repressive, suspicious about the willingness of the population to withstand the pressures of war and incompetent in relieving the suffering caused by bombing.

In 1940 extremes of poverty and wealth existed side by side in Britain. In January, 1,300,000 people were unemployed, despite rising industrial demand caused by rearmament. At the time of Dunkirk 645,000 were still out of work and the figure did not drop below 200,000 until June 1941. For the unemployed conditions were as bad as they had been in the 1930s. The hated household means test was continued even after Labour joined the government in May, despite their pledge in opposition to abolish it when they gained office. Unemployment was one of the main causes of poverty, but the outbreak of war worsened the position for many more families. In 1940 average prices were nineteen per cent higher than in 1939 but wages had risen by only eleven per cent. The government added to this burden by introducing a new regressive form of taxation in the first wartime budget. Purchase tax was set at thirty-three per cent for luxuries and just over sixteen per cent for essential items. The inequality of sacrifice was well demonstrated by a further series of measures. Only very limited food rationing was introduced in January 1940 and, although income tax was increased, excess profits tax on industry was set at only sixty per cent, enabling firms to retain a large part of the profits earned from armaments orders. Similarly, although no money could be found to abolish the means test, ailing industries could be given substantial help. In February 1940 the government guaranteed the four main railway companies a minimum revenue of £40 million, fifteen per cent higher than before the war, despite the fact that only one company had paid a dividend to its shareholders, and that of only half a per cent. Not surprisingly, the value of railway company shares rose by £200 million when the scheme was announced. The government achieved little in return and inadequate planning led to a major crisis on the railways in the winter of 1940-41.

The terrible conditions affecting a large part of the population were revealed in a series of surveys conducted in the late 1930s and the early part of the war. In York thirty-one per cent of working-class families (eighteen per cent of the total population and fifty per cent of all children) lived below the poverty line. In Middlesbrough in 1939 a third of all the houses were over seventy years old and only ten per cent had baths. Death rates in British cities were twice those of Holland and Glasgow's was higher than Tokyo's. The worst areas were in the industrial north, where child mortality was twice the level of that in the prosperous south-east. Even official Ministry of Health surveys were blunt about the state of the nation. In 1943 ten per cent of the population were described as 'ill-nourished' or worse: 'Many of the people had lived for years past in poverty and unemployment and had given up the struggle to maintain a decent standard of housekeeping and cooking.'[1] Two years earlier, an official health survey had revealed 'a state of affairs that is a disgrace to a civilized country'. Inequality was starkly revealed by the fact that public schoolboys were on average four inches taller than their working-class contemporaries, solely because of their better diet. The bulk of the population received no more than a very basic education. Less than one per cent of fourteen- to eighteen-year-olds completed

full-time secondary education and inequality of opportunity was
demonstrated by the fact that only half a per cent of elementary
school children went to university. Yet one of the government's
first actions on the outbreak of war was to postpone the planned
raising of the school leaving age to fifteen. The mass evacuation
of children in September 1939 brought home for the first time to
rural and middle-class districts the state of the inner cities. Of
those evacuated from Newcastle, one in eight did not have proper
shoes, one in five was deficient in clothing and half of the
children were infested with nits.

Extremes of wealth and privilege existed alongside such poverty
and deprivation. The battle for national survival made little difference to the lives of the rich and powerful. In the spring of 1940
there were still twenty different makes of car on sale for those
who could afford to buy them. During the summer of 1940 the
former deputy secretary to the cabinet, Tom Jones, could still do
the rounds of country house parties, taking in Cliveden, Gregynog
Hall and Stanley Baldwin's residence in Worcestershire. At each
place there were still plenty of servants to look after the guests.
In September the wealthy Conservative MP 'Chips' Channon had
to make do with what he described as a 'depleted' staff of six
(instead of the usual fifteen) at his town house in Belgrave
Square, although he was able to maintain the usual level at his
country home.

Social life continued with little alteration. At the height of the
Battle of Britain in August, John Colville, one of Churchill's
private secretaries, was able to maintain a full diary. Over one
period of eight days he went to two society lunches, dined out on
two evenings at an exclusive West End restaurant and went on to
the theatre or cinema followed by a night club, then spent the
weekend at Lord Bessborough's country residence playing tennis
before returning to London on the Monday morning. The Blitz,
too, had little impact on this style of life. Channon described the
scene at the Dorchester Hotel, where many ministers and senior
officials stayed, as the East End of London was battered by
German bombers and the population huddled in tube stations
and the homeless lived in squalid rest centres: 'Half London
seemed to be there ... I gave Bob Boothby a champagne cocktail
in the private bar ... our bill must have been immense for we had
four magnums of champagne. London lives well: I've never seen

more lavishness, more money spent, or more food consumed than tonight, and the dance floor was packed.'[2] Those in the government led similarly privileged lives. When Coventry was bombed in November, the Home Secretary, Herbert Morrison, was enjoying a champagne supper at nearby Himley Hall with the regional commissioner, Lord Dudley, and they both went out to watch the fires from a safe distance. Churchill regularly dined well. On 24 November it was champagne and oysters with Anthony Eden while they discussed the campaign in Greece. Five days earlier it was caviar, champagne and 1865 brandy in his private bomb-proof shelter in the disused Down Street tube station near Knightsbridge. Harold Nicolson, the junior minister at the Ministry of Information, spent most of his time eating in the clubs of St James's but on one occasion he had lunch in the refectory at Senate House, the ministry's headquarters. He was shocked by the inconveniences of mass catering: 'It is absolutely foul . . . It is run on the cafeteria system and we have got to queue up with trays with the messenger boys.'[3] Most of the time he was able to avoid such distressing experiences and was delighted to report a culinary highlight enjoyed as the threat of invasion reached its height in September: 'Dine with Guy Burgess at the Reform and have the best cooked grouse that I have ever eaten.'[4]

If pre-war habits in high society continued virtually unchanged in 1940, so did other ways of life in the government, society at large and the armed forces. When Colville joined the staff at No. 10 in October 1939, he was shocked to find that work started at the 'disgustingly early hour' of 9.30. All-out war for national survival, however, did not alter practices elsewhere. Until November 1940 the Foreign Office began work at 11 a.m. and at the Ministry of Economic Warfare Hugh Dalton had to issue special instructions that staff were to be at their desks by 10 a.m. after one civil servant did not arrive in time for one of Dalton's meetings at 10.30. Colville, apart from keeping up his active social life, was also able to fit in plenty of leave while at No. 10. He was on leave for eleven days from 5 September, at a time when invasion was expected at any moment. The Chief of the Imperial General Staff took a fortnight's leave in December 1940, which coincided with the first British offensive of the war in Egypt. Although workers in the aircraft industry put in very long hours, much of the rest of British industry also continued in the same old way. In July a *Daily Mirror* reporter entered the Vickers shipyard in Barrow in disguise. He spent a day there investigating what was happening in a key defence industry as the nation braced itself for invasion. What he discovered, as described by another member of the newspaper's staff, was so shocking that the paper felt it could not print the story:

> Seventy-five per cent of the workforce he saw were doing nothing at all. Many had done no work for weeks and some not even for months, and all the men were completely fed up. There was ample material, willing and skilled men and quantities of machinery, but practically no output. One gun, which had been completed, was out in the rain and had been out for at least two months. Fourteen men he found asleep in a pocket in a big gun mounting.[5]

There was a depressing similarity about other areas of social life. In 1940 Britain was experiencing the start of a rising crime wave that was to continue throughout the war. Despite a fall in the number of policemen available to investigate crime and the virtual elimination of traffic offences because of petrol rationing, crime rose by nearly sixty per cent during the war (three times the rate of annual increase before the war). With the imposition of rationing and the consequent black market, pilfering from work rose rapidly: threefold in Birkenhead docks during 1940. And shortly after the outbreak of war a special squad of 500 policemen had to be sent to France to try to stop mass thefts from the BEF for the French black market. The Blitz opened up new opportunities for looting. This was so bad that Scotland Yard had to set up a special anti-looting squad, and of those caught, nearly half were civil defence workers. Wartime social disruption also increased juvenile crime, which rose by forty-one per cent in the year after the outbreak of war.

In Whitehall those in charge of the armed forces spent a considerable part of their time discussing subjects that had little to do with operations and strategy. In February 1940 the Admiralty Board had to decide whether chaplains in the navy should be allowed to wear, at their own expense, a cap with a badge. There was also a long discussion about the names for the two new battleships about to enter service. 'Jellicoe' and 'Beatty' (both commanders in the First World War) were rejected as still too controversial and the board settled for safe names from the past: 'Anson' and 'Howe'.[6] At the same time the Army Board were deciding, despite protests from the Archbishop of Canterbury, that what were euphemistically called *maisons tolerées* should continue to be tolerated. Other examples of vital issues discussed at length in the spring of 1940 were whether the public should continue to be encouraged to knit socks for soldiers even though home-knitted socks were not impregnated against gas (the practice was allowed to continue in order to discourage people knitting for the navy or air force), and whether the kilt should be issued to all Scottish regiments in Britain or just to pipers and drummers.[7]

The armed forces were determined not to allow the pressures of total war to alter their pre-war social characteristics. In the autumn of 1940 public schoolboys still had fourteen times more chance of being selected as infantry officers than boys from state schools. The Royal Navy continued to reserve half the places on their officer cadet entry scheme for those from public schools. Even high-level civilian resistance could achieve little against the prevailing bias. Churchill, when First Lord of the Admiralty, intervened in the Royal Navy's selection system. In April 1940 he even went as far as personally interviewing three boys, placed fifth, eighth and seventeenth out of 400 candidates for officer selection, but who had all been rejected as 'unfit for naval service'. The reasons were that the first had a slight Cockney accent and the other two had inferior social origins, one being the son of a chief petty officer and the other having a father who was an engineer in the Merchant Navy. Churchill insisted that all three be accepted and he also allowed more sailors from the 'lower deck' to become officers. At the end of 1940, with Churchill safely removed from the Admiralty, the admirals decided to go back to a pre-1913 arrangement to restrict 'lower deck' promotions to no more than seven and a half per cent of the officer entry after the war. As early as April 1940, the army was expressing its concern that post-war officers should continue to reflect the old traditions. They decided to keep the system for permanent officer appointments which allowed colonels of regiments to nominate officer candidates who had 'either territorial or family claims for appointment to a particular regiment'.[8]

Pre-war distinctions and prejudices within the armed forces

also continued unchanged. During the Battle of Britain an officer pilot would receive the Distinguished Flying Cross for gallantry and was entitled to first-class rail travel. An equally heroic pilot who happened to be a sergeant could receive only the Distinguished Flying Medal and travel third-class. Although Churchill was keen to widen the social background of naval officers, he intervened to limit the number of black sailors. He told Admiral Phillips, 'Not too many of them please.'[9] Churchill's wife, Clementine, would not invite the officers of the guard at Chequers to dine with them when they came from the socially downmarket Oxford and Bucks Light Infantry, but would do so when they came from the exclusive Coldstream Guards. The Army Board agreed in February 1940 that, even in war, social traditions should be maintained by allowing only officers of General rank to take their wives with them at public expense on overseas postings in order to cope with the amount of entertaining involved. Other officers could do so at their own expense, but other ranks only if quarters were available, which normally they were not. Pay in the armed forces was often very poor: after deductions a private had 5p a day to spend and his wife was allowed just 6p a week more than wives in the First World War. The children's allowance paid to wives of men in the armed forces was a maximum of 25p a week, reducing to 5p a week for the fourth child. The contrast with the allowance for those taking in evacuated children was striking. At 42½p a week without exception, it reflected the fact that it was paid mainly to middle-class families in rural areas.

Evacuation, both within Britain and abroad, demonstrated clearly the distinctions between rich and poor, but also the government's indecision and lack of consistency. Before the war the government had drawn up an elaborate plan to evacuate mothers and children from large cities, which were expected to be targets for heavy enemy bombing, to the countryside. The plan was put into action at the end of August 1939, and about one and a half million mothers and children were officially evacuated. This number was exceeded by the two million who could afford to pay for their own evacuation, often to hotels in the north and west of Britain. Three-quarters of the children who were evacuated did not receive full-time education and, when the expected bombing did not materialize, over one million returned to the cities by early 1940. But it was not until April 1940 that compulsory education was reintroduced. The threat of invasion in the summer revived the question of evacuation. On 3 July the chiefs of staff asked for the compulsory evacuation of all residents from most of the east coast, from Felixstowe to Folkestone, in order to facilitate military operations. Ministers refused the request, preferring instead to rely on voluntary movement (although there had been a hurried decision in mid-June to evacuate 100,000 children from London). Along the east coast about half the population had already left by the end of June, fleeing the expected battle zone. To encourage further evacuation the government decided to close all state schools so that children who remained would receive no education. At the beginning of September the war cabinet decided to extend the existing 'voluntary' evacuation scheme to Kent and Sussex (where a landing also seemed likely), although they were worried about alarming the public and Churchill insisted that 'it was essential that ... it should be kept out of the press'.[10] Once the prospects of invasion receded, the population gradually drifted back to their homes.

Evacuation from one part of the country to another could be only a temporary expedient to avoid the worst of the war and would be to no avail if the Germans were able to invade Britain. A more drastic alternative was to leave the country altogether. Over 5,000 people fled Britain in forty-eight hours at the end of August 1939 when war seemed imminent, but during the war an exit permit was required. The rapid collapse of France in May 1940 raised the spectre of invasion and defeat and convinced some among the establishment that it was time to leave the country. Naturally, those who went did not tend to publicize their departure or the reasons for it, and there was also a reluctance on the part of the government for news of such an exodus to become widely known. Instances of the governing classes leaving the country were viewed with contempt, but the contempt was expressed in private rather than publicly. When Sir Samuel Hoare was sacked by Churchill, he was at first extremely reluctant to accept the post of ambassador in Madrid. Once the news of the French collapse at Sedan had arrived in London, however, he rapidly changed his mind. He went round to the Foreign Office and told officials there that Churchill wanted him in Madrid immediately, which the officials knew was not true. Sir Alexander Cadogan shrewdly assessed Hoare's real motives when he wrote in his diary: 'Dirty little dog has got the wind up and wants to get out of this country! However, they all want to be disembarrassed of him and agreed to send him out.'[11] The next day, Sir Samuel and Lady Hoare were again at the Foreign Office trying to speed up their departure. When Cadogan, making polite conversation, commented on the difficulty of settling into a new country, Lady Hoare made it clear what she expected to happen in Britain when she replied: 'It may be easier than to adapt oneself to serving in an old country in new conditions.' Cadogan contemptuously referred to them as 'rats' leaving the ship and expected Hoare to be the Quisling of Britain.[12]

At the beginning of July, government ministers found out that at least three MPs had fled the country. Only one of them was named in a private note by Churchill. The official cabinet papers, widely circulated within Whitehall, were careful not to name names. The MP identified by Churchill was Captain Alex Cunningham-Reid, the Conservative member for St Marylebone since 1932, who had left for Canada, ostensibly to evacuate his two sons, and was not expected to return. Two others were in the United States and not expected to return either.[13] Churchill asked the Home Office to prepare a Bill to allow the seats of those MPs who left the country without government permission for more than six months to be declared vacant. When this was discussed at the home policy committee of the cabinet on 16 July, Ernie Bevin argued that the MPs should be stripped of their British citizenship too.[14] Later that morning, when the war cabinet discussed the issue, they agreed that introducing such a Bill would create too much undesirable publicity and alert the public to what had happened, and that it was better to do nothing about the absent MPs. Cunningham-Reid eventually returned to Britain in 1942, but was quietly disowned by his local Conservative Association, sat as an independent MP and was not re-elected in 1945.

Although adults could not leave Britain in 1940 without an exit permit, this was not the case with children. If aged under sixteen, they were free to leave and could be accompanied by their mothers and, in a nice sense of social distinction, by their nurses and governesses. On the day France requested an armistice, the war cabinet agreed a scheme, which had been worked out in the previous couple of weeks, for government-assisted evacuation to the dominions. It was run by the tactfully entitled Children's Overseas Reception Board under a junior minister at the Dominions Office, Geoffrey Shakespeare. When the scheme was announced on 20 June the board's offices were immediately besieged by a crowd of over 3,000 people trying to secure places. There were similar scenes at the American embassy five days later when they announced arrangements to allow children to enter the country and staff were overwhelmed by crowds that filled all the waiting rooms. When the official British scheme closed for applications on 4 July, over 210,000 requests for places had been received in a fortnight. As Geoffrey Shakespeare wrote, the reaction was 'so instantaneous and overwhelming that it revealed a deep current of public apprehension'.[15]

Almost from the start some ministers, especially Churchill, wanted to stop official evacuation, regarding it as bad for morale. At the beginning of July the sinking of the *Arandora Star*, when it was carrying civilians and internees to Canada, provided a convenient excuse to put the scheme into abeyance as too dangerous. In fact the government was worried by the scale of the response and the widespread public anxiety about the prospects facing Britain. Official evacuation resumed in August, but the sinking in September of the *City of Benares*, carrying officially evacuated children, when only thirteen children but eighty-two of the crew were rescued, convinced the war cabinet to introduce what was described in public as a 'temporary suspension' of the scheme. In fact ministers had agreed to end official evacuation and the board was reduced to a small nucleus with the sole function of keeping in touch with children who had already left the country.

Although many in the government disapproved of the official scheme to evacuate children from Britain, it took the opposite view about private arrangements. These were available only to the wealthy and well-connected who could buy passages for their children (and mothers, nurses and governesses) and who had friends or relatives in the United States willing, under American immigration laws, to sponsor the evacuees. When the war cabinet first decided to suspend the official scheme on 10 July, the Home Secretary, Sir John Anderson, raised 'the more difficult question ... whether, in order to avoid any suggestion of class distinction in the matter ... the grant of exit permits ... should also be suspended'. His colleagues decided against such equality of treatment: 'The proposal virtually to ban the sending abroad of any further children by private arrangements was considered unduly drastic.'[16] Instead they settled for Chamberlain's suggestion that this discrimination might be made more tolerable by asking a few charities to sponsor passages (third-class) for a very limited number of poorer children. When the official scheme was discreetly abandoned at the end of September, the war cabinet again refused to stop private evacuation.

The consequence was that the privileged few were able to send their children to safety in North America while the rest of the population had to face the rigours of bombing and the threat of invasion. Chips Channon, who sent his son Paul (later a Conservative cabinet minister) to the United States, described the scene at Euston station on 24 June as the boat train for Liverpool and safety prepared to depart: 'There was a queue of Rolls-Royces and liveried servants and mountains of trunks. It seemed that everyone we knew was there.'[17] The list of those who left Britain for the United States covers every area at the top of British society.[18] Lord Mountbatten sent his wife and two children on 4 July. Members of the government such as Duff Cooper, who sent his son (John Julius Norwich), were prepared to take advantage of private arrangements while stopping publicly funded schemes. From the aristocracy, the names include the children of the Countess de Borchgrave, Lady Margaret Barry, Lord Radnor, Viscount Bayham, the Earl of March, many of the Guinness family and Viscount Bethell. The City of London was represented by four Rothschilds and the children of Sir Charles Hambro. The press baron Viscount Rothermere took his son, Vere Harmsworth, out of Eton and sent him to Connecticut. Minor politicians such as Hely-Hutchinson, the secretary of the backbench Conservative 1922 Committee, did the same. Other well-connected children such as Jeremy Thorpe (a later leader of the Liberal Party) and Vera Brittain's children (among whom was Shirley Williams) also left for the United States. Most of the children returned after 1942, once the danger of invasion and defeat had disappeared.

The result of the government's policy is clear from the statistics. The official scheme ended after some 2,600 children were evacuated because it was thought to be bad for morale. Similar considerations did not apply to the 17,000 children evacuated privately in the six months after June 1940. That other parents would have liked to do the same as the rich and well-connected is demonstrated by the huge demand for the government scheme that was stopped after just one per cent of those who applied to go were evacuated. The Ministry of Information, responsible for assessing the state of morale in Britain, estimated that the parents of about one million children wanted them to go abroad, but that most had been unable even to register them before the government closed the scheme. In the middle of July they reported that the government's decision to stop official evacuation but allow private arrangements to continue had 'provoked sharp recrimination against the rich whose children were enabled to sail'.[19]

Government concern over the morale of the British population is also illustrated by the measures it took to control the country. Legislation giving the government sweeping emergency powers was passed by parliament at the end of August 1939. These powers were based on those used in the First World War, but they were strengthened and widened in crucial areas such as detention without trial and the suppression of opinion. It became an offence to do anything prejudicial to the 'efficient prosecution of the war', the mere possession of certain books and articles was an offence and public meetings were strictly controlled. Individual movements were restricted and the government was able to detain people indefinitely without trial. Before 1939 the government had also decided that a large part of the Territorial Army could not be sent abroad as part of any expeditionary force. As General Ironside recorded in his diary: 'The Cabinet have decided behind closed doors that the Territorial Army is required to keep the peace in England and restore law and order in air raids. They daren't give this out because it would be unpopular.'[20] A new level of government was also introduced in 1939: regional commissioners. This idea had originated in the 1920s with the aim of co-ordinating the response to any widespread strikes, but it was now used to provide the framework for control in a crisis. The first role of the commissioners was to ensure effective planning between local councils and the emergency services but, in the event of invasion or major dislocation following bombing, they would take over all the functions of central and local government in their area. The men chosen by the government to fill these posts reflected the desire to ensure extensive Conservative political control. Of the sixteen commissioners in place in 1940, seven were Conservative politicians and the rest safe members of the establishment: four were former senior civil servants, two were military personnel, one was a peer and prominent local business-man, one a university vice-chancellor and just one was a Labour MP (in Scotland).

The unexpected collapse of France after the breakthrough at Sedan and the prospect of a speedy German military victory sent a wave of panic through Whitehall. In the last fortnight of May a whole series of draconian measures were introduced, some of them kept secret, to give the government almost total control over the lives of British citizens and allow them to intern enemy aliens and censor opinion. These measures were to have profound conse-quences, not just for the rest of 1940 but for the remainder of the war. On 18 May the war cabinet met to consider what additional powers they wanted. Chamberlain, who dominated the discussion, said that it was 'imperative' for Britain to abandon what he described as its 'present rather easy-going methods' and adopt a form of government 'which would approach the totalitarian'. He continued: 'Powers should be given to the Government to enable them to exercise complete control over property, business and labour.' He recognized that sanctions might be needed and argued that the best plan might be to establish labour corps, under prison discipline, to which recalcitrants could be compulsorily assigned. The war cabinet agreed to introduce legislation to 'require persons to place themselves, their services and their property at the disposal of His Majesty'.[21] It was rushed through parliament in two hours by Clement Attlee on 22 May. At the same time additional power was taken to control all forms of labour by giving the government the authority 'to direct any person in Great Britain to perform such services ... as may be specified'. When the war cabinet had discussed this power earlier in the day, strong views had been expressed that even this sweeping degree of control was inadequate and that more drastic measures would be needed shortly.[22] On 24 May MI5 asked ministers to ban all strikes immediately. Ernie Bevin, the new Minister of Labour, persuaded his colleagues to go for a semi-voluntary scheme instead. By early July he secured TUC agree-ment and Order 1305 was issued; it made binding arbitration compulsory in any labour dispute and effectively made any strike illegal. Although there were some strikes in the autumn of 1940, the government decided against prosecuting a large number of workers, although it did so later in the war.

In 1939 there were about 74,000 enemy aliens in Britain, the vast majority of whom were refugees from Nazi Germany and Austria. At the start of the war a few hundred possible Nazi sympathizers were interned, and at the beginning of March 1940 the Home Secretary told the House of Commons: 'There would be no justification for a policy under which all aliens of German and Austrian nationality were treated alike, without regard to the fact that the majority of them are refugees from Nazi oppression and are bitterly opposed to the present regime in Germany.'[23] Within ten weeks that unjustifiable policy was introduced. Beginning on 11 May, all enemy aliens, including the elderly and infirm and excluding only women in MI5's least suspect category, were interned. In public the measure was justified on the grounds of possible danger to aliens caused by hostile public opinion. Government papers reveal no such apprehensions; the measure was introduced simply because of a military fear about a possible 'fifth column', although there was no evidence to justify such a panic reaction. The result of this hasty and ill-thought-out decision was chaos, squalor and bitter resentment. The refugees were held in conditions far worse than those of genuine Nazi sympathizers, such as Oswald Mosley and his wife. Twenty transit camps were set up with hopelessly inadequate facilities. At Wharf Mills camp 2,000 internees were held in a disused, rat-infested factory with eighteen taps for washing, sixty buckets in the yard for toilets and straw mattresses available only for the chronically sick. When the deputy director-general of the Ministry of Information, Sir Walter Monckton, investigated conditions at Huyton camp he reported a tragic outcome to British policy: 'The two men who succeeded in committing suicide had already been in Hitler's concentration camps. Against these they held out, but this camp has broken their spirit.'[24] In July, compulsory deportation was started. Those deported were not dangerous internees with Nazi sympathies but simply selected at random; many were strongly anti-Nazi. One thousand three hundred of them died when the *Arandora Star* was torpedoed in the Atlantic on its way to Canada. The government held an investigation into what by now was becoming an embarrassing fiasco, but when the war cabinet read the highly critical report by the investigating committee it refused to allow its publication. Some releases from detention were authorized in October 1940, but the government decided that the process should be gradual so as to try to create the impression that the original decision had been well thought out rather than a last-minute panic.

The new emergency powers also significantly extended the role of government censorship. In the last ten days of May, the government spent a considerable amount of time deciding how to introduce censorship of opinion. From the outbreak of war, all mail leaving the country was opened and read by government censors and on 20 May test checking of mail to Northern Ireland and Eire was started. After just two days the government, alarmed by the opinions expressed, decided to introduce censorship in this area too. A warrant was signed by the Home Secretary to authorize all mail bound for Ireland to be intercepted. A few days later the military asked for extensive powers to prohibit the sending of telegrams and the making of long-distance telephone calls. Total censorship of both areas was considered but ruled out, not on grounds of principle, but purely because of the amount of work that would be involved. Instead, on 30 May the cabinet civil defence committee authorized random interception of any telegram or trunk telephone call, regardless of who sent the telegram or made the call. As a safeguard against abuse, the normal practice was for the Home Secretary to issue warrants to authorize the interception of individual telephone numbers or mail to a particular address, but this decision required a blanket authority to intercept every phone in the country and every telegram. The Home Secretary, Sir John Anderson, warned the committee:

> The action which it was now proposed to take in this matter was quite unprecedented, that the only way in which effect could be given to what was proposed was under the authority of a *General Warrant* signed by the Home Secretary, and that the only safeguards would be administrative safeguards.

He ended with a further warning that there might be 'questions as to the legality or constitutional propriety of the action taken'.[25] Nevertheless, mass interception went ahead.

Powers to intercept communications were designed to enable

the authorities to gauge the state of public opinion and identify individuals whose opinions were unsatisfactory. But powers were also needed to act on these findings. Other measures were therefore taken to deter people from expressing unwelcome views. On 11 June it was made a criminal offence 'to make or report any statement likely to cause alarm and despondency'. Such a wide-ranging power led to a rush of prosecutions. On 17 July a man was sent to gaol for a month for saying that Britain had no chance of winning the war. For proclaiming that 'the rotten government holds 390 million Indians in slavery' a man was given two months in gaol and a sentence of three months was passed on someone who told two New Zealanders: 'You don't want to get killed in this bloody war.' By early August the number of prosecutions was getting out of hand, so the Home Office issued instructions to magistrates that prosecutions should be brought only in really serious cases. Nevertheless in June 1941 a woman was given five years in gaol for saying that 'Hitler was a good ruler, a better man than Mr Churchill'.

Attempts to control the media raised difficult problems. In war there was an obvious need to control information that might be useful to the enemy, but government controls went far beyond this category. By November 1940 nine newspapers or periodicals were subject to a general export ban. The main reason for the restriction was not to keep information from the enemy but to withhold 'matter which endangers or brings into disrepute the war effort of this country or its allies'. Direct government censorship of news within Britain had been introduced at the start of the war, but it was not compulsory. A newspaper could publish whatever it liked, although there was the risk of prosecution under the emergency regulations. It could not be prosecuted, however, for printing a story which had been approved beforehand by the Ministry of Information. In the rapidly worsening circumstances of late May 1940 the government became worried that the existing system of censorship was inadequate. On 31 May the Ministry of Information considered imposing total government control, which would mean that only official news could be published, no speculation about events would be allowed and all comment would have to be agreed by the government before publication. On 3 June the war cabinet asked the ministry to start planning for the introduction of a scheme on these lines, and consultations were started with the Newspaper Proprietors Association. On 11 June Duff Cooper, the Minister of Information, submitted his proposals to the war cabinet. He ruled out total censorship, not on principle, but because it was judged to be administratively too difficult to control about 900 provincial newspapers. Instead he proposed a variant of the earlier scheme under which a Censorship Board would issue legally binding directives to the press on what could be said about the war. The war cabinet drew back from these totalitarian schemes both because of the shock it might cause the public and the adverse effect it would have on American opinion at a time when Britain was supposed to be fighting for freedom and democracy. Instead, they finally decided to extend the voluntary D-Notice system (which issued 'guidance' to the press on what areas of information should not be discussed in public) and rely on the threat of introducing more draconian powers to keep the press in line.

It was in the autumn of 1940 that the government reacted particularly strongly to the merest hint of criticism in the press and again threatened more controls. On 2 October the war cabinet asked the Liberal leader, Sinclair, to use his influence with the *News Chronicle* to stop its criticism of the government. A few days later, the *Daily Mirror* printed an editorial critical of the government reshuffle that brought Morrison to the Home Office: 'The shifting or shunting of mediocrities or reputed successes appears to have been directed by no principle plain to the outsider, unless it be the principle that new blood must rarely be transfused into an old body.' This mild political comment sent the war cabinet, Churchill in particular, into a paroxysm of rage. A secret police investigation, launched to discover who held shares in the paper, discovered nothing of interest, although the papers on this embarrassing subject were withheld from the public until the mid-1980s. Attlee and Beaverbrook were deputed to contact the newspaper owners and threaten them with total censorship of news and opinion if criticism continued. Attlee also had a separate interview with the editor of the *Daily Mirror*. He tried to argue that the government did not mind criticism, but only what he described as 'irresponsible' criticism. He proved unable, however, to define what distinguished the latter category, accusing the paper of endangering the war effort but without giving any examples. Eventually the storm died down and the government decided that the threats made against the press had brought them back into line.

The other part of the media that caused the government problems was the BBC. It is a long-held myth that during the war the BBC was independent of government and able, within the inevitable constraints of censorship, to broadcast whatever news it liked. In fact, the government controlled most of the corporation's output. The Minister of Information confirmed publicly, at the end of September 1939, that the BBC was independent only as to 'the lighter parts of its programmes'.[26] In November 1940 Duff Cooper told the House of Commons that as Minister for Information he was responsible for the 'political statements, news bulletins and talks sent out by the BBC at present'.[27] This detailed control could extend to individual programmes. For example, the Ministry of Information stopped the BBC broadcasting a 4 p.m. news because it was worried that this might compete with the evening newspapers. MI5 vetting of staff, which had been introduced before the war, was extended to include all artists appearing on the BBC, not just those giving talks. Sir Hugh Robertson, for instance, was due to conduct the Glasgow Orpheus Choir in a Christmas concert in December 1940, but this was cancelled because he was a pacifist and privately critical of the government. Unofficial pressure could also be employed. Beginning around the time of Dunkirk, J. B. Priestley gave a series of talks on Sunday evenings in the 'Postscript' series arguing for better times and more social justice after the war. The government's response was to send Margesson, the Chief Whip, to the BBC to complain about the 'leftish' slant of the talks and apply pressure to have Priestley withdrawn. The series was quietly dropped in the autumn. On occasions the BBC was so anxious to be co-operative that it would take action before being asked by the government. For example, all racing results were stopped on 8 June, ten days before the government banned horse racing altogether, because the BBC did not want to broadcast frivolous programmes.

Despite the detailed control available to the government and the co-operative stance of the BBC, ministers still resented the limited amount of independence remaining to the corporation. At the beginning of November Lord Reith, the Minister of Transport and a former Director-general of the BBC, reported a war cabinet discussion which contemplated imposing direct state control: 'The

P.M. spoke most bitterly about the BBC – enemy within the gate; continually causing trouble; more harm than good. Something drastic must be done with them, he said. Duff Cooper ... agreed – more control probably and they ought to be civil servants.'[28] After further thought the government decided to keep the façade of BBC independence rather than make it a government department and its employees civil servants. At the end of 1940 the government achieved its aims via the back door by sending in two civil servants, described in public as 'advisers' on foreign and home news. In fact their terms of reference gave them 'supreme direction' over the news output of the BBC.

From September 1939 the BBC was part of the government's drive to manage the news and keep up morale but one of the major problems, particularly in early 1940, was the appallingly low quality of its broadcasts. On the outbreak of war the BBC was reduced to a single service broadcasting mainly official announcements, pep talks by ministers and civil servants and Sandy Macpherson playing popular music on the organ. After a major public outcry about quality, a gradual improvement occurred and a second programme was introduced. Nevertheless, in early 1940 the Mass Observation team of observers (an early form of opinion sampling) was reporting on 'the sometimes nauseatingly complacent air of the BBC news bulletins'. As a result, according to the BBC's own figures, at least half the country was listening occasionally and a third regularly to the propaganda broadcasts by William Joyce (Lord Haw-Haw) in an attempt to find out what was happening in the war. (These figures were as high as those recorded for the popular and inspirational broadcasts by J. B. Priestley.) Mass Observation also reported that men on RAF stations were listening to German radio and Joyce even obtained the ultimate accolade of having details of his programmes listed in *The Times*.

One of the reasons for the problems facing the government on the propaganda front was the inadequacy of the Ministry of Information. In the First World War, Britain had not had a ministry responsible for internal propaganda but a secret 1936 report, clearly based on German experience of propaganda under Goebbels, recommended that such a ministry should be established in wartime. Set up in September 1939, the new department suffered from three weak ministers in succession: Lord Macmillan, a retired judge without any relevant experience; Lord Reith, who had broadcasting experience but found it almost impossible to work within Whitehall; and Duff Cooper, who had administrative experience but was too lazy to be effective. The rest of the staff, from the first director-general, Lord Perth – a retired diplomat from the Rome embassy where he had carelessly allowed his valet to steal secrets for the Italians – through men like Kenneth Clark, the director of the National Gallery, came from such circumscribed backgrounds (bounded by the clubs of St James's and the intellectual world of Bloomsbury and Oxbridge) that they had little if any knowledge of the lives of ordinary members of the public and no idea of how to communicate with them. They also had a secret dread that the working class would prove unreliable and defeatist, when the exact opposite was the case. As a result most of the ministry's campaigns were little more than exhortations and instructions often cast in highly patronizing tones. Their first poster campaign was built on the extremely ambiguous slogan: 'Your courage, your cheerfulness, your resolution, will bring us victory.' Not surprisingly, it was a failure. This permanent cajoling of the public was linked with constant detailed regulation of life by the government. One outsider, a diplomat at the Canadian High Commission, reported that 'living in London is like being an inmate of a reformatory school. Everywhere you turn, you run into some regulation designed for your protection. The government is like School Matron.'[29]

The most enduring memory of 1940 is, undoubtedly, of the series of stirring speeches made by Winston Churchill, with the aim of inspiring the nation in its hour of greatest need, raising morale and creating national unity. They have become part of the essential mythology of 1940. The reality is very different: not all of his performances were universally hailed as great at the time. At some critical moments of the war there were long gaps between the speeches, some of the most famous speeches were never broadcast to the nation and some of the ones that did reach the airwaves were not in fact spoken by Churchill. He regarded the House of Commons as the true forum of the nation and stuck to a policy of not repeating speeches he made there over the radio to the mass of the people. His first speech as Prime Minister was on 13 May to the House of Commons. Using a phrase he had first tried out on a meeting of junior ministers earlier in the day, he said: 'I have nothing to offer but blood, toil, tears and sweat.' That speech was not broadcast to the nation at all but merely read out by a newsreader. Churchill's first radio address to the nation as Prime Minister did not take place until 19 May, nine days after he took office. In a now little-quoted speech he talked of the battle of France, the coming battle for Britain and ended with an obscure biblical quotation. His next two speeches were made only in the House of Commons. On 23 May he announced the German penetration of the Allied line, a week after it took place, and talked of a possible counter-attack. Five days later, he announced the Belgian surrender and, with the BEF almost surrounded, he told the House to prepare itself for 'hard and heavy tidings'.

When he spoke again in the Commons on 4 June he was able to build on the rescue of the British army from Dunkirk. He criticized King Leopold for the Belgian surrender, although in private a few days earlier he had been sympathetic to his plight. The speech also included the well-known passage beginning 'we shall fight on the beaches . . .' That evening, with no recording of the speech in the Commons available, the BBC asked Churchill to repeat it as a broadcast to the nation. Churchill refused and instead the BBC used an actor, Norman Shelley (who played Larry the Lamb in 'Children's Hour') to imitate Churchill's voice while pretending to the public that it was Churchill speaking. In 1940, when ministerial speeches on the radio were still a rarity, and with no broadcasting of parliament, few people were familiar with politicians' voices and the imitation passed unnoticed until Shelley confessed to the impersonation nearly forty years later.

Churchill did speak on the radio on 17 June, the day the French asked for an armistice. He broadcast in the early afternoon when few were listening and spoke for only two minutes, ending with the phrase 'we are sure that in the end all will come right'. Churchill had not intended to broadcast until 19 June and he made the speech only after press pressure on the Foreign Office for some immediate statement of British policy at such a crucial time in the war. Cecil King of the *Daily Mirror*, for one, was far from impressed by the speech, calling it a 'miserable 119-word address' and describing it as: 'a few stumbling sentences to the effect that the situation was disastrous, but all right. Whether he was drunk or all-in from sheer fatigue, I don't know, but it was the poorest possible effort on an occasion when he should have produced the finest speech of his life.'[30]

On 18 June Churchill gave a thirty-six-minute speech in the Commons, which included the memorable passage that if the British Empire lasted for a thousand years men would say: 'This was their Finest Hour.' Not every member of the government was enthusiastic about his performance at the time. Lord Reith wrote in his diary: 'Churchill made a statement in the House of Commons this afternoon. Not very good.'[31] On this occasion, too, the BBC failed to persuade Churchill to repeat the speech on the radio and they had to fall back on using Norman Shelley again. Even those close to Churchill did not know about the impersonation but felt the broadcast was poor. Harold Nicolson wrote: 'As delivered in the House of Commons, that speech was magnificent, especially the concluding sentences. But it sounded ghastly on the wireless. All the great vigour he put into it seemed to evaporate.'[32] Two of Churchill's private secretaries were unimpressed and puzzled. John Colville thought 'it was too long and he sounded tired', and John Martin was struck by the 'halting delivery' at the start and thought the voice sounded funny.[33] The staff at No. 10 also received a large number of letters asking what was wrong with the Prime Minister. Churchill did make a broadcast to the nation on 14 July, but it is not now regarded as one of his great speeches.

Churchill's next speech in the Commons was on 20 August, when he coined the phrase 'never in the field of human conflict was so much owed by so many to so few'. Lord Reith was still unmoved by the rhetoric and wrote: 'I listened to Churchill and thought little of him. Of course he made the usual revolting reference to Beaverbrook which was received in silence.'[34] That speech, like the 'blood, toil, tears and sweat' speech, was not broadcast by the BBC. Churchill did not speak to the nation until 11 September, when he compared the situation both to 1588 and the Spanish Armada, and to 1805 and Napoleon's attempt to invade. That was the last broadcast to Britain Churchill made in 1940. During all the Blitz and the gloomy winter of 1940–41, he gave no inspirational address to the people, but he found time to broadcast to Czechoslovakia and France in late September and October and to Italy in late December. He did not speak to the people of Britain again until February 1941.

Despite Churchill's speeches the general state of morale remained indifferent at best and poor at worst. The Ministry of

Information employed nearly 10,000 people to read letters intercepted from members of the public (at a rate of about 200,000 a
week), and these formed the basis for its assessment of the state
of popular morale. These morale reports are now available to the
public, and another important source is the archive of Mass
Observation, an organization which used people from all over the
country to note impressions and views. These contemporary
records paint a picture of Britain in 1940 that differs markedly
from the view popularly accepted today. The accepted view re-
flects the contemporary propaganda line rather than reality, yet it
has become so strongly entrenched that it has affected individual
memory about moods and morale in 1940. In the mid-1970s, when
the Mass Observation archive was catalogued, the organizers
contacted the people who had provided diaries and information
in 1940 and asked them to describe again how they had felt
during that dramatic year. Their later accounts are seen through
rose-tinted spectacles: they are full of received notions of unity of
purpose, high morale, calmness and valiant struggle. These
directly contradict both their contemporary impressions and the
reality of life in Britain in 1940, when boredom, apathy and
pessimism were widespread.

It is not surprising that morale was poor during the 'phoney
war' of the autumn and winter of 1939–40, with its minimal
military action, no clear statement of war aims or sense of purpose,
and civilian involvement in no more than the inconveniences of
war. What is more surprising, perhaps, was the rapid fall in
morale once fighting began in earnest in May 1940. On 18 May
the Ministry of Information reported that 'public morale is at a
low ebb'.[35] Four days later, an emergency committee was set up
on home morale. One of the members of that committee, Lord
Clark, wrote later: 'The only interesting feature was the amount
of evidence that came in on how low morale in England was,
much lower than anybody had ever dared to say. But there was
obviously nothing we could do about it.'[36] Towards the end of
May, rumours swept the country that the royal family were
leaving for Canada, that a shadow government had already been
formed there and that the government was ready to leave the
moment invasion started. The Ministry of Information commented
on the significance of such fears: 'Rumour during the last few
days has tended to emphasize some aspect of our own feebleness

and futility ... This kind of rumour is clearly unhealthy for it is an unconscious reflection of privately held opinion.'[37] As the military situation in France worsened, the nation remained unmoved, and to some extent uninvolved. George Orwell commented on the day the Dunkirk evacuation started in earnest:

> People talk a little more of the war, but very little. As always, it is impossible to overhear any comments on it in pubs. Last night, Eileen and I went to the pub to hear the nine o'clock news. The barmaid was not going to have it turned on if we had not asked her. To all appearances nobody listened.[38]

By mid-June there was a widespread belief in the inevitability of invasion and doubts as to whether Britain could go on to victory. There was also considerable resentment that the government was not telling civilians what they should do in the event of invasion. (This reflected the fact that the government had been unable to decide what to advise people to do.) The Ministry of Information intelligence reports concluded: 'There is no escaping the tenor of our reports: leadership is in jeopardy ... There is great restlessness, great depression at the fall of France. Home morale is still being bungled. The appeals of the leadership are failing to register.'[39] By early July Cecil King was writing in his diary that 'the country is already reconciling itself to the idea of a Nazi conquest' and the war cabinet, concerned at what it described as the 'growing mood of pessimism', issued instructions for ministers and civil servants to stop the spread of 'defeatist talk'.[40] On 3 July, after an air raid on Newcastle, the war cabinet were worried about the publication of detailed casualty figures (eleven dead, 109 injured) on the grounds that they might have 'a demoralizing effect in this country'. They agreed that in future no detailed figures should be published and comments on air raids would merely describe them as 'slight', 'considerable', or 'heavy'.[41] A month later, the Ministry of Information intelligence reports from the provinces were even suggesting a widespread view that Churchill was 'played out' and should resign.

With morale still low in the summer of 1940, the Germans launched what should, according to the military theorists of the 1930s, have been a devastating blow to British willingness to continue the war: the Blitz. Until August 1940 both sides had done their best to avoid all-out bombing of population centres. In August 1939 Hitler announced that he would bomb only military targets and Goering, the head of the Luftwaffe, used a Swedish intermediary, Dahlerus, to obtain similar assurances from the British. Early in September both sides accepted President Roosevelt's appeal to avoid civilian bombing. The Germans made no attempt during the campaign in France to use the Luftwaffe strategically and restricted its use to tactical support of the army. During the German attack on Holland, however, Rotterdam had been bombed to assist army operations. This, not surprisingly, was misinterpreted by Britain as an end to the German policy of restraint and the RAF was authorized to bomb what it thought was the Ruhr, although given its navigation techniques it was almost certainly somewhere else. Despite this widening of operations, neither side was prepared to authorize the bombing of the other's capital. On 24 August Hitler repeated his instructions that London should not be bombed. The next day, during a raid on oil tanks at Rochester in Kent, one plane overshot the target and dropped some bombs on an outer suburb of London without causing any casualties. Churchill then authorized a raid on Berlin, which had been in preparation from early August. Few bombers found the target and there were no casualties. Hitler ignored the attack and the Luftwaffe continued to concentrate on RAF airfields. Churchill refused to agree to the RAF's suggestion of Leipzig as a target and insisted on a repetition of the Berlin raid. This was carried out on 29 August and ten civilians were killed. At this point Hitler ordered preparations to be made for raids on London in retaliation. These were approved on 4 September and began three days later.

The day and night raid on the London docks on 7 September marked the beginning of the Blitz on British cities. London was raided for fifty-seven successive nights and on 14 November major attacks also began on provincial cities. The large-scale raids ended on 10 May with a massive raid on London, after which the Luftwaffe was redeployed to the east for the attack on the Soviet Union. During this eight-month period 40,000 civilians were killed and about 800,000 houses were damaged beyond repair. Although the scale of destruction was large, it needs to be kept in proportion, compared with the weight of the Allied air attacks on Germany later in the war. In total 590,000 German civilians were killed (nearly fifteen times the British figure), 800,000 were seriously injured, and 7,500,000 were made homeless. The weight of bombs dropped by the Luftwaffe on Britain was just three per cent of the amount the Allies dropped on Germany. Individual raids reflect the same pattern. The attack on Coventry in November 1940 killed about 550 civilians. In August 1943, when the Allies attacked Hamburg, firestorms in the centre of the city, with temperatures of 1,000°C and winds of 150 m.p.h., killed about 50,000 people and destroyed sixty per cent of the houses. Just before the end of the war, the bombing of Dresden (which received seven times the weight of bombs dropped on Coventry) resulted in the deaths of about 130,000 people and destroyed all but ten per cent of the houses.

The advent of large-scale bombing was the event most dreaded by the government, since it believed that the population would not withstand such pressure for very long. Almost immediately some of the feared signs emerged. As Harold Nicolson, junior information minister, commented: 'Everybody is worried about feeling in the East End, where there is much bitterness. It is said that even the King and Queen were booed the other day when they visited the destroyed area.' [42] At the beginning of October, John Colville accompanied Clementine Churchill to her husband's constituency of Chingford to view bomb damage and found the same bitter feeling. He recorded one refugee saying: '"It is all very well for them" (looking at us!) "who have all they want; but we have lost everything."' [43] A fortnight later he noted that the intelligence report given to No. 10 reported that 'the morale of Londoners has deteriorated. There is less of "We can take it" and an inclination to say "This must stop at all costs".' [44]

If morale was poor, people learnt to adjust to the new reality of raids, destruction, sleepless nights and disruption. One reaction was to escape from the affected areas. People left the East End for Epping Forest, and the West End of London for department store basements or Chislehurst caves (where a regular community of 8,000 people was rapidly established). By the middle of September, about half the population of Stepney had gone and by October a quarter of London's citizens had left the capital. Those who stayed behind often had to cope with appalling conditions. Some of the worst were at the 'Tilbury' shelter near Liverpool Street station. This old warehouse, still full of food, accommodated nearly 15,000 people every night. Queues formed early in the morning and police were needed to control the crowds when the gates were opened at 4 p.m. Inside, conditions were squalid in the extreme. There were just two water taps and no toilets and the floor was soon awash with urine and faeces. Conditions were also primitive in the tube stations, where about 200,000 people a night took shelter. Nevertheless, only a minority used these facilities: about a third used domestic shelters and those in less vulnerable parts of London did not bother to take shelter.

When the attacks shifted to provincial towns the same reactions were seen. Here conditions could be more difficult, because the short sharp raids rather than the long series of attacks on London gave people less time to adjust. Official reactions in bombed cities showed a consistent picture:

Coventry – there was great depression, a widespread feeling of impotence and many open signs of hysteria ... terror, neurosis ... women were seen to cry, to scream, to tremble all over, to faint in the street, to attack a fireman and so on.

Bristol – much talk of having been let down by the Government, and of the possibility of a negotiated peace.

Portsmouth – on all sides we hear that looting and wanton destruction had reached alarming proportions. The police seem unable to exercise control ... The effect on morale is bad and there is a general feeling of desperation ... their nerve had gone.

Plymouth – the people cannot stand this intensive bombing indefinitely, sooner or later the morale of other towns will go even as Plymouth's has gone.[45]

Unofficial reports reveal the same picture. At the beginning of December 1940 the Bishop of Winchester visited Southampton and found it 'broken in spirit'. He reported: 'For the first time, morale has collapsed. I went from parish to parish and everywhere there was fear.'[46] After the bombing of Liverpool in early 1941 one Mass Observation member reported: 'An atmosphere of ineptitude seemed to oppress the town ... The general feeling – it is difficult exactly to express it, but residents spoken to felt it too – that there was no power or drive left in Liverpool.'[47]

The population of the provincial towns reacted in the same way as those in London: they left in large numbers, a phenomenon rapidly christened 'trekking'. In parts of Southampton after the bombing only one in five of the people were left, with the Mayor setting an example by leaving promptly every day at 3 p.m. for his rural retreat. Even three months after the bombing, 'trekking' still dominated life in Southampton and commercial life in the city took a long time to recover. In Portsmouth during the heavy bombing about 90,000 people a night were leaving the city; during quieter periods it was about a third of that figure. By March 1941, in some areas, two-thirds of the population had left and a survey showed that of those remaining three-quarters would go if they could. In Liverpool about 50,000 a night left and in Clydebank after the first attack the overnight population fell from 50,000 to 2,000. 'Trekking' highlighted the differences between rich and poor. Those with their own car and a country place or the ability to rent one could leave easily. Others had to walk and sleep out in the open.

In the decade before the outbreak of war the government had been planning how to respond to a bombing offensive. Yet when it happened the official reaction proved inadequate, confused and unco-ordinated. It was not until the bombing was over that an effective response on civil defence, shelter policy, and provision of emergency help was created. At a military level, there was no effective defence against night bombing because of the difficulty the fighters had in finding the enemy. The impotence of the defence can be judged from the fact that in September and October Fighter Command shot down only fifty-four bombers out of the several hundred a night flying over Britain. Once the Blitz began, the government moved large numbers of anti-aircraft guns to London, but that was largely to improve civilian morale by giving an impression of defence. At other levels civil defence was often inadequate, even after months of raids. On the night of 29–30 December 1940 a small force of 150 bombers, using a large number of incendiaries, caused widespread fires in the City of London. One of the reasons the raid was so effective was that it was carried out on a Sunday night, when buildings were closed and there were no firewatchers to douse the incendiaries as soon as they landed. Only after devastation on this scale did the government institute a system of compulsory firewatching, but

administrative difficulties meant that it did not become operational until after the Blitz was over and proved of little long-term
value. The same deplorable sequence happened on firefighting.
Despite all the pre-war preparations, there were still 1,668 separate fire brigades in Britain in 1940. Much of their equipment was
not interoperable, and so assistance could not be given to hard-
pressed brigades during attacks, with the result that fires often
got out of control. Not until two days before the end of the Blitz,
in May 1941, did the war cabinet agree to set up a national fire
service. By then it was too late.

The government attitude to shelter problems was ambivalent.
Before the war Whitehall decided that it did not like deep shelters
such as tube stations because they feared that once people entered
them they would be reluctant to come back above ground and
continue normal life. Public shelters had been provided in basements, and 'Anderson' shelters, which could withstand the effects
of blast but not a direct hit, were issued for people to place in
their gardens. When the bombing started in September, the government ordered London Transport not to allow people to use the
tube stations as shelters. Underground station staff found, however, that it was impossible to stop people entering and setting up
their own primitive squalid camps below ground. By early October
the government was on the brink of dealing with this manifestation of civil disobedience. Churchill's private secretary reported
that, although the Prime Minister was happy to use a disused
underground station as a refuge himself, he was 'thinking on
authoritarian lines about shelters and talks about forcibly preventing people from going into the underground.'[48] The inept government response to the effects of bombing and growing anger
among Londoners led directly to the appointment of Herbert
Morrison, the boss of the London Labour Party, as Home Secretary
in early October. Slowly the government began to admit that they
were wrong about the need for deep shelters. Grants were given
to local authorities to build them and effective management of the
tube stations as shelters was introduced involving tickets, proper
bunks, chemical lavatories and canteen facilities. At the beginning
of November the government announced the construction of deep
shelters for 100,000 people, although by the time they were built
the Blitz was over and they were used only as billets for troops
before the Normandy invasion. Not until January 1941 did the

war cabinet authorize construction of the so-called 'Morrison' shelters (though he had little to do with the project apart from gaining publicity from it) for better protection inside houses.

The government was also ambivalent about whether or not to evacuate the areas most at risk from bombing. After four days of bombing in the East End, the Minister of Health, Malcolm Mac-Donald, was prepared to agree to the total evacuation of the worst-hit area – Silvertown – but only on a voluntary basis. After another three months of bombing, the war cabinet civil defence committee was on the point of agreeing to the compulsory evacuation of all children from London. Only the decline in raids as the Luftwaffe switched its attention to the provinces and the end of the Blitz ensured that the scheme was not implemented. The residents of vulnerable boroughs in the East End were not the only ones who left London during these difficult days. Many who had second homes in the country left London altogether in the autumn of 1940. Others left at crucial times. The King and Queen normally left each evening for Windsor and the Princesses Elizabeth and Margaret stayed there permanently. Queen Mary, the Queen Mother, lived at Badminton. Churchill often left London for Chequers but moved on to Ditchley Park near Blenheim on moonlit nights when the Luftwaffe might be able to find his official residence.

The most acute problem facing the authorities was how to cope with the social dislocation caused by bombing. Two difficulties were at the core of the problem. Government planning before the war assumed a high casualty rate and envisaged disposal of bodies and control of the population in the event of mass panic as the main priorities. In fact the death and casualty rates were far lower than expected and social control was not a problem. Unexpectedly, homelessness, which affected one in six people in London, became the intractable issue. By the middle of October over 250,000 were waiting to be rehoused and, despite a large number of empty houses, only 7,000 had been found new homes. The second difficulty was administrative. Too many government departments, agencies and local authorities were involved in providing assistance and there were inadequate mechanisms to co-ordinate their work. In London six Whitehall ministries, the London County Council (LCC), the regional commissioner, twenty-eight local boroughs and seventy other agencies were involved, and all jealously guarded their privileges and independence. Within Whitehall, for example, the Ministry of Food was responsible for communal feeding centres at which people paid, but the Ministry of Health ran food and rest centres where free food was provided. Local boroughs resented interference, particularly from the LCC – their long-standing political rival – but were often lethargic one-party administrations that had lost contact with the local community long before the war. They could billet people only within the borough boundary and the worst-affected boroughs had no spare accommodation. The LCC was similarly hamstrung because it could billet only within London. There were long arguments over the appointment of the ARP controller, responsible for the civil defence effort, in many of the boroughs. The local council often wanted the mayor appointed for reasons of prestige, whereas the regional commissioner preferred the more administratively competent town clerk. In some cases local disagreements got out of hand. The argument in West Ham had to be resolved by the Ministry of Home Security. In Stepney the local administration was so bad that Morrison took away all its powers and placed them in the hands of commissioners.[49]

Everywhere it took a long time to improvise even basic facilities. In September 1940, after the first few weeks of bombing, West Ham had no canteens, lavatories or lighting in public shelters, and in many cases the local council refused to recognize impromptu shelters and provide any facilities. Neither were there any mobile canteens or communal feeding centres for people who had lost their homes or means of cooking. Much of the relief had to be provided by voluntary bodies, particularly the Society of Friends. Many companies, such as the Port of London Authority and the London and North Eastern Railway, refused, despite government requirements, to provide works canteens so that workers could obtain at least one hot meal a day. West Ham council discouraged self-help schemes for the repair of houses and insisted on doing all the work itself, leading to long delays and an increase in homelessness.

The most acute problems occurred in the rest centres, where those made homeless by the bombing were accommodated until they could find a new home. These centres starkly illustrated the difference between rich and poor. They were administered under the old poor law system for the destitute, and most people preferred to avoid them and make their own arrangements if at all possible. Nevertheless, by the end of September 1940 over 25,000 people were living in these so-called rest centres and nearly half spent more than ten days there waiting to be moved. They were improvised in converted schools and derelict buildings, and conditions were dreadful. In one centre in Stepney nearly 300 people who had been bombed out of their houses had to use ten pails or old coal scuttles as lavatories and make do with seven basins (but no soap and towels) to wash in. Food was bad, based as it was on poor law allowances. For the whole of London there were only 25,000 blankets available when the estimated requirement was two and a half million, and the War Office had to lend one million from army stores. The main reason for the shortage was that before the war the Treasury had refused to sanction the purchase of blankets because they were worried that it might tempt people to stay in the rest centres. Under strict government financial rules, some of those taking refuge were not even entitled to receive any assistance at all: about a third were there because of unexploded bombs either in or near their houses. Under the strict rules inherited from the poor law administration they had to pay for any help. 'Trekking' was always discouraged and the war cabinet civil defence committee consistently refused to provide any facilities or assistance to such people.

Not until the end of 1940 was a competent system to deal with the effects of bombing even beginning to emerge in London. Perhaps the most depressing fact about the official response to these problems is that none of the lessons being painfully learnt in London was applied in the provincial cities, with the result that they, too, suffered from all the same failings. The war effort did not galvanize the bureaucracy into action. For example, it took the Ministry of Health a year before it finally got round to issuing a circular to local authorities, in August 1941, suggesting the appointment of welfare officers. Even the official war historian was forced to admit:

The same story for each of some thirty cities. The same monotonous and insufficient food in the rest centres, the same meagre provision of clothing, blankets and washing facilities, first aid, lavatories, furniture and information and salvage facilities, the same inadequacy of unsupported public assistance officials

and of casually organized volunteers, the same weak liaison
with the police and civil defence controls ... All these faults
were constantly in evidence ... as one city after another was
bombed.[50]

An official Ministry of Home Security enquiry into the failures
during the attacks on Birmingham found that 'more heavy bombing would have led to a dissolution of the civic entity' and that
there were 'grave deficiencies' in the local system, inadequate co-
ordination between the fire service and the auxiliary service,
serious looting and disorderly scenes. It concluded that the local
authority had failed to help the local people.[51] Indeed the most
distinctive feature of life in all the bombed cities was the gap
between the administrative elite and the people. A Mass Observation reporter in Liverpool spoke of the 'almost complete divorce'
between the politicians and officials and the local population and
'the unprintably violent comments on the local leadership' by the
latter.[52] In Southampton there was much criticism of the local
council and its exhortations to carry on, compared with the lack
of practical help. A visit to the city by the King and Queen was
greeted with general indifference. In Portsmouth, where the communal feeding facilities for those made homeless by bombing
were dreadful, a government report said: 'The attitude of the
official in charge appears to be largely responsible ... Apart from
a personal horror of communal feeding, he expressed the opinion
that it encouraged parasitism and laziness and he did not see
why "workers probably earning more than I do should be encouraged by the government".'[53]

The most difficult problem, both in the provinces and London,
for people affected by bombing was how to obtain the help they
needed. Few boroughs provided a central point where all the
elements of the local bureaucracy could be contacted. In Plymouth,
for example, a person bombed out would have to go to fifteen
different offices scattered throughout the city for such essentials
as a new ration book, a gas mask, a meal, temporary accommodation, a new identity card, compensation, death registration, help
with a burial and a billet out of town. Even if the person knew
where the different offices were located, getting to them could be
a major problem in a city recovering from bombing and with little
public transport.

Despite all these problems, morale did not 'crack' as many in authority before the war, and when the bombing started, had expected. This should not, however, be seen as an example of uniquely British courage and resilience. No society subjected to massive bombing has disintegrated; indeed in many respects they have achieved greater social cohesion in the face of adversity. Germany and Japan later in the war suffered far heavier bombing without social breakdown, as did North Vietnam under an intensive American onslaught in the 1960s and early 1970s. Even if people were tired of bombing and disruption and yearned for an end, it is difficult to see how those feelings could be effectively expressed in Britain in late 1940. There were no avenues, short of mass demonstrations in the streets, through which views could be made known in the media or in politics. As Churchill admitted earlier in the year: 'In time of war the machinery of government is so strong it can afford largely to ignore popular feeling.'[54] The rumours circulating in the Midlands during May 1941, as reported by Mass Observation, show how bad the situation seemed to many people and what could be believed. It was rumoured that trainloads of corpses had left Liverpool for mass burial, that martial law had been declared in a number of big cities, that food riots had broken out and homeless and bombed people were on hunger marches with white flags.

In fact, most people did not want to demand an end to the war. They tried to carry on with their lives as best they could because they had little alternative. Despite the bombing, lack of interest in the war actually rose from a figure of about ten per cent who admitted not following the war news in May and June to nearly a third by the end of the year. Other surveys found that, when questioned about what depressed them most, people put the weather first, followed by war news and then air raids. In practice the Blitz made little difference to the underlying reality of life in wartime Britain. There were no major social changes and the poor and less privileged continued to bear the brunt of the problems. There was no fundamental political change either: the sense of disillusionment with politicians and those in power, already well-established, was only confirmed by the inept reaction of the authorities to the Blitz. The feelings of the majority of people, as they tried to cope with bombing and the disruption of their lives, were well summed up by a letter from a young Manchester resident to her husband in the Far East: 'You will hear a lot of talk about Manchester carrying on. I suppose we are ... but as one who lives here it's a rather weary carrying on. We are carrying on because we've got to.'[55]

9

Impotence

In the summer of 1940 Britain could wield just enough military power to avoid immediate defeat. Pre-war governments, by concentrating on the air defence of Britain, had provided the vital margin of safety. But all the problems that the pre-war policy-makers had been unable to resolve – an over-extended Empire, too many enemies, too few allies and inadequate industrial, economic and financial resources – not only remained unsolved but now came together, exacerbated by the pressure of all-out war, to leave Britain largely impotent militarily and diplomatically. The Empire survived 1940 largely intact because the Germans lacked the means to deploy significant forces outside Europe; the Italians, who did have the means, were weak and incompetent; and the Japanese had not yet decided to attack the Western nations.

The British Empire lay sprawled, almost defenceless, across the globe and the nightmare of facing three enemies simultaneously, which had seriously alarmed ministers and military planners in the 1930s, was now close to reality. Germany dominated most of western and central Europe and the Italian declaration of war in mid-June extended the conflict into the Mediterranean and the Middle East. In the Far East, Japan could be expected to take advantage of growing British weakness. After the debacle of Dunkirk, Britain hardly had an army left, and naval and air strength had to be concentrated on home defence, leaving other areas intensely vulnerable. Lacking significant military power Britain had little diplomatic power. The collapse of France left Britain without allies at a time when the Soviet Union was a hostile neutral and the United States friendly but unwilling to offer substantial assistance.

The crisis facing Britain in the summer of 1940 meant that emergency action had to be taken and existing plans for a long

war abandoned. The armaments programme was therefore radically recast. The planning assumption in September 1939 had
been for a three-year war, and production plans were based on
British forces reaching their peak size and efficiency in 1942, the
time when the final attack on Germany was expected. Rejecting
this timescale, the chiefs of staff told the war cabinet at the
beginning of June that 'this is manifestly too far ahead to be
acceptable as a programme in present circumstances'.[1] The war
cabinet agreed to accelerate the rearmament programme so that it
would be completed by June 1941, accepting that if the war went
on into 1942 then the quality of British forces would start to
decline, because it was impossible to sustain arms production at
this level in the long term. Even this accelerated plan, however,
would take time to bear fruit and in 1940 forces would have to be
provided within existing, limited resources. Many of the new
armaments were needed simply to re-equip the army after Dunkirk. The chance of substantially reinforcing any of the overseas
garrisons now likely to be attacked was remote, given the immediate German threat just across the Channel. In view of this overwhelming weakness, the British army was lucky not to be fighting
any part of the German army, only the far weaker Italians, until
the spring of 1941.

The pre-war dilemma of whether to give a higher priority to the
Mediterranean and Near East or to the Far East was finally
resolved when the Italians declared war. Even so, in June 1940
the forces immediately available to face the Italians were weak in
both manpower and equipment. Middle East Command, which
stretched from Cyprus to Somaliland and from the western desert
to Iraq, consisted of two divisions, two brigade groups, an under-
strength armoured division, sixty-four field guns and a 500-man
camel corps. The RAF presence in the area was thin (Malta, for
example, had three obsolete aircraft for its defence) and the initial
reaction of the First Sea Lord, Admiral Pound, to the Italian
declaration of war was to urge the withdrawal of the fleet from
Alexandria and the eastern Mediterranean altogether, thereby
leaving Egypt undefended. Churchill had to overrule his advice.[2]
When the Italians did attack, the British were unable to provide
effective resistance. By mid-August all British troops had been
forced out of Somaliland and a further Italian attack on Kenya
seemed imminent. In the western desert, when the Italians moved

sixty miles into Egypt in mid-September, the British forces were unable to drive them out again.

A counter-attack could not be mounted unless reinforcements were sent from Britain. In mid-August ministers agreed to send three regiments of tanks to the Middle East, together with nearly 70,000 troops. This was a brave decision with Britain facing the threat of invasion; it illustrates, though, just how overstretched British military resources had become. Churchill, however, was unable to persuade the Royal Navy to escort the convoys through the Mediterranean, which meant that much time was wasted sending them via the Cape. Not until the beginning of December could a small British force, made up of an Indian infantry division and an armoured division – a total of 36,000 men – attack the Italians in western Egypt. Within three days, aided by extensive intelligence gained by breaking the Italian air force code, they had defeated two Italian corps and taken 36,000 prisoners at the expense of just over 600 British casualties. In early January 1941, British forces crossed the border into Libya, having destroyed eight enemy divisions, and on 21 January Tobruk was captured, followed a couple of weeks later by the fall of Benghazi. Hitler, however, had already decided to move in German troops to support his routed allies and under the brilliant command of General Rommel they were to regain most of what the Italians had lost.

In the autumn of 1940, before the attack on the Italians, the British were being drawn into south-east Europe. Between July and August Britain had to watch helplessly as Rumania, whose independence it had guaranteed in the spring of 1939, was dismembered by Hitler and his friends and allies and the map of south-eastern Europe redrawn. At the end of June the Soviet Union demanded the return of the provinces of Bessarabia and Bukovina. Hitler advised Rumania to agree and, with the British only offering sympathy for the plight of Rumania, the Soviet Union extended its frontier further westwards. A pro-German government took over in Bucharest, but the Hungarians forced Hitler to award them the province of Transylvania in August and the dismemberment of Rumania was completed when Bulgaria received the Dobruja province in September. In the autumn, after a coup, German troops entered Rumania.

Mussolini created a difficult dilemma for the British. He was jealous of Hitler's success and determined to launch his own unexpected assault on a neighbour and obtain some glory. Unfortunately, he picked on Greece. The Italian attack on 28 October was not only successfully resisted but turned into a counter-attack as Greek forces advanced into Italian-held Albania. At this stage the Greeks turned to Britain for military assistance. The British wanted to help, particularly with American public opinion watching how Britain reacted to yet another unprovoked attack on a small state, but had few military resources to spare. Conscious of the fate of other states, such as Poland and Rumania, which had been given guarantees by Britain, Churchill told the war cabinet on 4 November: 'If Greece were overwhelmed it would be said that in spite of our guarantees we had allowed one more small ally to be swallowed up.' But as Halifax put it, 'The difficulty was to find a way of heartening the Greeks without disclosing our weakness in the Middle East.'³ Luckily, the Greeks had not asked specifically for the British army to provide help and so the war cabinet agreed to send two squadrons of Blenheim fighter-bombers and a small military mission as a token of British support. It was the most they judged they could spare from the forces in the Middle East, already fully stretched against the Italians in Egypt.

Although the immediate military threat to British interests in the second half of 1940 came in the Mediterranean, the Far East still posed major strategic problems and remained a contentious political issue throughout 1940. Churchill's government faced essentially the same situation as its pre-war predecessors. The vulnerable dominions of Australia and New Zealand, together with British trade and other possessions such as Hong Kong and Singapore, needed defending against any threat from Japan. But Britain had no forces in the Far East capable of doing this: the fleet in the area consisted of three modern and two old cruisers together with five old destroyers, while the army had three brigades available to defend Malaya and the RAF could muster eighty-eight front-line aircraft.

The basis of British strategy in the Far East from the early 1920s was to send the bulk of the Royal Navy to Singapore in the event of any threat from Japan. By early 1939, the chiefs of staff were having doubts about the feasibility of this deployment, given the threat of war with Germany and Italy. As a result, the size of the fleet planned to go to Singapore was reduced and the time it would take to reach the base was increased. The dominions, who were not told of this change of strategy, continued to rely on the assurance given by the British at the 1937 imperial conference that the existence of the Empire depended on the ability to despatch the fleet to the Far East. On the outbreak of war, Australia began to raise an army to send abroad, probably to the Middle East as it had done in the First World War. Before sending their only military forces out of the country the Australian government sensibly asked the British to reaffirm the assurances they had received about imperial protection against Japan. This demand caused acute embarrassment in London. At the end of November 1939 the war cabinet met to decide how to respond. They decided against giving an assurance to send seven capital ships to Singapore in the event of war with Japan, but did agree to a pledge to give up the Mediterranean if necessary. Chamberlain was reluctant to go along with the pledge but Churchill convinced his colleagues that the commitment to the dominions would be 'more elastic' than that given in 1937 and would come into effect only if there were an 'invasion in force' of the dominions rather than just war with Japan. As Churchill cynically added, the important point was to 'reassure the dominions, so that they would consent to the despatch of their forces'.[4] On this basis dominion troops were sent to the Middle East.

The collapse of France and the entry of Italy into the war transformed the situation as far as Britain's Far East commitments were concerned. There was now no chance that a fleet could be sent to Singapore; it was needed at home to deal with any invasion, as well as in the Mediterranean to counter Italy. On 13 June the Australians were told that it was 'most unlikely that we could send adequate reinforcements to the Far East'.[5] In August the 1939 'reassurance' on the fleet was redefined. Churchill told the dominion Prime Ministers that he did not expect Japan to go to war unless there were a successful German invasion of Britain, and in a passage very carefully drafted to provide plenty of escape clauses for the British about when they might react and in what strength, said that if Japan 'set about invading Australia and New Zealand on a large scale ... we should then cut our losses in the Mediterranean and sacrifice every interest, except only the defence and feeding of this island' and send a fleet to the

Far East which would 'parry any invading force' and try to cut its links with Japan.[6] In the autumn, when the chiefs of staff took another look at what forces could be sent in the event of war with Japan, they identified only one battle cruiser and one aircraft carrier, both of which would be based not in Singapore but in Ceylon, well out of the way of the Japanese and too far away to defend Australia or New Zealand. In July and August the British also tried to decide what interests they would fight to defend in the Far East. Neither Indo-China nor Thailand was regarded as central (no action was taken when the Vichy French government allowed Japan to station troops in northern Indo-China in September). The Dutch East Indies were considered more important because they were close to the route from Singapore to Australia and provided a significant amount of Britain's oil, but without a guarantee of American help the British were reluctant to protect them. A gloomy chiefs of staff assessment in August warned the war cabinet that Britain was almost powerless in the area: at best it might be able to limit the damage Japan could cause the Far Eastern Empire and: 'in the last resort ... retain a footing from which we could eventually retrieve the position when stronger forces become available'.[7]

As Britain's strategic position collapsed, the only chance of defending the Empire was to turn to the Americans. As early as May the chiefs of staff told the war cabinet, 'We must rely on the United States of America to safeguard our interests in the Far East.'[8] The dominions were given the same message when the British informed them in June that no fleet could be sent to defend them. In November the chiefs of staff could still say that: 'It is only the US Navy which can provide the reinforcement of the naval forces in the Far East necessary to contain the Japanese fleet and provide for the security of all Allied territories and communications.'[9] As Halifax told the war cabinet at the end of June, the problem was that the United States was 'unlikely to use force in defence of British or French interests in the Far East'.[10] None the less, the British continually hoped for a firmer American policy. In particular they wanted the US Navy to deploy to Singapore as a clear signal of their willingness to defend imperial interests in the area. They were also anxious to hold staff talks involving the Americans, British, Australians and Dutch on planning for a possible war with Japan. The US government would not, however, agree to either suggestion.

This American failure to respond left the British unable to withstand Japanese diplomatic pressure, backed up by the threat of military force. In 1939 the government had been forced to settle the dispute at Tientsin on unfavourable terms and on the outbreak of war to withdraw gunboats from northern China in order to avoid antagonizing Japan. At the end of June 1940, the Japanese decided to exploit British weakness and preoccupation with the threat of invasion: they demanded the withdrawal of all British troops and warships from Japanese-controlled areas of China, the cessation of supplies to the Chinese via Hong Kong and the closure of the Burma Road, the main supply route to the national-ist Chinese fighting the Japanese. What is interesting about the war cabinet debates on how to respond to these far-reaching demands is that, despite his pre-war criticisms of appeasement, it was Churchill who favoured appeasement of Japan while Halifax, the supposed appeaser, wanted to stand firm. Once in office Churchill found that he too was unable to solve Britain's strategic problem: too many commitments and too few resources.

In his paper for the war cabinet at the end of June, Halifax warned that acceding to the Japanese requests would 'deal a severe blow' to Chinese morale and that 'it would be taken to mean that Great Britain had deserted Chiang Kai-Shek'. Halifax concluded that 'there is little doubt that we cannot, in fact, accede to this demand'.[11] This feeling was widespread in Whitehall. John Colville, Churchill's private secretary, took the same view: 'It is a moral defeat to sacrifice in one part of the world the principles we are defending in another.'[12] And Cadogan, the head of the Foreign Office, wrote in his diary: 'I am convinced we must stand out against closing of Burma Road, even at the risk of war. If we give way, Americans will give up, with hopeless results, not only in Pacific but also on this side [sic]'.[13] The ambassador in Tokyo did not think that rejecting the Japanese demands would lead to war, but the chiefs of staff favoured reaching a deal: 'If we are not in a position to stand fast on all Japanese demands, accepting the risk of war, we must go for a sufficiently wide settlement to satisfy the Japanese.'[14] At the war cabinet on 5 July, Halifax, despite the military advice, still argued for a firm line and added that 'we should lose less by standing up to Japanese blackmail than by relinquishing our principles'. It was Churchill who argued strongly for accepting the Japanese demands, saying that he 'did not think that we ought to incur Japanese hostility for reasons mainly of prestige'. He hoped to be able to put the blame for any concessions on the United States, and his colleagues agreed to send a telegram to Washington saying that 'unless we received a clear assurance of American support, we should be compelled to bow to *force majeure*'.[15] But as Cadogan commented: 'It's hopeless to do as Winston suggested – try to put the US on the spot. They simply won't stand there.'[16]

Cadogan's prediction was fully justified when the Americans deftly refused to advise the British one way or the other. The ambassador in Tokyo then reported that the Japanese had been very offended by the British reluctance to accept their demands and that any rejection would have 'deplorable effects' on relations. He urged an immediate three-month closure of the Burma Road and suggested using the time gained to try to reach an agreement with Japan. On 10 July the war cabinet, worried by the 'grave risk' of war, agreed to the immediate closure of the link to China.[17] The next day, when discussing the scope for negotiations, they agreed that 'no time ought to be lost in coming to terms with Japan' in order to avoid a possible declaration of war.[18] At the beginning of August ministers agreed, under continuing Japanese pressure, to withdraw British garrisons from Shanghai, Tientsin and Peking, a move justified in public on the grounds that they were needed in Singapore.

The negotiations with Japan proved fruitless and at the end of September the Japanese signed a tripartite pact with Germany and Italy. By then, though, British prestige and self-confidence had risen with the failure of the Germans to mount an invasion. This, together with American pressure, convinced the war cabinet that they could afford to reopen the Burma Road at the end of the three-month closure period. The decision to do so was taken at the beginning of October, although Halifax's comment that Britain 'had no option but to carry out our duties as a neutral in the Sino–Japanese conflict' by supplying the Chinese might have seemed a little odd to anybody who chose to remember the decisions taken at the beginning of July.[19]

The British Empire in the Far East survived in 1940 only because the Japanese had not decided in favour of military means to achieve their expansionist aims. Had they adopted that policy then the Empire, virtually undefended and with no American help, would have collapsed even more ignominiously than it did under the eventual Japanese assault at the end of 1941 and in the early months of 1942. But already in 1940 Britain's perceived inability to defend the Empire made an impact both in the dominions and in Washington. There were the first signs of the reorientation in Australian and New Zealand defence policy that culminated after the war in the defence treaty with the United States, excluding Britain. The dominions were actually told by London that their security depended on the US fleet and Robert Menzies, the Australian Prime Minister, told his war council: 'The United Kingdom might be defeated in the war, and a regrouping of the English-speaking peoples might arise.'[20] Similar thoughts about Britain's decline were also being expressed in Washington. One member of the State Department wrote: 'Britain is a small country of 45 million population and may not be able to hold the far-flung empire together. Should it go under, it is a very fair question whether the United States might not have to take them all over, in some fashion or other.'[21]

British military weakness, the growing threat from Japan and the actual threat from Italy left Britain highly vulnerable in both the Mediterranean and the Pacific. The military view, expressed throughout the 1930s, that Britain was strong enough to face only one enemy was proving correct. And facing Germany and a hostile continent without allies could be sustained only for a short period unless outside help became available. In this catastrophic situation, as the fabric of British power across the globe was steadily unravelled, the Churchill government had to try, with meagre military and diplomatic resources, somehow to improve Britain's strategic position. In the summer of 1940 Britain had little influence or prestige to wield, given the widespread expectation that it too would either be defeated or forced to come to an understanding with Germany. By the autumn, though, successful resistance produced a marginal improvement in the situation by giving the first indication that Germany might not be invincible after all.

Throughout the second half of 1940, relations between Britain and its ex-ally France were fraught with difficulty. On both sides the French collapse provoked bitter feelings of betrayal and recrimination, which were brought to boiling point a fortnight after the French armistice when the British attacked the French fleet at Oran. With the British fleet fully stretched in home waters (on convoy duty and anti-invasion work), in the Mediterranean against Italy and with no ships available for the Far East, the fate of the French fleet, which was larger than the German or Italian navy, was of vital concern. Added to the German fleet it might overwhelm the Royal Navy. In the days just before the armistice request the British asked their ally to send the navy to British ports. For the French, however, the fleet represented one of their few bargaining counters with Germany and they consistently refused to give away their last asset. (Churchill later took the same view when the Americans asked for the Royal Navy to sail to North America in the event of a German invasion.) The French moved the fleet from ports most likely to be taken by the Germans to safer harbours in north Africa and the south of France. On 18 June the Pétain government decided that the fleet would not be surrendered, whatever the consequences for the armistice negotiations. In fact Hitler was shrewd enough to realize that a demand for the fleet would not be accepted and after the armistice the Germans were content for it to stay in French ports under light German supervision.

The French assured the British that the fleet would never be handed over to Germany or Italy and insisted that orders would be given for their ships to be scuttled in the event of danger. The British also knew, from intercepted French naval signals, that such orders had been issued. (When the Germans took over the unoccupied zone of France, in November 1942, seventy-seven French ships, including all the capital ships, were indeed scuttled.) The British, however, felt that they could not rely on these French assurances. Their doubts were reinforced by two factors. The first was a mistake in the English translation of the terms of the Franco–German armistice, which instead of 'supervision' of the fleet used the stronger word 'control'. Second, Churchill was determined to demonstrate as clearly and publicly as possible British determination to go on fighting. In doing so he sought to undermine those in his administration who wanted a compromise peace (the British peace feelers via Sweden had gone out at the time of the French armistice) and at the same time to consolidate his own political position.

The first discussion on whether to attack the French fleet in the event of an armistice took place a week after Dunkirk. At this first meeting a small group, including the First Sea Lord, Admiral Pound, decided in favour of military action.[22] A fortnight later, as the armistice came into effect, Pound and the Admiralty argued strongly against the use of military force, and their reluctance to attack their old ally was to carry through into the operation itself. It took six days of intensive argument between 22 and 27 June before the war cabinet decided to use force, and ships were despatched from Gibraltar to French north Africa. Ministers decided that a series of alternatives should be offered to the French, ranging from sailing the fleet to the UK or to the French West Indies to scuttling themselves. If the French suggested demilitarization of the ships, this option would also be accepted. Only if all these alternatives were rejected were the French to be attacked. The commander of the British force (Admiral Somerville) tried to exclude the use of force, but was overruled from London and ordered to complete the operation during daylight on 3 July.[23]

On that day those French ships which were in UK ports were seized and agreement was reached to demilitarize those at Alexandria in Egypt. After a day of fruitless negotiations at Oran, the British finally attacked late in the evening. It was a botched operation. One French battleship (*Bretagne*) was sunk with over 1,000 casualties but another (*Strasbourg*) escaped, together with five destroyers, and reached Toulon. At Algiers seven ships also managed to escape to France and later attacks on the battleships *Dunkerque* and *Richelieu* at Oran and Dakar in west Africa respectively were also abortive. Some of the explanation lies in the attitude of the Royal Navy to the task. Admiral Somerville wrote to his wife: 'The truth is my heart wasn't in it ... I think it was the biggest political blunder of modern times and I imagine will rouse the whole world against us.'[24] Some in the Vichy government wanted to declare war on Britain in retaliation, but Pétain was more circumspect. The French reaction was restricted to a formal break in diplomatic relations (which only regularized the de facto break since the armistice) and a token air attack on Gibraltar. Elsewhere the British action had the impact that Churchill wanted. The United States and President Roosevelt in particular were impressed by this show of determination and began to calculate that Britain might not go the way of France.

During the second half of 1940, the British still had difficult problems to resolve over their French policy. In particular they had to decide whether to reach an agreement, official or informal, with the Pétain government at Vichy or work with de Gaulle, who had fled to Britain at the time of the armistice. Gradually, as the year wore on, de Gaulle was pushed to the sidelines as the attractions of a deal with Vichy, which still controlled the unoc- cupied zone of southern France and the colonial empire in Africa and the Far East, became increasingly obvious.

From the beginning the British regarded de Gaulle as no more than a temporary expedient, a useful symbol of continuing resist- ance. He was an army officer who had been made a junior minister after the start of the German attack in May and wielded little or no influence in France. On 18 June he was allowed to broadcast over the BBC about continuing the war after the French request for an armistice, but the government quickly realized that this had been a mistake while they still hoped to influence the French government, then in Bordeaux, to continue the fight from north Africa. Only after the armistice was signed was de Gaulle allowed to broadcast again, with a strictly censored text about maintaining the struggle. The next day, 23 June, the war cabinet agreed to recognize the French National Committee in London as the group forming a nucleus of forces to fight with the British, but they did not recognize de Gaulle as its head. They still intended to find someone more influential and hoped that the former Prime Minister Paul Reynaud would oblige. On 24 June Duff Cooper and Lord Gort flew to Morocco to try to contact the French politicians who had arrived by boat from Bordeaux. Their mission failed when the local authorities obeyed orders from Vichy and kept the Frenchmen on the boat. On 28 June, with no alternative in sight, Britain recognized de Gaulle as the 'leader of all free Frenchmen' who rallied to the Allied cause. Although this was a formula designed to enhance the status of de Gaulle, it deliberately stopped short of recognizing him as a head of govern- ment. He was useful merely as a military leader. In their agreement with de Gaulle the British also refused to guarantee pre-war French frontiers or the continuation of the French empire. De Gaulle's role was to show that Britain was not completely isolated in the summer of 1940, but to the outside world he looked more like a British puppet. At the beginning of August he commanded just 2,000 troops and a navy of a similar size. The British were so doubtful about the loyalty of these men that they refused to let them fight as separate units (unlike the forces of the other governments in exile), believing that the navy in particular would sail for home at the first opportunity. In September the British tried to get rid of de Gaulle. General Catroux, the Governor-General of Indo-China, was brought to London and twice offered the leadership of the Free French by Churchill. He refused, preferring to work under de Gaulle.

At the end of August de Gaulle achieved his first success when the administrations of the strategically unimportant French colonies of Chad, Cameroons and the Congo defected from Vichy. By then, however, the British were engaged on an operation designed to install de Gaulle in the important colony of Senegal in west Africa by seizing the capital and main port Dakar. This was a vital base for the British as well as de Gaulle. It was on the Gibraltar to Cape Town route, and if the German navy operated from it they would be able to dominate much of the south Atlantic. The British colonies in west Africa were virtually defenceless – Freetown in Sierra Leone had no shore defences, no aircraft and two anti-aircraft guns – and therefore vulnerable to any threat from German forces that might be established in the area. The French also held at Dakar £60 million of gold belonging to the Belgian and Polish governments, which the British, desperately short of foreign currency, wanted to borrow.

From early August plans were being laid to seize Dakar. As a military operation it bore an uncanny resemblance to the fiasco in Norway in April, revealing once again depths of incompetence in the direction of the war that the replacement of Chamberlain by Churchill had done little to alter. The fundamental flaw in the Dakar operation was that the British and French never decided whether the objective was to attack and capture the town or, through a show of force offshore, to induce the French administration of the colony to rally to de Gaulle. On 5 August the war cabinet approved a Free French expedition to west Africa using only French troops. The next day Churchill and de Gaulle agreed on Dakar as the objective and on the use of Polish forces to assist the French. But on 8 August Churchill instructed the chiefs of staff to prepare for what was an essentially British expedition, using the Royal Marines to seize Dakar. This plan was accepted by the war cabinet on 13 August. When discussing the plan with Churchill, de Gaulle had said that he would only take over already friendly territory and not attack fellow Frenchmen. The British chose to ignore that consideration until the military planners discovered, a fortnight after the expedition was first approved, that Dakar was heavily defended. On 20 August the chiefs of staff and de Gaulle agreed that when the Anglo-French expedition arrived an emissary would be sent ashore to try and persuade the garrison to defect and only if he failed would an attack be carried out. The expedition sailed despite a chiefs of staff warning to the war cabinet that the force was inadequate to overcome full-scale opposition by the Dakar garrison.

This inept planning was compounded by still more mistakes. The troops and their supplies were badly loaded and the ships had to sail past Dakar to Freetown to reload and refuel. De Gaulle's security was abysmal and the destination of the force was hardly a secret. Certainly Vichy knew and sent naval reinforcements through the straits of Gibraltar, where the Royal Navy made no attempt to stop them. On 16 September, two days before the planned attack, Churchill persuaded the war cabinet to abandon the operation and send de Gaulle to Chad instead to consolidate his control there. After three cabinet meetings during the next two days, that decision was rescinded under pressure from de Gaulle and the British commanders of the expedition. The operation eventually started on 23 September, when de Gaulle's emissaries were arrested and the troops that tried to land got lost in fog. The next day the British tried a naval bombardment, but it was ineffective and the ships were driven off by the shore batteries. On 25 September, after HMS *Resolution* was torpedoed, the British force withdrew and the operation was abandoned.

Dakar was yet another blow both to Britain's tottering prestige and to the shaky relations with the Free French, rather than a significant military defeat. The official communiqué tried to pretend that 'serious warlike operations' against Vichy had never been intended, but Churchill admitted to the war cabinet that 'a fiasco had undoubtedly occurred and it was to be hoped that it would not too much engage public attention'.[25] De Gaulle went on to establish control over Gabon in October, despite the British refusal of any help. But the colonies under his control remained economically dependent on Britain, as did de Gaulle to a large extent. Britain continued to refuse to recognize him as more than the leader of the Free French and as being in control of some French colonies (they could hardly do less) and consistently rejected all his attempts to establish himself as the legitimate government-in-exile. Indeed the British were secretly in touch with the Vichy government and hoping to reach a wide-ranging agreement with them at de Gaulle's expense. As Churchill told his private secretary on 1 November: 'De Gaulle is definitely an embarrassment to us now in our dealings with Vichy.'[26]

These contacts with the Vichy government had begun in the autumn of 1940. At the time, relations between Vichy and Germany were not close. Pétain met Hitler on 24 October but the meeting was a failure and no long-term settlement was agreed. Britain's successful resistance had increased the options open to Vichy and enabled them at least to consider the possibility that Germany might not prove victorious. Despite their support for de Gaulle, the British had a major interest in co-operation with Vichy since they were anxious to ensure that the Germans were kept out of the French empire. In addition, Britain did not want Vichy to attack de Gaulle's colonies, since it might force them to come to his aid, stretching limited British military resources still further.

Although Britain did not recognize the Vichy government, both Canada and South Africa within the Commonwealth did, as did the United States. There were, therefore, plenty of secret diplomatic channels available. The deal the British negotiated with Vichy in the autumn of 1940 is still regarded as highly sensitive: it undermines the myth that Britain always put resistance to Germany as its top policy priority. Papers have been withdrawn from private archives and the main British file on the contacts is closed until 2016.[27] Those involved, however, have left accounts and some of the French papers used in the post-war trial of Marshal Pétain reveal what happened. On 20 October Churchill authorized the ambassador in Madrid, Sir Samuel Hoare, to open contacts with the Vichy ambassador.[28] The other channel used was a French-Canadian academic, Professor Louis Rougier, who saw Churchill twice during 25–26 October as well as paying secret visits to Vichy. Churchill personally annotated the papers Rougier took to France. These discussions continued until December. The fact that no formal agreement was ever signed enabled Churchill after the war to deny any 'deal' had been done with Pétain, but both sides accepted and acted upon the under-

standings reached via Rougier. Churchill accepted Pétain's offer
not to sign a separate peace before the end of hostilities between
Britain and Germany, not to give the Germans naval bases in the
colonies, to resist any attempt to seize the empire and to accept de
Gaulle's existing control of the unimportant colonies in central
Africa. In return the British agreed not to take military action
against Vichy territory (which meant keeping de Gaulle under
control), to stop the BBC's attack on Pétain and to ease the
blockade on trade with France. In 1940, therefore, Britain was far
from committed to de Gaulle and the idea of resistance within
France. The simple fact was that Vichy had more to offer than de
Gaulle and the British preferred to reach an accommodation that
would bring immediate tangible benefits rather than some specula-
tive gains in a more distant future. De Gaulle, however, a difficult
colleague obsessed with his mission to save France, never forgot
or forgave the way he was treated during the war either by
Churchill or, later, Roosevelt, and this wartime experience undoubtedly coloured his attitude towards Britain and the United
States after the war.

In 1940 Britain's strategic position was so desperate that every
effort was made to seek some improvement. Although the war
cabinet were willing to consider ceding Gibraltar as part of a
compromise peace with Germany, it was too important as a naval
base at the entrance to the Mediterranean to give up during the
conflict. On 21 June, Hoare at the Madrid embassy suggested to the
Foreign Office that Britain should offer to discuss the future of
Gibraltar at the end of the war if Spain would guarantee to
remain neutral. Churchill vetoed that idea because the offer meant
nothing. If the British won they would not agree to any transfer,
and if they lost Spain would probably get Gibraltar anyway.
When, at the end of September, Churchill agreed to ease the
severity of the blockade of Spain in order to help sustain their
neutrality, he encouraged them to gain French territory instead.
He suggested that Spain should be told that Britain would be 'no
obstacle to their Moroccan ambitions', a position he was prepared
to justify on the basis that 'the letters exchanged with de Gaulle
do not commit us to any exact restoration of the territories of
France'.[29]

In other areas, though, Britain did consider making significant
concessions in order to obtain support. British possession of the

Falkland Islands had long been a sore in relations with Argentina,
an important source of wheat and beef for Britain's wartime food
supply. Argentina had never recognized Britain's claim to sovereignty over the islands. In the decade before 1940, the British
consistently refused to submit the issue to any international
tribunal because of doubts as to whether their claim would be
upheld. As one senior Foreign Office official wrote in 1936: 'The
difficulty of our position is that our seizure of the Falkland
Islands in 1833 was so arbitrary a procedure as judged by the
ideology of the present day that it [would not be] easy to explain
our position without showing ourselves up as international ban-
dits.'[30] Exactly what happened in 1940 is yet another closely
guarded secret, since all the relevant Foreign Office files remain
closed. It seems clear, however, that the Churchill government did
consider giving the title of the islands back to Argentina under a
leaseback scheme. The contemporary index to the closed files
refers to '[an] offer by HMG to reunite Falkland Islands with
Argentina and acceptance of lease'.[31] Doubts about the British
title are confirmed by the use of the word 'reunite' to describe the
transfer of the islands to Argentina.

Nearer home, the Churchill government was to make even more
fundamental concessions, which went as far as offering the Dublin
government a united Ireland, and they brought themselves to the
point of forcing Ulster to accept the deal made behind their
backs. The reason for the policy was the British desire to obtain
the key Irish ports of Cobh, Berehaven and Lough Swilly as naval
bases in order to extend the range of the Atlantic convoy escorts.
When Ireland was partitioned in 1922, these so-called 'treaty
ports' in the south were left under British control. The return to
power in the 1930s of the more extreme nationalist de Valera led
to a dilution of Eire's dominion status and negotiations about the
future of the ports. The British were prepared to hand them over
to the Irish as long as they could continue to use them in the
event of war. The Irish consistently refused these demands and
eventually, in 1938, the Chamberlain government agreed to the
unconditional transfer of the ports to Irish control. The British
may have hoped this would produce a co-operative attitude in
Dublin, but they also had to take into account the fact that it
would be very difficult to operate the ports in the face of outright
Irish hostility. Churchill in opposition attacked this deal as a

strategic blunder and once in office remained scathing about the Irish government. In the autumn of 1939 he was wrongly convinced that the Irish population as a whole was really loyal to Britain: he continued to argue, despite legal opinions to the contrary, that Ireland as a formal dominion could not be neutral, and he wanted to seize the ports as soon as possible.

The rapid German conquest of France made the Irish government worried that they too might be attacked and on 16 May they asked for British arms. The British were also worried that a German invasion of Ireland would bring about a catastrophic deterioration in Britain's already weak strategic situation. Fantastic British intelligence assessments fed these fears. At the end of May MI5 suggested that the Germans had a shadow government of 2,000 gauleiters in place ready to take over the country and that a large number of secret airfields had already been constructed for use by glider-borne troops. On 23 May the first highly secret military discussions took place on how Britain would help the Irish in the event of a German attack. The Irish insisted that British forces could not move south until the Germans had attacked and Dublin had asked for help, but the British plans envisaged seizing the ports at the first opportunity. On 5 June Chamberlain, who was in charge of British policy towards Ireland, asked the unionist leader in Belfast, Craigavon, to put forward some ideas on unity to make de Valera more co-operative. Craigavon simply refused to respond. On 12 June the British issued invitations to both leaders to discuss the joint defence of the island. Neither accepted.

It was the final collapse of France in the middle of June that forced the pace of discussions. Between 17 June and the end of the month, the British government sent Malcolm Macdonald, the Minister of Health (who as Dominions Secretary had negotiated the 1938 deal on the ports with the Irish), on three missions to Dublin. Churchill regarded Macdonald as 'rat poison' for his role in giving away the ports, but realized that he had the trust of the Irish government.[32] At each meeting with de Valera the concessions Britain was willing to offer to secure Irish co-operation were increased. In the end a formal offer of unity with Ulster was made, even though the British government knew that immense pressure would have to be put on the Ulster government to force them to accept the deal.

At his first meeting with de Valera on 17 June, Macdonald opened by suggesting the Irish declare war on Germany, that British troops be deployed in Eire and the Royal Navy allowed to use the ports. He must have known that there was no chance of the Irish accepting such a package and, predictably, it was rejected. De Valera made it clear that the Irish wanted arms and British assistance if the Germans invaded and hinted that a united Ireland would radically alter attitudes. Macdonald responded with the idea of a joint defence council for the island with representatives from both north and south, which, he argued, might lead on to something more. De Valera insisted that a British declaration in favour of a united Ireland was essential but Macdonald told him that this was impossible, adding, 'A great majority of Ulsterman would object strongly.' With nothing agreed, the meeting broke up.[33]

The war cabinet considered the outcome of this first exchange on 20 June. At this point, desperate for help and assistance as its only ally went out of the war, Britain decided to propose a united Ireland. But it was one thing to propose and another to deliver such a wholesale reversal of British policy. There was the problem of the Ulster unionists, who would never willingly accept union with the south, and the fundamental issue of how far the British would go to force them to accept the deal. The majority of ministers in the government and the war cabinet had been elected as unionists, pledged to maintain Ulster's separate status. In the dreadful circumstances of June 1940, however, those pledges were quickly forgotten. Churchill underwent another of his many changes of mind on the issue. During the 1914 Home Rule crisis he had been one of the ministers in a Liberal cabinet in favour of taking a tough line with Ulster, and as First Lord of the Admiralty he had deployed elements of the Royal Navy to Belfast to try and overawe the unionists. On his return to the Conservative and Unionist Party he had become a strong unionist, declaring in September 1939 that 'we cannot in any circumstances sell the loyalists of Northern Ireland'.[34] In 1940, although he continued to reject the idea of military coercion of Ulster (which was not a feasible operation anyway), Churchill accepted that intense political and moral pressure should be put on Ulster to force them into union with the south in Britain's wider interests. As Chamberlain informed his colleagues on 20 June, the unionists would have to be told 'that the interests of Northern Ireland could not be allowed to stand against the vital interests of the British Empire'.[35] Cadogan, the head of the Foreign Office, who was at the meeting, was under no illusions about where British policy was heading. He wrote in his diary that this 'looked like coercion of N. Ireland'.[36]

Immediately afterwards Macdonald had another meeting with de Valera in Dublin. The first part of the discussion went over the same ground as the previous exchange four days earlier. Only then did Macdonald introduce the idea of unity, suggesting a declaration of unity in principle, a joint defence council, British supply of arms and use of the ports, but with Ulster a belligerent and Eire remaining a neutral. De Valera countered by suggesting a united but neutral Ireland guaranteed by Britain and the United States, with the Americans using Irish ports for their warships. Predictably, each side once again rejected the other's proposals. Macdonald ended the meeting by proposing going beyond a mere declaration in favour of a united Ireland to the idea of working out a detailed plan. De Valera expressed interest, but cautiously insisted that the details would have to be agreed first and only then might Ireland join the war.[37]

On 25 June the war cabinet agreed that Macdonald should return to Dublin with a formal plan for unity and Irish entry into the war, although Chamberlain commented that he did not expect the Irish to accept it. Macdonald took with him a six-point plan incorporating an immediate declaration by Britain accepting the principle of a united Ireland, a joint body of representatives from north and south to work out the details with Britain assisting if necessary, an immediate joint defence council, Irish entry into the war, British use of the ports, internment of German and Italian citizens in Eire and British arms for the Irish.[38] The question of Ulster's intransigence remained unresolved, although Chamberlain told his colleagues: 'I do not believe that the Ulster Government would refuse to play their part in bringing about so favourable a development.'[39]

Doubts about Ulster dominated the next round of discussions between Macdonald and de Valera on 26–27 June. The Irish knew that Ulster would not willingly join a united Ireland and that the key question was how much pressure Britain was prepared to apply. When the Irish cabinet met on 27 June, they rejected the

British proposals because Ireland was expected to make all the immediate concessions without an absolute guarantee of unity. When Macdonald saw de Valera and two of his colleagues after the meeting, he tried to reassure them that it was 'absolutely definite that if the plan were accepted as a whole, a united Ireland would come into actual being within a comparatively short period of time ... the establishment of a united Ireland was an integral part of our plan, from which there would be no turning back'. Then, without authority from the war cabinet, he made a fundamental concession by suggesting that an Irish declaration of war might not be necessary if Britain could use the ports. When questioned about dealing with Ulster, Macdonald explained that only military coercion was ruled out and that 'the United Kingdom Government would take full responsibility to the Eire Government for seeing that our obligations under the plan were carried out in full'.[40] The next day Chamberlain wrote to de Valera confirming that no declaration of war by Eire was now required, only British use of the ports, and adding more concessions, including a 'solemn undertaking' to achieve union, a meeting of the two parliaments and a joint body to establish at 'as early a date as possible' the machinery of government for a united Ireland.[41]

This was still not enough: Eire formally rejected the British proposals on 5 July. They were not prepared to trade the fact of neutrality for the promise of unity. The Irish leaders had long been accustomed to British duplicity, particularly over the drawing of the border with Ulster in the 1920s, and they did not trust them to keep their word. The Irish made no concessions during the negotiations; that was done by the British, who moved within a week from rejection of unity, because of the likely opposition from Ulster, to a 'solemn undertaking' to achieve it and, in the process, even dropped the demand that Eire should enter the war. Understandably, what really interested Eire's politicians was the extent of political will to end Ulster's separate status, against the wishes of its government and most of the population.

In 1940 Ulster was given special treatment within the United Kingdom. Conscription did not apply (for fear of alienating the minority Catholic community) and the Belfast government refused to raise a Home Guard, as in the rest of Britain, because this might involve arming Catholics. Instead, they insisted that the all-

Protestant paramilitary 'B Specials' should take on the volunteer home defence role. The Ulster government was told nothing about the negotiations with de Valera until 26 June, when Macdonald left for his third meeting with the Irish, taking with him a firm offer of unity. Chamberlain then wrote to the Ulster Prime Minister, Craigavon, to tell him what was proposed about the future of the province. He was invited to 'make your own comments or objections as you may think fit'. This was carefully drafted to avoid giving Ulster the right to veto the unity plan. Craigavon sent a strongly worded telegram to Chamberlain the next day, saying, 'Am profoundly shocked and disgusted by your letter making suggestions so far-reaching behind my back and without any pre-consultations with me. To such treachery to loyal Ulster I will never be a party.' In his reply Chamberlain made it clear that Ulster would play a limited role if the Irish government accepted the plan and that the British felt Ulster would have to sacrifice itself for the wider interests at stake: 'You can be assured that you will have every opportunity of making your views known before any decision affecting Ulster is taken. Meanwhile please remember the serious nature of the situation which requires that every effort be made to meet it.'[42] At this stage Irish rejection of the deal put an end to the exchange and meant that the British government avoided what promised to be some vicious arguments about a 'loyal' Ulster putting its own interests before the desperate situation facing Britain by refusing to commit suicide.

During the time that Britain stood alone against Germany and Italy in 1940 it was largely impotent, incapable of improving its strategic and diplomatic position. Its military strength was so low that until the end of the year it could do little in the Mediterranean, the one area, apart from the defence of the United Kingdom, where any fighting was taking place. In the Far East it was unable to promise effective defence for Australia and New Zealand and unwilling to resist Japanese pressure for concessions. The future of the Empire in the Far East depended on whether the Japanese decided to attack. In Europe, Britain had little influence to deploy against the overwhelming power of Germany and Italy. The possibility of backing de Gaulle against the Vichy government was never taken very far, given the fact that Vichy had far more to offer Britain than the uncertain prospects of a minor French politician. Elsewhere, major concessions in Ulster and the Falkland Islands were considered in a desperate attempt to gain some extra strength. This incapacitating military and diplomatic weakness in the face of two actual opponents and one likely enemy had been predicted in the 1930s as the outcome of a major war. But even this desperate situation was overshadowed by a potentially fatal threat that had also been forecast before the war: the exhaustion of Britain's gold and dollar reserves, heralding financial collapse and inability to continue the war.

10

The End of Independence

Before 1939 the government had become increasingly worried that the strains imposed by a major war, particularly if prolonged, would drive Britain into dependence on the United States. These fears reflected the experience of the First World War, when American loans and government assistance had played a vital role in financing the war effort. On that occasion the effects on Britain's post-war prestige and international position had not been too dramatic or long-lasting, partly because of the American retreat into quasi-isolation. Although, after the war, Britain had to take account of the strategic interests of the United States, particularly by conceding naval supremacy and ending the Anglo–Japanese alliance, the British were left with most of their economic and diplomatic freedom intact. That situation began to change with the outbreak of war. In 1939 the Treasury estimated that Britain's reserves of dollars and gold might last for three years if carefully husbanded, but the inability of British industry to produce the variety and quantity of armaments required by the armed forces and the need for large amounts of raw materials increased reliance on American sources of supply. In early 1940 the Treasury still hoped that, despite the growing volume of orders being placed in the United States, the reserves would last for another two years. While those reserves lasted Britain would remain independent of the United States and be able to continue the war on its own terms.

These calculations were undermined by the rapid collapse of France. Within a fortnight of the start of the German attack, the British government was forced to consider if it could continue the war on its own against a German-dominated Europe, with Italy in the war too and with Japan increasingly hostile. Churchill asked the chiefs of staff to give their views. Their report, euphemistically entitled 'British Strategy in a Certain Eventuality', was blunt.

It contained one fundamental assumption: that the United States

> is willing to give us full economic and financial support, *without which we do not think we could continue the war with any chance of success* [italics in original].[1]

The moment dreaded by pre-war governments had now arrived. This was an admission that Britain could no longer guarantee its independence, but would have to rely on American assistance to avoid a humiliating compromise peace with Hitler. The war cabinet accepted the chiefs of staff report. The problem facing Churchill's government was that although they had been forced to admit that survival, let alone a successful outcome to the war, now depended on the Americans, there was no guarantee that the necessary assistance would be forthcoming. Throughout 1940 Churchill hoped that the United States would enter the war, in June during the collapse of France, in the autumn after the German bombing of British cities and in November after the presidential election. This expectation was his strongest argument for continuing the war and not considering a compromise peace. For the remainder of 1940, Britain's fate would be decided by the answers to two key questions: would the Americans save Britain and would Britain's dwindling resources hold out until the Americans made up their minds what to do?

Both at the time and later, many in Britain, particularly Churchill with his frequent references to 'the English-speaking peoples', sought to romanticize Anglo–American relations. They wanted to assume an identity of interest between the two countries and chose to believe that the Americans finally did come to the rescue because they were impressed by Britain's heroic resistance and courageous stand against tyranny. In reality, the Americans were making some cool calculations about where their national interests lay and whether or not they should be drawn closer into what was still a European war. Although from the start of the war President Roosevelt made it clear that his sympathies were with the Allies and never adopted the even-handedness shown by President Wilson in the early stages of the First World War, the American decision, made at the end of 1940, to save Britain was based, in the same way as its policy earlier in the year, on self-interest.

During the inter-war years the United States had seen itself as detached from Europe's quarrels, and even after 1939 the overwhelming majority of the country was opposed to any intervention in the war. (As late as May 1941 an opinion poll showed eighty per cent against the United States voluntarily joining the war.) During 1939 and most of 1940 the American government limited itself to expressions of sympathy for the Allied cause and allowing massive armaments orders to be placed. These orders had the welcome domestic benefit of boosting the American armaments industry and helping lift the United States out of the long depression of the 1930s (at the end of the decade there were still ten million unemployed and two-thirds of steel plants were idle).

The United States in 1940 had only very small, ill-equipped armed forces: an army of 200,000 men and 1,800 aircraft. Although in the summer of 1940 extensive plans were laid to develop large, modern forces – a navy capable of operating in the Atlantic and Pacific simultaneously, an army of two million men (with armaments production to be based on an eventual size of four million) and an air force of 7,800 front-line aircraft with annual production set at 18,000 – they would not be available until at least early 1942. This rapid build-up of forces was not intended to help Britain or rescue Europe, but to defend the United States. However, the United States needed time to rearm. Keeping the Allies in the war helped to buy that precious commodity and kept the Germans fully occupied in Europe rather than the western hemisphere. American actions throughout 1940 were based on this policy of self-interest. At best, if Britain and France could be kept going through US arms supplies and moral support, they might defeat Hitler without the need for American military intervention. At worst, even if they were defeated, they would have gained time for the United States to be ready to meet any challenge. As the war developed, the Americans always carefully assessed the balance of advantage and where their own interests lay. Normally the administration decided that they should help the Allies and only once, in the first month that Britain fought alone, did they come close to adopting a radically different policy of concentrating all their efforts on the defence of the western hemisphere.

Churchill was always to make much of his personal relationship with President Roosevelt. Certainly this proved of vital importance once the United States entered the war after Pearl Harbor. In 1940, however, the relationship was far from close. The two men had met only briefly at the end of the First World War. Churchill forgot the occasion and Roosevelt only remembered it for Churchill's rudeness. An occasional correspondence was initiated by Roosevelt in September 1939 after Churchill had taken over at the Admiralty. Until May 1940 the President sent only three messages, none of any importance, and although Churchill sent twelve, they were all confined to naval affairs and details of operations and did not touch on any wider strategic or diplomatic concerns. In 1940 contacts between the two countries were still tenuous. There was no 'hot-line' for communications, Churchill and Roosevelt's correspondence was sent by diplomatic telegram, and few of the senior policy-makers had even met.

Within days of taking office, Churchill sent his first message as Prime Minister to Roosevelt. It was a wide-ranging appeal for help, asking for destroyers, aircraft, steel, free supply of US goods and visits by US warships to Singapore and southern Ireland. Roosevelt sent a reply on 16 May ignoring all of Churchill's concrete requests. Nevertheless, as the situation deteriorated in France, and particularly after the British army lost most of its equipment at Dunkirk, Roosevelt did his best to provide military supplies. Arms sales, together with rhetorical appeals to the French to keep fighting, constituted the US policy of trying to keep the Allies in the war for as long as possible to buy time. The US government was legally prohibited from selling arms to other countries and so Roosevelt had to arrange for key items to be sold back to the manufacturers so that they could then sell them to Britain and France. In this way, in the month after the start of the German attack the Americans were able to supply the British with 250,000 rifles, 130 million rounds of ammunition (a quarter of the US stocks) and 80,000 machine guns. But relations between the two heads of government still remained distant. Churchill sent ten messages to Roosevelt between 15 May and 15 June while Roosevelt sent only three. The first was the dismissive reply to Churchill's appeal for help, the second was a copy of a message sent to Reynaud and the third made it clear that the US was not committed to military support of the Allies and that the message to Reynaud, couched in vaguely encouraging terms, was not for publication.

The French armistice made the Americans reconsider the wisdom of continuing to provide arms. There were widespread doubts in Washington, shared by Roosevelt, about whether

Britain could survive. Since May, many had been arguing that providing arms was the wrong policy, since they would only fall into German hands, and that the United States should keep everything for its own defence. On 2 July Roosevelt signed an Act which allowed the supply of arms to other countries only if both the head of the army and the navy certified equipment as 'not essential for US defence'. Earlier in June Roosevelt had discussed with his cabinet the possible loan of about fifty old destroyers to Britain. They agreed not to go ahead because they were worried that the deal might anger Hitler. The rapid deterioration in Allied fortunes had reinforced a mood of caution. As Roosevelt said: 'We cannot tell the turn the war will take, and there is no use endangering ourselves unless we can achieve some results for the Allies.'[2] During the six weeks from 15 June until 31 July, during the first stages of the most difficult period when Britain was facing Germany and Italy alone, there was almost total silence between Churchill and Roosevelt. Churchill sent one unimportant message about the appointment of the Duke of Windsor as Governor of the Bahamas. Roosevelt sent none.

In the early summer of 1940, one of the most important aspects of Anglo–American relations was the future of the Royal Navy if Britain were driven to make peace with Germany. The arguments were remarkably similar to those between Britain and France over the French fleet. If the British fleet fell into German hands, then American control of the Atlantic would be imperilled and there would be a direct threat to the United States. Roosevelt therefore sought an assurance that in the last resort the fleet would sail for North America. Churchill was opposed to giving such an undertaking because it would lessen the pressure on the President to ensure that Britain survived. He argued, in the way the French had earlier with him, that the navy might be the last national asset and a future government might well have to use it to secure the best possible peace terms from a victorious Germany.

Roosevelt first raised the subject on 17 May, just a week after the German attack in the west. He suggested to Lord Lothian, the British ambassador in Washington, that in the worst case the fleet should sail for North America. Lothian replied that it would depend on whether or not the United States was in the war by then. On 20 May Churchill repeated this message strongly to

Roosevelt. The President's reaction was to ask the Canadians to send an envoy secretly to Washington for staff talks about the future defence of North America. At the meeting that followed, Roosevelt suggested that Britain and France were finished and that the Canadians should put pressure on the British to sail the fleet to safety in North America. The Canadians refused. The British were probably aware of the President's opinions because at their meeting on 24 May the war cabinet minutes describe Roosevelt as 'taking the view that it would be nice of him to pick up the bits of the British Empire if this country was overrun'.[3] On 17 June Roosevelt proposed secret Anglo–American staff talks. This might have seemed an encouraging sign of growing co-operation, but the President was interested only in the defence of North America. Churchill was strongly opposed to the idea of holding talks and it took long arguments from Halifax before he would agree. Even then the talks did not take place until the end of August, by which time the situation had changed significantly. During August, negotiations on the exchange of fifty old American destroyers in return for the grant of bases on British possessions in the western hemisphere were reaching a conclusion.

Churchill had raised the subject of a loan of about fifty ex-First World War destroyers in his first message to Roosevelt as Prime Minister, on 15 May. The pre-war shipbuilding programme had been heavily biased by the Royal Navy in favour of large capital ships and on the outbreak of war Britain found itself short of vessels for vital convoy escort work. Roosevelt rejected Churchill's request, saying that the US navy needed the ships and pointing out that Congressional approval would be required, which would probably not be given, and that the whole process would take so long that the ships would not reach Britain in time to be of any use. Behind this array of excuses lay a reluctance to be helpful, stemming from doubts as to whether Britain would survive, in which case the ships would pass to the Germans.

The idea of offering the Americans bases was first raised by Lothian with London on 25 May, as a way of increasing US backing for Britain. Although the Foreign Office and the chiefs of staff favoured the idea, the Dominions Office, the Colonial Office and, most important, Churchill opposed it, so no action was taken. Lothian returned to the subject on 23 June, but with the

same result. The Foreign Office resurrected the idea a month later
in a major paper on the future of relations with the United States.
The paper's thesis, in the tactful and understated language of
Whitehall, was that 'the future of our widely scattered Empire is
likely to depend on the evolution of an effective and enduring
collaboration between ourselves and the United States'.[4] This
paper reflected the growing official recognition that Britain could
no longer function as a fully independent state and that American
support was vital in the future. It argued that Britain would
have to help bring this relationship into existence and that,
as a result, it was not in a position to drive hard bargains
with the United States. A spontaneous offer of bases in three
colonies – Jamaica, Trinidad and British Guiana – was therefore
suggested.

In parallel with the discussions in London about possible US
bases, the question of destroyers was again back on the agenda.
On the advice of Lothian and the US ambassador in London,
Joseph Kennedy, Churchill had dropped the subject until the end
of July. The delay was deliberately timed to avoid the delicate
period when Roosevelt was waiting to be nominated by the
Democrats for an unprecedented third term as President. On 30
July Churchill again asked Roosevelt specifically for the destroyers, which, he argued, would be vital during the autumn
until new British construction became available. At a cabinet
meeting on 2 August the Americans concluded that Britain needed
the ships but that a loan or sale would not be accepted by
Congress without a transfer of bases and a declaration about the
future of the Royal Navy. Churchill's reaction to this proposed
package deal was that 'we must refuse any declaration as is
suggested and confine the deal solely to the Colonial bases'.[5]

On 8 August Lothian gave Roosevelt details of the deal as put
forward by the British: an exchange of ninety-six destroyers for
bases in the Caribbean colonies. Five days later, Roosevelt sent
Churchill the American terms. In exchange for fifty destroyers
the British would have to give a private assurance about the
future of the fleet and allow long-term US bases (on ninety-nine-
year leases) on Newfoundland, Bermuda and in five West Indian
colonies. The war cabinet reluctantly agreed on 14 August to
what they thought was a very hard bargain on the grounds that
Britain's need for US help was so great that it could not afford to

reject the deal. Their one condition was that the two sides of the deal were not to be linked together, but represented in public as free gifts. The US immediately rejected this formula and insisted on formal linkage, in order to demonstrate to Congress and the American public that specific advantages were being gained in return for the destroyers. On 21 August the war cabinet decided that 'a formal bargain on the lines proposed was out of the question'[6] because it would make the unequal nature of the deal starkly apparent. Four days later, Churchill told Roosevelt that what the Americans wanted amounted to 'a blank cheque on the whole of our transatlantic possessions'.[7]

Despite the British protests, the United States, at the end of August, laid down its final terms for the deal. They were prepared to accept bases in Newfoundland and Bermuda as a gift, but insisted that the five West Indian bases had to be presented as a direct exchange for the fifty destroyers. To offset this minor concession they also demanded that the British commitment, that in the last resort the fleet would sail to North America, had to be made public. The British felt they had no option but to accept these American terms. As Chamberlain wrote to Churchill: 'The American attitude simply infuriates me, but we can't win as we would wish without their help.'[8] The deal was signed on 2 September. During the long negotiations on setting up the US bases, which were not complete until March 1941, the US continued to drive a hard bargain and more concessions had to be made by the British on the exact sites the Americans were to occupy and the powers they were to exercise. By early 1941 Britain was dependent on the US for financial support and Churchill recognized that this inevitably meant making further sacrifices. As he told his private secretary John Colville in March: 'We cannot afford to risk the major issue in order to maintain our pride and to preserve the dignity of a few small islands.'[9]

Although both sides gained from the destroyer-for-bases deal, it was the British who had to make all the significant concessions, a fact that demonstrated their diminishing independence and increasing reliance on the United States. The number of ships they received was half that requested, the number of bases acquired by the US was twice the initial British offer, the two elements of the deal were firmly linked together and the British had to make a public declaration about the future of the Royal

Navy. The tangible results for the British were few. The destroyers were of limited operational value and in poor condition. Only nine were in service by the end of 1940 and only a further twenty by May 1941 because of a shortage of crews and the navy's insistence on giving every vessel long refits before they became operational. The intangible benefits were, however, immense, for the deal was not a neutral act by the United States. It could be seen as the start of a commitment to the British side and was presented as such by the British. The Americans undoubtedly gained the most. In return for handing over some almost obsolete ships they obtained a string of bases in an area of vital importance for the defence of the United States. As one State Department official wrote in his diary: 'In a single gulp we have acquired the raw material for the first true continental defense we have had since the sailing ship days.'[10] Despite the British gloss, the deal demonstrated that Roosevelt was still hedging his bets about Britain's future. The destroyers might provide some assistance but in return he had gained the long-desired pledge about the future of the fleet if Britain was defeated; the bases also improved the defence of the United States.

In public Churchill was fulsomely optimistic about relations with America throughout these difficult negotiations. In his speech in the House of Commons on 20 August he compared the growing co-operation with the Mississippi rolling on 'full flood, inexorable, irresistible, benignant, to broader lands and better days'. In private he was deeply disillusioned about the limited help being given to Britain in its hour of greatest need. Apart from the destroyers-for-bases deal and allowing Britain to buy armaments and raw materials, the Americans had done nothing. Just before Christmas he told Halifax, after his appointment as ambassador in Washington: 'We have not had anything from the US that we have not paid for and what we have had has not played an essential part in our resistance.'[11] Churchill's sense of bitterness about the United States was reinforced by the fact that Britain had already given the Americans crucial scientific and intelligence information in an attempt to build confidence between the two nations. On 14 August one of Britain's top scientists, Sir Henry Tizard, had left for the United States, taking with him samples and information about recent discoveries vital for the war effort. His baggage included miniaturized valves, a cavity magnetron, information on microwave radar, chemical warfare and explosives formulae, together with designs of the jet engine and the German magnetic mine. A month earlier, Roosevelt's friend Bill Donovan, who was later to head the precursor of the CIA, had visited the British codebreaking centre at Bletchley Park, where the first successes against the German Enigma codes were being obtained. Donovan was given complete access to this closely guarded secret at a time when most members of the war cabinet were unaware of the existence of this vital breakthrough and of the information obtained from it. From the end of August Roosevelt was also sent a copy of the daily intelligence report issued by London to the dominions.

Although the British had conceded much to try to build a relationship with the Americans, in the summer and autumn of 1940 they still had no promise of action in the area identified as crucial to Britain's future: finance. The state of the gold and foreign exchange reserves, how long they would last and whether the United States would rescue Britain before financial collapse forced a compromise peace with Germany, was the key issue facing the British government in the second half of 1940. After Dunkirk, when rifles and ammunition had to be bought at short notice and major additional armaments orders placed in the United States, Britain's financial situation deteriorated rapidly. British imports of raw materials from the United States were already rising at an alarming rate. In 1939 they made up just eight per cent of Britain's total, but in 1940 rose to twenty-four per cent and were expected to rise still further. Orders for steel in 1940 amounted to about £13 million, but by the middle of the year a total of over £100 million was already forecast for 1941. When France collapsed Britain took over all the orders its ally had placed in the US, increasing the strain further. By July the Treasury thought that Britain's assets might last out for about another year, until the early summer of 1941.

Although unprecedented and open-ended American support was seen in London as essential for Britain's survival as early as May 1940, the government was undecided about how to approach the Americans and unsure about what reaction to expect when they did. Churchill alerted Roosevelt to the looming financial problem in his first message as Prime Minister on 15 May, when he told him: 'We shall go on paying dollars for as long as we can, but I should like to feel reasonably sure that when we can pay no more, you will give us the stuff all the same.'[12] Roosevelt's reply completely ignored the financial problem. In the middle of July a senior official at the Treasury, Sir Frederick Phillips, was sent to Washington, where he met both Henry Morgenthau, secretary of the treasury, and President Roosevelt. His message was that Britain would need some help until the end of the year in selling its holdings of US securities, but he warned them that from the middle of 1941 Britain would have no assets left and that extensive credits would be required. Morgenthau made some suggestions about how Britain could improve its position, but kept an eye open for US national interests by advising the sale of assets in South America, where Americans would be able to buy at what were likely to be knockdown prices. Phillips told London that the Americans would not be willing to provide large-scale credits until they were 'satisfied that our existing resources are in fact exhausted or near exhaustion'. When he saw Roosevelt on 17 July, he reported that the President 'said nothing that could be regarded as a commitment' and that the United States was 'not prepared to make promises now'.[13] Phillips was told to come back for further discussions 'in the late fall', which meant after the presidential election at the beginning of November. The British had achieved little apart from alerting the US government to the problems they would have to meet within a few months. Meanwhile Britain, with no guarantee of help obtained, carried on and acted on the assumption that the United States would come to the rescue in time.

Almost immediately after Phillips's visit to the United States, Britain's financial position deteriorated sharply. Between mid-July and mid-August the gold and dollar reserves fell by £80 million, leaving only £300 million, together with about £200 million of securities. At this rate it was doubtful if Britain would have enough assets to last to the end of the year, when the Americans might be in a position to take action. Britain's future now depended on the outcome of the presidential election. Chancellor of the Exchequer Kingsley Wood told the war cabinet in the third week of August: 'We are faced with the immediate practical problem of holding out till well into November in the case of a Democratic victory, or until after the 20th January, when the new President takes office, in the case of a Republican victory.'[14] If the

Republicans won, Wood was 'very doubtful' as to whether British assets would last long enough. Ministers decided that they had no option but to wait and hope that the essential American rescue would materialize in time.

Despite the mounting financial crisis, the war cabinet had to decide, at the beginning of September, what aircraft orders to place in the United States. Beaverbrook, as Minister of Aircraft Production, proposed two schemes: the first for US production of 1,250 aircraft a month and the second for 3,000 a month. Although the initial costs until the end of 1940 would be similar, the smaller scheme would eventually involve expenditure of £300 million a year in dollars, and the larger £800 million. Britain did not have the money to fund either option, even though the aircraft were vital to the war effort. As Kingsley Wood explained: 'There is no prospect of our having dollars to pay these sums, nor of our ever repaying those amounts, if lent to us by the USA.' Even the expenditure of the £75 million in dollars required by December would make it 'doubtful whether on our own resources we can last out the current calendar year'.[15] On 6 September the war cabinet decided to go ahead with the larger, more expensive scheme on the basis that whatever happened Britain could not pay and in the meantime the order might increase pressure from American industry for the government to bail out Britain. At this stage the only immediate cost the British government could calculate was the steadily mounting debt. After just over a year of war, British orders in the United States amounted to $10 billion – far beyond even the debts incurred in the whole of the First World War – and there was nothing with which to pay these huge bills. The war cabinet were aware that there would be a price to pay for American help but they had no way of knowing what that price would be:

It was now fairly widely appreciated in the United States that there was no prospect of our ever having dollars to repay the colossal sums for which we were becoming indebted to them ... We had no knowledge of what conditions the United States were likely to attach to the credits which we assumed they were about to extend to us.[16]

One of the problems the British faced was that both Roosevelt and his advisers took the British Empire at its face value. They believed that a country that controlled a quarter of the world must have the resources to match and they simply could not believe that Britain was on the point of collapse. Even when the collapse came, many in the US government were convinced that Britain must be concealing key resources in order to obtain free assistance. The scale of the American illusions about Britain can be judged from the fact that in the late 1930s Roosevelt thought that Britain had assets worth at least $7 billion in the United States, roughly ten times the actual figure. This belief in British power died hard. Towards the end of September 1940, Lord Lothian in Washington was worried that the Americans had not begun to understand the scale of the problems facing Britain or the appalling consequences of a failure to act. He reported: 'Public opinion here has not yet grasped that it will have to make far-reaching decisions to finance and supply us and possibly still graver ones next spring or summer unless it is to take the responsibility of forcing us to make a compromise peace.'[17]

But the British too had plenty of illusions. The worst was that the presidential election on 5 November would quickly resolve all the outstanding problems. The Treasury assumed that full-scale credits would be granted within a fortnight of the election and Churchill, together with many other senior ministers, thought that the United States would quickly enter the war. The British paid too much attention to what Roosevelt said, which was mainly aimed at keeping up their morale, and did not take enough notice of the small amount of action he was prepared to take. Their misunderstanding of what was still, in 1940, the unfamiliar world of American domestic politics was almost total. They assumed, quite wrongly, that if Roosevelt were re-elected, he would have a majority in Congress to do whatever he wanted. Roosevelt's re-election by a popular majority of five million and an electoral college vote of 449 to 82 proved a great disappointment to the British, because nothing happened as a result. No action was taken about Britain's problems; indeed most of Washington was away on holiday for the rest of November, recovering from the strain of the election campaign. With financial collapse only a matter of weeks away the British felt they must take some action to bring home to the Americans the urgency of their plight.

Lord Lothian had returned to Britain in early November for

various consultations about future policy. While in London he convinced a reluctant Churchill that the only way forward was for the Prime Minister to write to Roosevelt, setting out the full gravity of Britain's position. The first draft produced by Lothian on 12 November was blunt about the situation and the consequences of an American refusal:

> It is only a question of weeks before the resources we have available with which to pay for our requirements and the munitions ordered from the United States are exhausted. Unless we can get financial assistance from the United States on the largest scale, it is obvious that our capacity to carry on the war on the current basis must abruptly come to an end.'[18]

This proved too blunt for Churchill. By 8 December, when the letter, described by Churchill as one of the most important he ever wrote, was finally sent to Roosevelt, it had been altered in tone and balance, but the basic message remained the same. Over half the letter now concentrated on shipping problems and only four hundred words at the end dealt with finance. As a whole it was a dismal catalogue of British inadequacy, which Churchill tried to disguise by talking about an identity of British and American interests and a 'common purpose'. He warned Roosevelt that without US merchant shipping, naval escorts and patrolling in the Atlantic the supply routes to the UK and other battlefronts could not be kept open and that without US munitions, especially aircraft, Britain could not arm either itself or its allies. Turning at last to finance, he pointed out that the value of British orders in the United States 'many times exceed the total exchange resources remaining at the disposal of Great Britain. The moment approaches when we shall no longer be able to pay cash for shipping and other supplies.' He argued that it would not be morally right to strip Britain of all its saleable assets nor would it be in the United States' own interest to do so, if it wanted a stable post-war world. The letter ended by saying that Britain placed itself in American hands to resolve these fundamental problems.[19] The message in this begging letter was expressed more succinctly by Lothian on his return to the United States at the end of November when he told reporters: 'Well boys, Britain's broke: it's your money we want' (an indiscretion for which he was later rebuked by Churchill).

Churchill's letter was the first comprehensive statement to the Americans of the serious crisis facing Britain. Previous British hints about a looming threat had not suggested an immediate collapse. In November Roosevelt thought that Britain still had assets of about $2½ billion in the United States that could be sold and that any financial problem was at least six months away. The US Treasury thought the same. Now the crucial turning point in Anglo–American relations had arrived. Britain's cards were at last on the table: it no longer had the power to continue the war or maintain its independence unaided. The United States, which was still relying on Britain to stay in the war while its own rearmament programme was completed, had to decide whether it should extend its policy of aiding Britain.

The United States recognized its new power and Britain's dependence very quickly. An official at the US embassy in London sent Washington his assessment of the situation just after Churchill's message to Roosevelt:

> Willy-nilly the United States holds one end of the Scales of Fate on which balances precariously the future of the British Empire ... The British government is aware that it is not in a position to resist quid pro quo demands from the United States ... The British are not ready givers ... But the fact remains that they will in the last analysis stand and deliver.[20]

The British sent Sir Frederick Phillips back to Washington at the beginning of December to negotiate the terms for American help with Morgenthau. They decided to try and achieve a number of aims in the talks.[21] They wanted the US to finance all British war purchases from 1 January 1941 in the form of gifts rather than loans. The UK was to retain a minimum gold reserve of £150 million to operate the sterling area and, finally, American demands for Britain to sell off its overseas assets were to be resisted. Given the weakness of Britain's negotiating position, this was a completely unrealistic set of objectives and in fact only one was secured – the use of gifts rather than loans – and that only because the US wanted to avoid a repeat of the acrimony over the repayment of war loans that had followed the First World War.

When the talks began on 10 December, Phillips rapidly found that Britain could not negotiate and that the United States would decide the terms on which they would provide assistance. This was a lesson that still had to be painfully learnt in London. Morgenthau did not like the British attitude of trying to dictate the terms of US assistance and Phillips had to pass on his somewhat equivocal and not altogether reassuring message that: 'Mr Churchill must put himself in Mr Roosevelt's hands with complete confidence; if he trusts him, he will not find him in any bargaining mood.'[22] Roosevelt was certainly not in a bargaining mood. He was determined to lay down American terms for supporting Britain. At the outset Morgenthau demanded a complete statement of Britain's financial position and all its assets, including those overseas, that could be sold to the Americans. All the niceties of drafting that had still preoccupied the British only a month before were no longer relevant. The Americans wanted to look at Britain's balance sheet and draw their own conclusions. Phillips could only advise London to comply in words that encapsulated the new power structure between Britain and the United States: 'It should be for them to allow us to keep our assets, not for us to withhold them.'[23]

The US administration made up its mind quickly how to respond but the assistance itself did not arrive for another three months. At a press conference on 17 December, using a vivid metaphor of a man lending his neighbour a hose to put out a fire and getting it back when the emergency was over, Roosevelt outlined the idea of 'Lend-Lease' for supplies to Britain. After Christmas, in a radio address to the nation, he put this help in the context of America's new role in the world, speaking of the United States as the 'arsenal of democracy'. Although the British, relieved that a way had been found of maintaining supplies, welcomed Roosevelt's general ideas as the best solution to their problems, they had not been consulted about what the Americans intended, another sign of the new balance of power between the two nations. Roosevelt never replied to Churchill's long letter of 8 December and there was no bilateral discussion either of the contents of the 'Lend-Lease' Bill to be presented to Congress or of the detailed terms for US assistance. The US simply decided unilaterally what it was prepared to do. The Bill, entitled 'An Act to promote the defense of the United States' and numbered 1776 (the date of the declaration of independence) as a deliberate snub to Britain and a symbol of the new relationship, was not published until early January. Britain then had to wait helpless on the sidelines while Congress spent the next two months in hearings. 'Lend-Lease' finally became law on 11 March.

The period between December 1940 and March 1941 was one of humiliation for Britain. Its collapse as a great power was laid bare to the American public – the US administration insisted on the publication of a full statement of Britain's financial condition – and its fate depended on the passage of American legislation. Behind the scenes there were a series of painful encounters with American officials as the British government sought to tackle three crucial issues which were not resolved by the American decision to rescue Britain. How many British assets would have to be sold? What was to happen to British orders placed before the Lend-Lease Bill became law and how were these orders to be paid for? In each case the British found themselves unable yet again to do anything other than meet American demands.

Throughout December the Americans kept up the pressure on Britain to sell its assets to pay for military orders. They were keen for sales in Latin America and Canada, where US companies would be able to pick up shares in companies at low prices. By the middle of January the US government was slowly becoming convinced that the British had few assets left. As Roosevelt told a member of his cabinet: 'We have been milking the British financial cow which had plenty of milk at one time but which has now about become dry.'[24] Nevertheless the American government still wanted an assurance that all remaining British assets in the US would be pledged against military supplies. When Britain refused to give the assurance, Morgenthau, convinced that such a bargain was essential for domestic political reasons, simply announced it to Congress anyway in mid-January 1941:

> Every dollar of property, real property or securities that any English citizen owns in the United States, they have agreed to sell during the next twelve months, in order to raise money to pay for the orders they have already placed, they are going to sell – every dollar of it.

The British were still reluctant to embark on selling their last remaining assets and on 10 March Morgenthau gave Halifax, the new ambassador in Washington, an ultimatum. An important

British company was to be sold within a week in order to demonstrate good faith. Britain had no choice but to obey and the American Viscose Corporation, a subsidiary of the British firm Courtaulds, the largest remaining British holding in the US, was sold. Because of the terms of Morgenthau's ultimatum it was bought by an American consortium at half its market value.

Although the Lend-Lease Bill took over all the existing UK orders in the United States – amounting to some $10 billion – the British also wanted the US to assume responsibility for all payments after 1 January 1941. Roosevelt consistently refused. His unalterable position was that the US could not make any payments until the Lend-Lease Bill became law. The problem was that Britain had hardly any money left to pay for existing orders during this interim period. Morgenthau, now aware of Britain's financial straits, refused to allow any new orders to be placed after 19 December. But this veto did not solve the problem of how to pay for orders already placed. At the end of the year the British told the Americans that at least $540 million was due before 1 March but that they had less than half that sum available and a proportion of that would be needed for orders placed outside the USA. British default on its contracts seemed the most likely outcome because of the time needed to pass the Lend-Lease Bill. Both governments wanted to avoid such a disaster. All the British could do was come up with various ideas under which the US government might advance money. In mid-January Roosevelt agreed that the US government would take over the funding of new armaments factories being built to supply British orders. But the price for this deal was that Britain was forced to place orders only for equipment to US specifications and not its own. In this way Roosevelt was able to justify the expenditure as being for US defence. The financial crisis continued to worsen and eventually Morgenthau had to step in at the end of January and take control of all British arms orders. He unilaterally restricted Britain to spending no more than $35 million a week until the Lend-Lease Bill became law.

In parallel with these unilateral American moves, Britain was still desperately searching round for other ways of avoiding default on its US contracts. To do this it was necessary to scrape the barrel of its remaining gold and dollar reserves and those of its allies. In October 1940 the Czech government-in-exile lent

Britain £7.5 million of gold in order to fund purchases in the US, a noble gesture since Britain did not recognize the Czech government as legitimate. In early 1941 the Canadians began selling British investments in the country in order to pay for goods ordered by Britain from the US. The Dutch and Norwegian governments in London refused to lend Britain any gold, despite begging appeals. Eventually it was a loan of £60 million of gold on 4 February from the Belgian government in London that avoided disaster. Without these loans Britain would have defaulted on its payments in the United States, because by the beginning of 1941 it had less than £3 million left in its gold and dollar reserves. This was as near to bankruptcy as it was possible to go without actual default.

The most dramatic moment in the financial crisis came at the end of December 1940, when Britain's last gold holdings were taken by the United States in a secret operation. On 23 December the British were told by Roosevelt that a US warship had already been despatched to Cape Town to pick up £50 million of gold, Britain's last tangible assets. The government at first wanted to protest at the high-handed way in which the US was acting but on reflection they decided they could only acquiesce. Churchill went as far as drafting a telegram to Roosevelt complaining (quite accurately) that the US attitude was like that of 'a sheriff collecting the last assets of a helpless debtor' but the embassy in Washington persuaded him not to send it.[25]

When more South African production became available in March 1941, the US sent another warship to collect that too. The British were only told after the warship had sailed and although they needed the gold to pay for orders outside the US, they again had no choice but to accept the US action and hand over the gold.

As a bankrupt nation, Britain had to learn the hard lesson that the United States would dictate the terms on which it was prepared to provide help with little regard for hurt pride. Britain was saved from complete financial collapse, inability to continue the war and the humiliation of seeking a compromise peace only through American intervention. The United States gave help, quickly and generously, because it was in their national interest to do so. The longer Britain could keep fighting, the longer the United States had to complete its own preparations. British arms orders also played an invaluable role in mobilizing the American economy and converting it to war production. Lend-Lease was simply a way of ensuring that this process continued. It was, as the Bill said, 'an Act to promote the defense of the United States'.

The financial crisis at the end of 1940 marked the end of Britain as an independent power. Such a crisis had been foreseen as a distinct possibility by the government before the war and expected, sooner or later, by the war cabinet from early 1940 as Britain's attempt to fight a war for national survival proved too great a strain for its limited resources. Even so, the process of adjustment to subordinate status as a client of the United States was painful. In public the harsh reality of the relationship was heavily disguised by talk of the common purpose of the English-speaking peoples. Even in the corridors of power British policy-makers took time, and found it hard, to accept that they could no longer make demands, but only do what the Americans wanted. 1940 marked the final and decisive shift of power in the world from Britain to the United States.

11

The Client State

Britain's great achievement in 1940 was to survive. That was vital, not just because it saved the country from the horrors of a Nazi conquest, but because in terms of the grand strategy of the war it preserved a base from which Allied armies could later invade the continent and help defeat Germany.

On 8 February 1941 Churchill, hoping to create a sense of optimism about Britain's chances not just at home but also in the United States, where the Lend-Lease Bill was still passing through Congress, said, 'Give us the tools and we will finish the job.' But the job was to defeat Germany and Italy and, by the end of the year, Japan too. That was something Britain could not hope to do on its own, even with American help in the form of military equipment, raw materials and food. The factors that enabled Britain to survive in 1940 – the building of an effective air defence system by pre-war governments, the waters of the English Channel which stopped Hitler from deploying overwhelming military strength against a depleted British army, the ill-equipped and badly led Luftwaffe and, most important, rescue by the United States – would not be enough to bring about victory.

Despite the grim satisfaction of having survived the worst year in British history, the outlook at the end of 1940 was one of almost unrelieved gloom. In an end-of-year assessment, Cecil King of the *Daily Mirror* wrote in his diary of a government dominated by over-age men with no idea of how to win the war; he expected Britain to be defeated, followed by a collapse of the political system, as had occurred in France. Others did not abandon all hope, but even they could not see how Britain was going to win the war. Sir Alexander Cadogan wrote in his diary, on the last day of 1940: 'Everything – on paper – is against us, but we shall live. I don't, frankly, see how we are going to win, but I am convinced that we shall not lose.'[1] A few months later the Chief of the Imperial General Staff, General Dill, told a visiting American, General Arnold, that privately he saw no hope of victory apart from a repeat of the sudden and unexpected collapse of morale that overwhelmed Germany in 1918. In the autumn of 1940 Churchill too could not see clearly the way through to victory. His private secretary, John Colville, recorded that Churchill told two senior RAF commanders that he 'felt sure we were going to win the war, but he confessed he did not see clearly how it was to be achieved'.[2]

The United States remained the key to British hopes of ultimate salvation and victory. Churchill's strongest argument for fighting on in the summer of 1940 had been the expectation of American entry into the war, which he confidently assumed could not be later than after the November presidential election. By the end of 1940, though, it was clear that these expectations had been unfounded. The United States might provide large-scale aid but a declaration of war still seemed remote. The British, therefore, had no choice but to struggle on into what seemed a very bleak future.

In the absence of allies and with little military power, Britain had no alternative but to adopt an indirect strategy aimed at weakening Germany rather than defeating German forces on the battlefield. Despite all the efforts in the course of 1940 to boost production, the gap between the two powers remained huge. For example, at the end of 1940 British steel-making capacity was eighteen million tons a year, whereas the Germans controlled an output of 212 million tons. Although the prospect of large American supplies through Lend-Lease could compensate for some of Britain's financial and industrial inadequacies, Britain could not deploy large military forces. Churchill told Roosevelt in December 1940 that Britain was unable to match 'the immense armies of Germany in any theatre where their main power can be brought to bear'.[3] Indeed until the end of 1942 the British army never fought at any one time more than four weak German divisions out of a total of over two hundred.

Britain's indirect strategy, which was adopted in the summer of 1940 after the fall of France, had three main elements: economic pressure, bombing and subversion. The most effective Allied weapon of the First World War had been the economic blockade, which had drastically reduced the level of raw materials and food available for Germany. But by 1940 Germany controlled so much of Europe and therefore its economic resources that blockade was no longer a powerful weapon. The controls established in 1939 were maintained, though, in the hope that it might have some marginal effect. Churchill admitted its futility to Beaverbrook in early July 1940: 'We have no continental army which can defeat the German military power. The blockade is broken . . .', adding that Britain would be unable to stop Hitler turning eastwards and conquering still more territory. He believed that the only possible hope was a massive bombing campaign on Germany, without which he frankly admitted, 'I do not see a way through.'[4] He was also enthusiastic in the summer of 1940 about the likely results of a campaign of subversion and resistance. The British could do no more than hope that a combination of these three elements would make it difficult for Germany to control occupied Europe and place increasing strains on the German economy, leading to economic and political collapse. This would be followed by a relatively easy reinvasion of the continent, by a numerically inferior British army, and eventual victory. Most of the hopes about the effectiveness of this strategy were unfounded.

The belief that the German economy would collapse stemmed from intelligence assessments made before the war. These assumed that Hitler had already fully mobilized the German economy for war in the 1930s, that there was no spare capacity available and that existing levels of output could not be maintained indefinitely. With little fresh intelligence available from Germany, Britain stuck with this belief throughout 1940; indeed it was one of Churchill's arguments for fighting on as France fell. At the end of May the Ministry of Economic Warfare viewed the German economy as highly vulnerable: 'It has long been foreseen . . . that Germany would reach her maximum strength in May 1940. But even this great strength is brittle . . . by April 1941, she should be down to one million tons of oil. This was her dying out figure in the last war.'[5] An intelligence assessment sent to the Prime Minister at the same time emphasized the growing strains they believed the war was imposing on German output and morale:

The difficulties there are increasing and the Nazis are terrified of failing to win the war this summer. There is general apathy at home in Germany, the casualties have been heavy, the shortages of food and raw materials are making themselves felt, and the production of tanks and aircraft is falling off by forty per cent.

It was on this basis that, when the chiefs of staff were asked by Churchill at the end of May to consider whether Britain could continue the war with any chance of success, they stated that 'upon the economic factor depends our only hope of bringing about the downfall of Germany'.[7]

Such assumptions badly misjudged the actual state of affairs. The German economy had not been geared for war in the 1930s, and Hitler was to continue his attempt to achieve conquests in short campaigns, using minimum industrial resources, until the defeat at Stalingrad at the end of 1942 forced the beginnings of full-scale economic mobilization. He did not think it necessary to prepare for a long war and was determined to try to avoid military production interfering with domestic consumption. In 1940 consumer expenditure was greater than military expenditure and the German standard of living was to remain higher than Britain's until 1944. Military output was actually reduced in 1940: tank production was just forty a month (compared with 2,000 a month achieved in 1944). The result of this policy was that the German army remained a ramshackle, ill-equipped force. Of the 150 divisions that attacked the Soviet Union in June 1941, only forty-six were fully equipped with German arms; the rest were either short of equipment or using captured French and Czech weapons. For most of the war, therefore, there was plenty of spare capacity available in the German economy, which made it almost impossible for Britain to apply enough pressure to bring about a collapse of the war effort.

British hopes about the fragility of the German economy were also one of the factors behind the decision, taken in the summer of 1940, to embark, on a strategic air offensive. The main reason, though, was that it was the only way in which Germany could be attacked, despite the considerable limitations on the offensive. In 1940 the RAF did not have suitable aircraft and a new generation of four-engined bombers capable of carrying a substantial load to

Germany would not be operational for nearly two years. Daylight bombing was not a feasible operation against a determined defence, as the RAF found out in the early days of the war. (This was a lesson that was learnt again by the Luftwaffe in the summer of 1940 and by the United States in 1942–3.) It forced the adoption of night bombing, and the RAF was untrained and ill-equipped to cope with the enormous difficulties in navigation and target-finding it involved. They had no adequate bombsight until 1942 and their primitive navigation guidance systems were ineffective. In August 1939, during a carefully planned training exercise, forty per cent of the bombers involved could not find a designated 'target' in broad daylight in a friendly city with no fighter defence. Given this level of competence, it was not surprising that night flying proved even more inaccurate. The official historians of the bomber offensive were forced to admit the fundamental constraints on the RAF: 'When war came in 1939 Bomber Command was not trained or equipped to penetrate into enemy territory by day or to find its target areas, let alone its targets, by night.'[8]

When the air offensive began in 1941, the only feasible policy was therefore to attack German cities, because these were the only targets the RAF had even a remote chance of finding. The best that could be hoped for was that under these attacks German civilian morale might crack. The early stages of the offensive were little short of catastrophic for the RAF. During 1940 and 1941, more RAF personnel than German civilians were killed during the attacks. One reason for the low level of German casualties was poor navigation by the RAF. An official survey in August 1941 showed that one-third of the aircraft despatched did not attack any target at all, and that the best third only managed to drop their bombs somewhere within five miles of the target.

As time went on, techniques gradually improved and American entry into the campaign in 1942 increased the weight of the air offensive beyond anything the British could have imagined in 1940, but nevertheless strategic bombing contributed little towards final victory. It cost the RAF a total of 8,000 aircraft and 50,000 dead, yet it failed to damage civilian morale or reduce significantly German industrial output. In fact, German war production reached its peak under the full weight of the bomber offensive. Between 1942 and 1944 German munitions output trebled, with the production of tanks increasing five-fold. Aircraft production also doubled to 40,000 in 1944 (fifty per cent higher than the British level). The official Allied survey after the war estimated that, overall, the Germans lost just under four per cent of their productive capacity to the bomber offensive; in 1945 German machine tool capacity was actually higher than in 1939. Production collapsed at the end of 1944 only because the Allied armies overran the main sources of German raw materials. The official historians of the air offensive were forced to conclude:

Area attacks against German cities could not have been responsible for more than a very small part of the fall which had occurred in German production by the spring of 1945, and ... in terms of bombing effort, they were also a very costly way of achieving the results they did achieve.[9]

The same disappointing results were experienced with the third prong of the strategy devised in 1940 to try to win the war: resistance and subversion. At the end of May the chiefs of staff identified subversion as a key element in Britain's future strategy and one of the few ways available of undermining German power. An organization (Special Operations Executive), combining parts of MI6 and the War Office, that had studied subversion before the war, was established by the war cabinet on 22 July to run this new form of warfare. Churchill chose Hugh Dalton, the Labour Minister of Economic Warfare, as the political head of SOE, mainly in order to balance Conservative control of MI5 and MI6.

Delton took a bold view of what SOE should do in carrying out semi-terrorist warfare:

We have got to organize movements in enemy-occupied territory comparable to the Sinn Fein movement in Ireland ... This 'democratic international' must use many different methods, including industrial and military sabotage, labour agitation and strikes, continuous propaganda, terrorist acts against traitors and German leaders, boycotts and riots.[10]

Churchill told Dalton to 'set Europe ablaze'; they both hoped that campaigns of subversion would make it impossible for Germany to rule Europe and in the ensuing chaos the British army might be able to reinvade the continent and defeat Germany. This was a hopelessly optimistic scenario for a number of reasons. The men chosen to run the new outfit – Sir Frank Nelson, a former Conservative MP who had moved to the City, and Gladwyn Jebb, a diplomat – were not the best choices for organizing such an unorthodox and aggressive campaign, Moreover, many of the governments-in-exile in London were opposed to the idea of SOE stirring up trouble in their countries for fear of attracting reprisals against the civilian population. SOE also found it difficult to obtain from the other services the military resources necessary for a major campaign. In addition, certain political restrictions were imposed on SOE activity. For example, no agents could be dropped into Vichy France before the German take-over in November 1942 because of the desire to maintain good relations with the Vichy government. Increasingly the British government altered its views about the benefits of a Europe in a state of continuous revolt. They developed a preference for the well-organized 'secret armies' of Yugoslavia and Poland and other groups prepared to co-ordinate their activities with Allied military operations rather than more sporadic action by individuals and irregular forces across occupied Europe. The greatest drawback of all to SOE operations was a chronic lack of support on the ground. In 1940 Britain did not have a single agent in western Europe and the thirty or so in the Balkans lasted only until the German invasion in the spring of 1941. Not until May 1941 did the first British agent parachute into France. Although the agents showed great courage, their impact on the outcome of the war was marginal. The simple fact was that in the early years of the war there was little active resistance to the Germans for the British to back. Not until the Allies started to achieve military success in 1942 and 1943 and German defeat seemed likely did the resistance become a significant force that, supplied with agents and equipment, could disrupt German communications and tie down large numbers of troops.

None of the British strategic options – economic warfare, bombing and subversion – therefore provided a successful route to winning the war. Even the great intelligence breakthrough in the summer of 1940 could not transform this situation. By developing previous French and Polish work on the mechanics of the Enigma machine the British were able to read Luftwaffe signals with increasing frequency and speed from May 1940. In the spring of 1941, naval signals were also regularly broken and army codes were cracked a year later. Once a system had been developed to send this invaluable information quickly to front-line commands the British (and later the Americans) had a stupendous advantage over their opponents. In the period when the British fought alone, however, they were unable to take advantage of the information they were receiving because of their lack of military power. In this period Churchill and a handful of top advisers were increasingly well informed about German military intentions but could do little to counter them. Intelligence could play its full part only when British inferiority in manpower and equipment had been replaced by American superiority in both areas.

In late 1940 the war cabinet also had to face another developing threat to Britain's survival: a supply crisis. Between the outbreak of war and the end of 1940, Britain lost two million tons of shipping, although these losses were largely offset by acquisitions from Allied countries. Once imports from Europe and the Mediterranean came to an end, goods had to be carried over longer distances. By the autumn of 1940 this, combined with slower turn-round times in British ports affected by bomb damage and the blackout, reduced import capacity to only two-thirds of pre-war levels. At forty million tons this was the level the government considered to be Britain's minimum requirement for survival. (In 1937 imports had been sixty million tons.) Food imports were reduced from twenty-three to sixteen million tons and other goods cut by almost a third to twenty-four million tons, of which a significant part had to be armaments and raw materials to maintain the war effort. The threat facing the war cabinet in the winter of 1940–41 was that continued sinkings and the inability of the shipbuilding industry to construct sufficient merchant ships, linked with the fact that no more supplements could be expected from the fleets of Allied nations, were already reducing imports below even minimum survival levels. In the last four months of 1940 less than twelve million tons was imported, equivalent to only thirty-five million tons in a full year. If this shortfall of over ten per cent were to continue or worsen, then Britain's war-making capacity would have to be cut back because food imports were already near the minimum. In January 1941, the Americans were given full details about this growing menace and asked to rescue Britain from yet another potentially fatal threat.[11]

At the beginning of 1941 none of the fundamental strategic problems facing Britain had been resolved. The country had been saved from bankruptcy by the United States, but Europe was dominated by Germany and Italy, the situation in the Mediterranean was precarious and in the Far East threatening, as a Japanese attack seemed increasingly likely. Britain could not deploy enough military power to win the war on its own Most of its efforts in 1941 had to be devoted to ensuring sur vival through maintaining air defences, escorting convoys across the Atlantic, combating the U-boats and keeping a hold on Egypt. This strategy might avoid immediate defeat, but the chance of victory depended on the United States' entry into the war. The year 1941 was to be a grim one as Britain, committed to a war it could not win, waited on the Americans who seemed determined not to enter the war. Britain was now reduced to the status of an American client, kept in the war in order to buy the time needed for its patron to complete rearmament.

Anglo–American relations in 1941 remained, as they had been in 1940, distant, with the Americans the dominant power, still determined to maintain their own national self-interest. Military staff talks between the two countries held in Washington in early 1941 brought home the inequalities in the relationship. They could agree that defeat of Germany was the overriding aim if the United States entered the war, but there was no agreement in other areas. The Americans, for example, still refused to send part of their fleet to Singapore to defend British territory. American domination was made painfully clear when they forced the British to reveal all their secret treaties and commitments before the talks got down to issues of substance.

Although the Americans were prepared to hold these secret discussions on hypothetical joint military plans, they were not prepared to provide much direct practical assistance. In the spring of 1941 there was a crisis in Anglo–American relations. In the

Mediterranean the British suffered another defeat with the German conquest of Yugoslavia, Greece and Crete, together with very heavy merchant shipping losses which deepened the supply crisis. The Americans were unmoved. Churchill wrote to Eden that it seemed 'as if there has been a considerable recession across the Atlantic, and that quite unconsciously we are being left very much to our fate'.[12] Churchill even considered using the threat of making a compromise peace in an effort to shift the American attitude, but Eden counselled against the move. Roosevelt refused to provide US escorts for convoys in the Atlantic and only agreed to tell the British about U-boat sightings in the area off the American coast. The sinking of a US merchant ship by a U-boat in May produced no response from the Americans. The German attack on the Soviet Union at the end of June took some of the pressure off Roosevelt to aid Britain, because any immediate threat of defeat was lifted while the German army and air force were fully occupied in the east. In July American troops relieved British forces occupying Iceland, but this was compatible with the policy the Americans had followed, since the summer of 1940, of strengthening their defences in the western hemisphere. American convoys were sent to Iceland escorted by US warships but the US navy was not allowed to escort British or even neutral shipping, nor to attack German ships.

Churchill and Roosevelt met for their first wartime conference in Newfoundland at the beginning of August 1941. The results were a great disappointment for the British. In the summer of 1940 they had fought on alone in the hope that Germany might collapse and that the United States would soon enter the war. Now neither seemed likely; Hitler was stronger than ever and looked likely to defeat the Soviet Union before the winter, and Roosevelt showed no sign of wanting to enter the war. Apart from reaching agreement on a statement about common aims for the post-war world, little was achieved in the way of immediate help. Churchill thought he had obtained an assurance that the Americans would start escorting convoys in the western Atlantic and attacking U-boats, but in the weeks after the meeting it became clear that Roosevelt had been speaking only about a contingency plan. At the end of August there was acute depression in the war cabinet: they no longer expected imminent American entry and they faced the prospect of a long war ahead and little chance of success without full US involvement.

In the autumn Roosevelt inched cautiously towards greater help to keep Britain in the war. Following an attack on the USS *Greer* by a U-boat, he extended the American defence zone to Iceland, but this was still far short of what the British needed in terms of convoy defence and assistance from US merchant shipping. At home, Roosevelt had to take account of the continuing lack of public support for greater US involvement and the limited support in Congress for any firm action (the draft was renewed by just one vote and parts of the Neutrality Act were repealed by the lowest majority on this subject since 1939). Although at the end of November Roosevelt authorized US merchant ships to sail to Britain, he exerted tight control of the numbers involved. Strict instructions were issued to the US navy to avoid any incident. Without the Japanese attack on Pearl Harbor the carefully limited American assistance in the Atlantic – enough to stop the British being defeated, but no more – would probably have continued for a considerable time.

In the Far East, Britain had little more than a spectator role in US diplomacy with Japan throughout 1941. Although the American attempt to strike a deal with Japan that would avoid war was vital to the future of British interests in the area, the US did not consult Britain about the substance of the talks. Churchill was not convinced that the Americans would join an Anglo–Japanese war and he remained determined to try to avoid a conflict by not provoking the Japanese. On the other hand, he always insisted that Britain would join any American–Japanese war immediately. Not until 3 December, when a Japanese attack somewhere in the Far East was expected at any moment, did the United States finally inform the British and Dutch that it would fight if Japan attacked either British territory or the Dutch East Indies. It was the Japanese attack on Pearl Harbor four days later that finally transformed a European war into a world war and ensured the eventual defeat of Germany, Italy and Japan.

Shortly after Pearl Harbor, in a moment of candour, Churchill described Britain's relationship with the United States as that of 'a client receiving help from a generous patron'.[13] That unbalanced relationship was to continue for the rest of the war. Although Churchill described Lend-Lease as 'the most unsordid act in the history of any nation' he was indulging in wishful thinking to disguise Britain's weakness and the pursuit of self-interest by the

United States. During the war the United States used the power acquired through Britain's dependence on Lend-Lease supplies to control British economic policy and ensure British acquiescence in American aims for the post-war world.

In total Britain received $27 billion of Lend-Lease assistance to keep its economy afloat and maintain the war effort. Although Britain did not have to pay dollars for these goods, they were not free. The Act passed by the US Congress only deferred payment and allowed the President to decide what 'consideration' should be required at some stage from recipients of aid. During 1941 and early 1942 there were detailed discussions between British and American officials over the terms to apply to Britain. The American negotiators proved to be tough and determined to extract a high price, not in money, but by forcing major concessions in British economic and financial policy which would have far-reaching implications for the position of both countries in the post-war world. At an early stage, in September 1941, the British were forced to accept severe restrictions on exports. Lend-Lease supplies were not to be exported, nor were goods made from raw materials supplied under Lend-Lease. In addition, Britain was stopped from exporting British goods to new markets or to areas where goods similar to Lend-Lease materials might be in competition with American exports. In this way US manufacturers were able to supplant Britain in many markets, particularly in Latin America. The US government unilaterally decided Lend-Lease munitions would be free, but that all American-supplied equipment that survived the war would have to be returned to the United States, and that in return for other Lend-Lease supplies changes in British economic and trade policy after the war would be required. The Americans had long wanted to dismantle the system of imperial trade preference built up by the British in the 1930s and the linked sterling area exchange controls. The end of these two features of British economic policy would leave the United States, which had by far the largest economy in the world, in undisputed domination of the world's trade and financial systems. In February 1942 the British had to make a commitment to end 'discriminatory' trade and finance systems after the war.

In other ways the United States also used its financial power ruthlessly to keep Britain in a state of dependence. During 1942 US air force units, followed by troops, began to arrive in Britain.

This resulted in a major inflow of dollars, which caused British currency reserves to rise. The Americans realized that if this continued, as more US forces poured into Britain before the invasion of Europe, it would enable Britain to become more independent and strengthen its financial position after the war. On 1 January 1943 the US government therefore decided unilaterally that 'the United Kingdom's gold and dollar balances should not be permitted to be less than about $600 million nor above about $1 billion'.[14] This level the Americans thought would be enough to stop Britain adopting a siege economy after the war, while not leaving them so strong as to be able to resist US economic demands. Despite continual protests from the British over the next two and a half years, including several personal appeals from Churchill to Roosevelt, the US refused to change its position. They continued, moreover, to manipulate the British economy and currency reserves by removing some goods such as tobacco from the Lend-Lease supplies, thus forcing the British to pay dollars for them, and by demanding free goods from the sterling area through 'reverse Lend-Lease'. This kept Britain within the arbitrary limits for currency reserves the Americans had decided upon at the beginning of 1943.

Although during 1941 and early 1942 the Americans were providing the assistance that enabled the British to continue the war, they did not provide the military effort that could compensate for British military weakness. The consequence was the final collapse of British power around the globe. The theoretical nightmare which had faced the government before the war became a reality, as Britain did have to fight three enemies simultaneously. In 1941 the key area was the Mediterranean and the adjacent Balkan countries. In the first two months of 1941, the British put an enormous effort into trying to construct a Balkan front against Germany. The aim was ambitious. As Churchill told Eden and General Dill, in the sealed orders they took with them for the various negotiations, it was 'to use the Balkan theatre as the stage on which to inflict a military defeat on the Germans when the will to resist of the German people was on the point of breaking down'.[15] The problem with achieving this aim was that both Greece and Yugoslavia, the only likely members of an anti-German front, were reluctant to take part for fear of precipitating a German attack. In early February the death of the Greek dictator, General Metaxas, led to a new government, which requested British assistance. On 24 February the war cabinet, influenced in part by elements in the US administration who thought the Balkans were vital, agreed to send British forces to fight in Greece. Yugoslavia proved more difficult to bring into an anti-German alliance. British pressure on the Belgrade government, after the decision to deploy to Greece, was unproductive and when the Yugoslavs allied with Germany and Italy (while refusing the passage of German troops through the country) SOE mounted a coup to install a new government. This new government was still reluctant to side with Britain and Greece. Ten days after the coup in Belgrade, the Germans attacked Greece and Yugoslavia simultaneously on 6 April. Within three days, the Yugoslav government had fled Belgrade and both countries were quickly overrun, with British troops being rapidly evacuated from Greece. The ignominious collapse of the Balkan front was followed by another disaster, this time in Crete. Although the British had almost complete information about German plans through intercepted Enigma messages and also had a four-to-one superiority in troops, they were ignominiously defeated within days by a German airborne invasion covered by local German air superiority. The remnants of the army were evacuated to Egypt, where the British were able to cling on precariously after German forces under Rommel also drove them out of Libya.

The German attack on the Soviet Union at the end of June 1941 provided only temporary relief for the British. Military and intelligence experts expected the usual rapid German victory against what was assumed to be a weak, badly equipped opponent. Churchill ordered British counter-invasion preparations to be brought to a state of full readiness by 1 September in the expectation of a rapid German redeployment to the west and a final assault on Britain. Even in the early autumn when, after a series of brilliant victories in the summer, the pace of the German advance slowed down, the accepted view in London was that a Soviet defeat was almost certain in 1942.

In the autumn of 1941, Britain's position was increasingly bleak. Germany controlled most of Europe and its armies were fighting in the suburbs of Moscow and Leningrad. In the Middle East Britain could just sustain its position in Egypt against a handful of German divisions. The Japanese attack in the Far East at the end of the year swept away most of the largely defenceless Empire. The only part of the fleet that could be scraped together for despatch to Singapore (*Prince of Wales* and *Repulse*) arrived just before the Japanese attack, but both ships were sunk within days of the opening of hostilities. The Japanese quickly overran Hong Kong, Malaya, Singapore, Burma and most of New Guinea. Australia faced the threat of invasion unprotected. The Japanese army was on the borders of an India in almost open revolt. The Royal Navy withdrew from its Indian Ocean bases to the east coast of Africa.

The British assessment in the 1930s that it could not withstand three enemies simultaneously was proved right. The consequences were devastating. A bankrupt Britain, dependent on American supplies to continue the war and barely able to ship the minimum level of food and raw materials into its ports, was left hanging on to the remnants of an empire. Britain was rescued from this parlous state and turned into a victorious nation, able to resume its control over large parts of the Empire, through the combined economic and military power of the United States and the Soviet Union. Only with American entry into the war was Churchill at last confident of victory. In his memoirs he recalled his thoughts on 7 December, the night Pearl Harbor was attacked: 'So we had won after all! . . . All the rest was merely the proper application of overwhelming force.'[16] But that overwhelming force was not Britain's to deploy. Victory depended on the ability of both the United States and the Soviet Union to mobilize enormous military strength, and in the American case the mobilization of the largest and most advanced economy in the world. The effort demanded of these two superpowers during the remaining three and a half years of the war shows just how marginal the British contribution had become.

The United States was able to deploy major naval, army and air forces in Europe and the Pacific simultaneously and equip them, together with a large part of the forces of their allies. The American economy coped with the war effort without any sign of strain: consumer expenditure actually increased by twelve per cent between 1941 and 1945, despite the huge increase of resources devoted to arms production. In 1940 British arms production was only half the German and Italian level, despite the fact that the German economy was not mobilized for war. By 1943 the Allies were outproducing Germany, Italy and Japan by three to one and US arms output was at four times the British level. The strength of the American economy can be judged from the fact that in 1939 the United States manufactured 2,100 aircraft and in 1944 96,300. British arms production reached a plateau in 1942 and could not be increased without redeploying men from the armed forces. Increasingly, Britain was dependent on US weapons for its forces. By 1944 two-thirds of the tanks and lorries in the British army were made in the United States.

US power was matched by Soviet military power and it was on the eastern front that the German war machine was finally destroyed. In 1941 the Germans claimed to have killed, wounded or captured three million Soviet soldiers, yet the Soviet Union was still able to deploy an army of over four million which had more tanks and aircraft than the Germans. Later in the war, Soviet casualties were often running at five or six times the German level without this affecting their capability to continue the war. In the great tank battle at Kursk in the summer of 1943, the Soviets lost 2,000 tanks in a week, but still destroyed seventeen German Panzer divisions. Soviet casualties during the war were twenty times greater than the total of British and American casualties. Of the roughly thirteen and a half million German casualties and prisoners during the war, ten million occurred on the eastern front. It was this enormous Soviet military effort that made possible the Allied landings in Normandy, for in June 1944 the Allies in France and Italy faced ninety German divisions while the Soviet Union was still fighting 250 divisions.

The British role in this display of economic and military power was minor. As the war continued, British influence over events and decisions also became correspondingly less significant. The scenario for an Allied victory, which had worried the British government before the war, became a reality. The Soviet Union was moving westwards and establishing its control over eastern Europe, and Britain had become a dependency of the United States. In 1942 the defence of Australia and New Zealand became an American responsibility and the United States dominated Allied strategy in the Pacific. In Europe, too, once American forces were deployed on a large scale British influence over strategy waned.

In 1945 the Allied victory, achieved mainly by the power of the United States and the Soviet Union, enabled British rule to be

re-established over the Empire. But it was rule without the substance of power. Although Britain emerged on the winning side
in the war, it had achieved a largely pyrrhic victory. The fact of
winning the war could not change Britain's economic and financial
circumstances, which were conditioned by the experience of bankruptcy in 1940 and nearly five years of dependence on the United
States. The wartime economy had been kept going only by massive
injections of American supplies and the willingness of the sterling
area countries to allow Britain to accumulate large debts.

At the end of the war, Britain's economic and financial position
provided both a poor basis on which to build the better future
people wanted after the deprivations and sacrifices of six years of
war, and weak foundations for the resumption of its role as a
world power at the centre of a vast Empire. In 1944 exports were
only a third of the 1938 level, whereas imports were over fifty per
cent higher. In addition to this enormous trade gap, overseas
capital assets worth £1.3 billion (a major source of income before
the war) had been sold. Britain's overseas debts had risen five-
fold to £3.4 billion, the largest in the world. Britain was even in
debt to parts of the Empire, such as India, Egypt and Iraq. The
total debt was seven times greater than the foreign currency
reserves, and could be controlled only by keeping sterling as a
non-convertible currency to stop holders of sterling from selling. In
the latter stages of the war the Treasury started to analyse
Britain's likely situation in the first years of peace. The prognosis
was horrific. They doubted that the sterling area countries could
be persuaded to go on holding vast assets in an almost worthless
non-convertible currency and they also forecast that the likely
balance of payments deficit would be a minimum of £1 billion
over the first five years. Even at this level, which was probably
too high to be financed, imports would not be sufficient to rebuild
the economy and unemployment was likely to be around three
million. In August 1945 the Treasury concluded that Britain was
facing 'an economic Dunkirk ... virtually bankrupt and the economic basis for the hopes of the public non-existent'.[17]

Once again Britain looked to the United States for help. The
British had assumed that American assistance would continue
after the war, but a week after the Japanese surrender Lend-Lease
was abruptly terminated, leaving Britain to pay cash for $650
million worth of goods already in the pipeline. To the government

the only available option seemed to be to ask the United States for a massive loan. John Maynard Keynes was sent to Washington to undertake the negotiations and after considerable haggling he was able to obtain a loan of $3.75 billion at two per cent interest (the British had wanted an interest-free loan). Again the Americans drove a hard bargain. They took the opportunity to obtain pledges from the British that they would accept US ideas for the structure of the post-war world that would enshrine American domination. In return for the loan, the newly elected Labour government was reluctantly forced to accept membership of the General Agreement on Tariffs and Trade (GATT), which was committed to the liberalization of world trade (a policy which was bound to be in the interests of the United States as the world's biggest trading nation). In addition, Britain had to agree to make the pound a convertible currency within twelve months of receiving the loan. With the United States holding two-thirds of the world's gold reserves and the dollar as the dominant world currency, this was bound to place the British in a subordinate position and put serious strains on an already weak economy. Britain's role as a client state of the United States, which had become reality in 1940, was once again brought home by the fact that it was powerless to resist American demands.

However, the Treasury's projections about the state of the British economy and the perceived need for an American loan were based on an assumption that Britain was still a world power and that it should, and could, continue in that role. After the negotiations in Washington, Keynes commented within White-hall on the significance of the arithmetic: 'The American loan is for £937 million ... estimated political and military expenditure [in the three years 1946–8] is £1,000 million. Thus, it comes out in the wash that the American loan is primarily required to meet the political and military expenditure overseas.'[18] This determination to maintain Britain's role as a world power, without the financial, economic and industrial base to support such a policy, was at the heart of the Labour government's strategic assumptions; and it was a continuation of pre-war and wartime attitudes. In May 1947 Ernie Bevin, the Foreign Secretary, told the House of Commons:

His Majesty's Government do not accept the view ... that we

have ceased to be a Great Power or the contention that we have
ceased to play that role. We regard ourselves as one of the
Powers most vital to the peace of the world and we still have
our historic part to play. The very fact that we have fought so
hard for liberty, and paid such a price, warrants our retaining
this position; and indeed it places a duty upon us to continue
to retain it. I am not aware of any suggestion, seriously
advanced, that by a sudden stroke of fate, as it were, we have
overnight ceased to be a Great Power.[19]

The tone of Bevin's words was perhaps rather defensive, but
the emotional force behind Britain's urge to remain a world power
was still potent and virtually unchallengeable. His argument that
because Britain had been on the winning side in the war it
followed it was still a great power and that the sacrifices of the
war somehow imposed a duty to go on with the illusion, regardless
of the harsh facts of life in a world dominated by the superpowers,
encapsulates the prevailing failure to accept the lessons of 1940.
It was as if all those military assessments of the impossibility of
defending the Empire made both before and during the war; all
those Treasury papers depicting economic and financial collapse;
all the experience of living on borrowed funds as a client of the
United States and the humiliation of having to open up the books
to prove to the American government that the great British Empire
was bankrupt, had all been forgotten.

Yet the lesson of 1940 was that Britain was no longer a great
power. In that year its rapidly growing strategic weaknesses – an
overstretched Empire, too many enemies, too few allies, an inadequate industrial base and impoverished finances – combined finally
to end its independent role in the world. On the surface, 1940 was a
heroic year of resolution and defiance in the face of disaster. A
powerful mythology grew up around the dramatic events of that year
which both reinforced that belief and embellished the picture. It was
easier for the public and the politicians who participated in those
events, including the members of the post-war Labour government,
to embrace the reassuring mythology than to contemplate the harsh
reality of what had happened behind the scenes. As a result, much of
Britain's post-war economic, defence and foreign policy was based
on an illusion; an attempt was made to reassert Britain's role as a
major power without the necessary foundations to sustain it.

What could not be admitted in wartime could not be revealed in peacetime either. The files gathered dust in departmental archives and no attempt was made to analyse Britain's real position in 1945 and take the necessary action to adjust policy to reality. The histories and war memoirs were published in a steady stream, but they stressed other, more heroic aspects of the war. The emphasis was on Dunkirk and the determination of Britain to fight on alone, not on the financial disaster that engulfed Britain at the end of the year nor the complete collapse of British power and outright dependence on the United States.

The determination to ignore what actually happened in 1940 became a permanent part of British post-war policy. The myth of great-power status was maintained and its trappings clung to, despite the strains imposed on a battered economy. The myth of the 'special relationship' with the United States was sedulously cultivated, in part to help support the dreams of strategic strength but also to disguise Britain's real role as a client state of the Americans. It was both convenient and comfortable to believe in the identity of interests between the two countries, the shared heritage of the 'English-speaking peoples' and American magnanimity. For the last fifty years Britain has cherished a mythology about the events of its 'Finest Hour', a mythology that has sustained many post-war illusions as well. The reality has never been accepted.

Notes

References for material in the Public Record Office at Kew are as follows:

ADM — Admiralty
CAB — Cabinet Office
DO — Dominions Office
FO — Foreign Office
HO — Home Office
INF — Ministry of Information
PREM — Prime Minister's Office
T — Treasury
WO — War Office

Chapter 1: 22 August 1940 (pp. 4–10)

1. CAB 66/11, WP (40) 324
2. CAB 16/209, Strategic Affairs Sub-committee (6.4.39)
3. CAB 24/287, CP 149 (39) (3.7.39)
4. CAB 66/5, WP (40) 45 (9.2.40)
5. CAB 65/14, WM (40) 232nd Conclusions (22.8.40)

Chapter 2: Façade of Power (pp. 11–40)

1. K. Burk, *Sinews of War*, p. 81
2. Ibid, p. 203
3. M. Gilbert, *Churchill Vol 5*, p. 105
4. CAB 53/1, COS 30th Meeting (27.5.26)
5. CAB 4/15, CID 701
6. Chatfield to Fisher, Chatfield Papers CHT/3/1 (6.6.34)
7. House of Commons, 27.1.42
8. R. Minney, *Private Papers of Hore-Belisha*, pp. 59–60
9. CAB 24/273, CP 316 (37) (22.12.37)
10. N. Chamberlain Diary, 6.6.34

11 CAB 4/24, DRC Third Report (21.11.35)
12 PREM 1/276, Eden to Chamberlain, 9.1.38
13 CAB 4/26, Comparison of the Strength of Great Britain with that of certain other Nations as at January 1938 (12.11.37)
14 PREM 1/276, Eden to Chamberlain, 31.1.38
15 K. Feiling, *Neville Chamberlain*, p. 324
16 CAB 53/37, COS 698 (28.3.38)
17 CAB 2/8, CID 341st Meeting (15.12.38)
18 C. Barnett, *Audit of War*, p. 95
19 CAB 24/274, CP 24 (38)
20 CAB 27/648, CP 247 (38)
21 CAB 132/28, Imperial Conference 5th Meeting (24.5.37), & CAB 53/51 (31.5.37)
22 CAB 16/209, SAC Paper No. 16 (5.4.39)
23 CAB 27/625, Foreign Policy Committee (20.6.39)
24 CAB 53/52, COS 946 (18.7.39)
25 FO 371/22814
26 CAB 24/282
27 CAB 24/287, CP 149 (39) (3.7.39)
28 Cadogan Diary, p. 182 (20.5.39)
29 A. J. P. Taylor, *Origins of the Second World War*, p. 262
30 Foreign Relations of the United States, 1939. Vol. 1 (Kennedy to Hull, 30.8.39)
31 CAB 66/1, WP (39) 15 (8.9.39)

Chapter 3: Failure (pp. 43–58)

1 CAB 66/1, WP (39) 42 (22.9.39)
2 CAB 66/5, WP (40) 45 (9.2.40)
3 CAB 65/5, WM (40) 40th Conclusions (13.2.40)
4 T 177/52, Minute by Sir F. Phillips, 28.2.40
5 Channon Diary, p. 215 (3.9.39)
6 J. Colville, *Fringes of Power*, p. 40 (13.10.39)
7 D. Carlton, *Anthony Eden*, p. 156
8 Foreign Relations of the United States, 1938. Vol. 1, p. 687
9 ADM 199/1928, Minute of 5.12.39
10 CAB 99/3, Supreme War Council meeting 28.3.40
11 CAB 83/1, Military Co-ordination Committee meeting 20.12.39
12 ADM 116/4471 (10.4.40)
13 Nicolson Diary, p. 70 (11.4.40)
14 Ironside Diary, p. 285 (26.4.40)
15 Nicolson, op cit, p. 74 (30.4.40)
16 Channon, op cit, p. 242 (25.4.40)

17 Ibid, p. 244 (1.5.40)
18 Harvey Diary, p. 326 (30.10.39)
19 Cadogan, op cit, p. 277 (8.5.40)
20 P. Addison, *The Road to 1945*, p. 103
21 Nicolson, op cit, p. 75 (4.5.40)

Chapter 4: The New Regime (pp. 59–77)

1   M. Cowling, *The Impact of Hitler*, p. 367
2   A. Howard, *RAB*, p. 64 (Butler Diary, 20–21.7.35)
3   C. King, *With Malice Towards None*, p. 76
4   Colville, op cit, p. 118 (8.5.40)
5   .A. J. P. Taylor, *English History 1914–1945*, p. 475
6   Cadogan, op cit, p. 277 (9.5.40)
7   Lord Birkenhead, *Halifax*, pp. 454–5
8   Ibid, p. 455
9   A. J. P. Taylor, *Beaverbrook*, p. 410
10 Ibid, p. 411
11 Channon, op cit, p. 248
12 Colville, op cit, p. 51
13 Ibid, p. 122
14 Butler Diary, 14.5.40
15 Ickes Diary, 12.5.40 (not in published version)
16 Butler Diary, 13.5.40
17 Channon, op cit, p. 252
18 Ibid, p. 268 (26.9.40)
19 M. Gilbert, *Churchill: Finest Hour*, p. 327
20 Chamberlain Papers, NC/2/24A (9.9.40)
21 Chamberlain Diary, 30.9.40
22 King, op cit, pp. 11–14 (3.1.40)
23 Ibid, p. 41 (15.5.40)
24 Lloyd George Papers, G/81, Memorandum, 12.9.40
25 A. J. Sylvester Diary, 3.10.40
26 Chamberlain Diary, 28.5.40
27 Ibid, 18.6.40
28 Colville, op cit, p. 321 (20.12.40)
29 Cadogan, op cit, p. 342 (20.12.40) & p. 343 (23.12.40)
30 Lord Avon, *The Reckoning*, p. 145
31 D. Irving, *Churchill's War*, pp. 477–8 (omitted in published version of Hopkins papers)

Chapter 5: Collapse (pp. 78–95)

1 A. Adamthwaite, *France and the Coming of the Second World War*, p. xv
2 CAB 65/13, WM (40) 120th Conclusions (13.5.40)
3 CAB 65/7, WM (40) 122nd Conclusions (14.5.40)
4 CAB 79/14, COS No. 133 of 1940 (15.5.40)
5 CAB 65/13, WM (40) 123rd Conclusions (15.5.40)
6 CAB 99/3, Supreme War Council 11th Meeting 1939–40 (16.5.40)
7 CAB 65/7, WM (40) 125th Conclusions (16.5.40)
8 CAB 66/7, WP (40) 159
9 CAB 69/1, Defence Committee 14 (40) (8.6.40)
10 Pownall Diaries, pp. 342–5 (26.5.40)
11 King, op cit, p. 85 (1.11.40)
12 Dalton Diary, p. 27 (28.5.40)
13 N. Harman, *Dunkirk*, p. 187
14 CAB 99/3, Supreme War Council 13th Meeting 1939–40 (11.6.40)
15 CAB 65/7, WM (40) 163rd Conclusions (12.6.40)
16 Ibid, WM (40) 165th Conclusions (13.6.40, 10.15 p.m.)
17 PREM 3/468, Message from President Roosevelt 15.6.40, 1.30 a.m.
18 Channon, op cit, p. 261 (10.7.40)

Chapter 6: Peace? (pp. 96–119)

1 Foreign Relations of the United States, 1939. Vol. 1, p. 45 (Kennedy to State Department 2.10.39)
2 PREM 1/395, Churchill to Chamberlain 9.10.39
3 House of Commons, 12.10.39
4 King, op cit, p. 25 (9.3.40)
5 Cadogan, op cit, p. 249 (24.1.40)
6 FO 800/324, Halifax to Lothian 2.2.40
7 D. Reynolds, *The Creation of the Anglo-American Alliance*, p. 82
8 Butler Diary, 13.3.40
9 CAB 65/2, WM (39) 107th Conclusions (7.12.39)
10 Foreign Relations of the United States, 1940. Vol 1 (Kennedy to State Department 15.5.40, 2 a.m.)
11 Chamberlain Diary, 15.5.40
12 W. Kimball, *Churchill and Roosevelt*, Vol. 1, p. 64
13 House of Commons, 13.5.40
14 W. Churchill, *Their Finest Hour*, p. 157
15 Reynolds, op cit, p. 103
16 CAB 65/7, WM (40) 137th Conclusions (24.5.40)
17 CAB 65/13, WM (40) 139th Conclusions (26.5.40, 9 a.m.)

18 CAB 65/13, WM (40) 140th Conclusions (26.5.40, 2 p.m.)
19 Ibid
20 CAB 65/13, WM (40) 142nd Conclusions (27.5.40, refers to discussion on 26.5.40)
21 Chamberlain Diary, 26.5.40
22 CAB 66/7, WP (40) 170 (26.5.40)
23 CAB 65/13, WM (40) 142nd Conclusions (27.5.40)
24 Cadogan, op cit, p. 291 (27.5.40)
25 CAB 65/13, WM (40) 145th Conclusions (28.5.40)
26 Beaverbrook Papers, D 414/3 (29.5.40)
27 Channon, op cit, pp. 257–8 (14.6.40)
28 US National Archives 740.0011 European War 1939 3882½
29 CAB 65/7, WM (40) 171st Conclusions Item 5 (18.6.40)
30 Cadogan, op cit, p. 304 (18.6.40)
31 B. Martin, *Friedensinitiativen und Machtpolitik im Zweiten Weltkrieg*, p. 272
32 CAB 65/7, WM (40) 172nd Conclusions Item 7 (19.6.40)
33 FO 800/326
34 CAB 65/7, WM (40) 172nd Conclusions (19.6.40)
35 Ibid, WM (40) 177th Conclusions (24.6.40)
36 M. Balfour, *Propaganda in War*, p. 197
37 B. Martin, op cit, p. 277
38 Cadogan, op cit, p. 309 (2.7.40)
39 B. Martin, op cit, p. 283
40 Nicolson, op cit (22.7.40)
41 PREM 4/100/3 (3.8.40)

Chapter 7: Survival (pp. 120–137)

1 CAB 65/7, WM (40) 172nd Conclusions (19.6.40) & CAB 66/8, WP (40) 208
2 Memo by General Jodl, 30.6.40
3 Halder Diary, 13.7.40
4 CAB 66/7, WP (40) 168

Chapter 8: Government and People (pp. 138–172)

1 C. Barnett, op cit, p. 193
2 Channon, op cit, p. 272 (5.11.40)
3 Nicolson, op cit, (21.10.40)
4 Ibid, p. 112 (12.9.40)
5 King, op cit, p. 62 (18.7.40)
6 ADM 167/109

7 WO 163/49 (OS7, OS30, OS48)

8 Ibid, (OS54)

9 M. Gilbert, op cit, p. 158

10 CAB 65/9, WM (40) 245th Conclusions (9.9.40)

11 Cadogan, op cit, p. 286 (19.5.40)

12 Ibid, p. 287 (20.5.40)

13 HO 45/24882

14 CAB 75/5, Home Policy Committee meeting 16.7.40 & CAB 75/8 HPC (40) 226

15 G. Shakespeare, *Let Candles be Brought in*, p. 265

16 CAB 65/8, WM (40) 199th Conclusions (10.7.40)

17 Channon, op cit, p. 259 (24.6.40)

18 DO 131/31

19 INF 1/264 Home Intelligence Report 16.7.40

20 Ironside, op cit, p. 46 (20.1.38)

21 CAB 65/13, WM (40) 128th Conclusions

22 CAB 65/7, WM (40) 133rd Conclusions

23 House of Commons, 1.3.40

24 A. Marwick, *The Home Front*, pp. 36–7

25 CAB 73/2, CDC (40) 19th Conclusions (30.5.40) & CAB 73/3 CDC (40) 29

26 House of Lords, 26.9.39

27 House of Commons, 13.11.40

28 Reith Diaries, p. 270 (6.11.40)

29 P. Lewis, *A People's War*, p. 18

30 King, op cit, p. 55 (18.6.40 & 20.6.40)

31 Reith, op cit, p. 257 (18.6.40)

32 Nicolson, op cit, p. 97 (19.6.40)

33 Colville, op cit, 18.6.40

34 Reith, op cit, p. 261 (20.8.40)

35 INF 1/264, Daily Report 18.5.40

36 T. Harrison, *Living Through the Blitz*, p. 288

37 INF 1/264, Daily Report 24.5.40

38 Orwell Diary, 28.5.40

39 INF 1/264, Daily Report 24.6.40; P. Lewis, op cit, p. 4

40 CAB 65/8, WM (40) 189th Conclusions (1.7.40)

41 Ibid, WM (40) 192nd Conclusions (3.7.40)

42 Nicolson, op cit, p. 114 (17.9.40)

43 Colville, op cit, p. 257 (4.10.40)

44 Ibid, p. 268 (18.10.40)

45 INF 1/292 Reports on Coventry 19.11.40, Bristol 4–11.12.40, Portsmouth May 1941. For Coventry see also HO 199/442 (19.11.40). Plymouth comment by H. Morrison 7.5.41 (Nicolson, p. 164)

46 Harrison, op cit, p. 154
47 Ibid, p. 242
48 Colville, op cit, p. 264 (12.10.40)
49 CAB 73/2 CDC (40) 45th Conclusions. See also HO 186/634
50 R. Titmuss, *Problems of Social Policy*, p. 309
51 Harrison, op cit, p. 252
52 Ibid, p. 245
53 INF 1/292 Report on Portsmouth, May 1941
54 King, op cit, p. 22 (8.2.40)
55 Harrison, op cit, p. 249

Chapter 9: Impotence (pp. 173–195)

1 CAB 66/8, WP (40) 193 (4.6.40)
2 Alexander Papers 5.4.26
3 CAB 65/13, WM (40) 282nd Conclusions (4.11.40)
4 CAB 65/2, WM (39) 89th Conclusions (20.11.39)
5 D. Day, *The Great Betrayal*, p. 55
6 Ibid, p. 75
7 CAB 80/16, COS (40) 592 (15.9.40)
8 CAB 66/7, WP (40) 168
9 CAB 80/18, COS (40) 704 (8.11.40)
10 CAB 66/9, WP (40) 234 (29.6.40)
11 Ibid
12 Colville, op cit, p. 200 (25.7.40)
13 Cadogan, op cit, p. 310 (4.7.40)
14 CAB 66/9, WP (40) 249 (4.7.40)
15 CAB 65/9, WM (40) 194th Conclusions (5.7.40)
16 Cadogan, op cit, p. 311 (5.7.40)
17 CAB 65/8, WM (40) 199th Conclusions (10.7.40)
18 Ibid, WM (40) 200th Conclusions (11.7.40)
19 CAB 65/9, WM (40) 265th Conclusions (3.10.40)
20 C. Thorne, *Allies of a Kind*, p. 72
21 D. Reynolds, op cit, p. 136
22 ADM 205/4 (7.6.40)
23 ADM 1/10321 (1.7.40)
24 A. Marder, *From the Dardenelles to Oran*, p. 267
25 CAB 65/15, WM (40) 250th Conclusions
26 Colville, op cit, p. 283 (1.11.40)
27 FO 371/24361
28 PREM 3/186A/2 (20.10.40)
29 PREM 4/21/1 (29.9.40)
30 FO 371/19763 (16–19.10.36)

31 PRO Foreign Office Index 1940, Vol. II p. 6
32 Cadogan, op cit, p. 341
33 PREM 3/131/1
34 M. Gilbert, op cit, p. 43
35 CAB 65/7, WM (40) 173rd Conclusions (20.6.40)
36 Cadogan, op cit, p. 305
37 PREM 3/131/1
38 PREM 3/131/2
39 CAB 65/7, WM (40) 178th Conclusions (25.6.40)
40 PREM 3/131/1
41 Ibid
42 PREM 3/131/2

Chapter 10: The End of Independence (pp. 196–215)

1 CAB 66/7, WP (40) 168 (25.5.40)
2 *Secret Diary of Harold Ickes Vol. III*, pp. 199–200
3 CAB 65/7, WM (40) 129th Conclusions (25.5.40)
4 CAB 66/7, WP (40) 276 (18.7.40)
5 FO 371/24241 (4.8.40)
6 CAB 65/8, WM (40) 231st Conclusions (21.8.40)
7 W. Kimball, op cit, p. 65
8 M. Gilbert, op cit, p. 758
9 Colville, op cit, p. 407 (5.3.41)
10 Adolf Berle Diary 31.8.40
11 PREM 4/25/8 (20.12.40)
12 PREM 3/468 (15.5.40)
13 FO 371/25209
14 CAB 66/11, WP (40) 324 (21.8.40)
15 Ibid, WP (40) 354 (3.9.40), WP (40) 355 (4.9.40)
16 CAB 65/15, WM (40) 244th Conclusions (6.9.40)
17 FO 371/24246 (21.9.40)
18 PREM 3/486/1
19 CAB 66/13, WP (40) 466 (8.12.40)
20 D. Reynolds, op cit, p. 93 (Telegram 13.12.40)
21 T 160/1051 (31.10.40)
22 FO 371/25209 (10.12.40)
23 Ibid
24 Ickes Diary, op cit, 19.1.41
25 PREM 4/17/1

Chapter 11: The Client State (pp. 216–235)

1 Cadogan, op cit, p. 346 (31.12.40)

2 Colville, op cit (13.10.40)
3 CAB 66/13, WP (40) 466 (8.12.40)
4 M. Gilbert, op cit, pp. 655–6
5 Dalton Diary, p. 20 (24.5.40)
6 Colville, op cit, p. 144 (31.5.40)
7 CAB 66/7, WP (40) 168 (25.5.40)
8 C. Webster & N. Frankland, *The Strategic Air Offensive*, Vol. 1, p. 125
9 Ibid, Vol. 4, p. 49
10 M. R. D. Foot, *SOE*, p. 19
11 CAB 66/16, WP (41) 17 (29.1.41)
12 PREM 3/469 (2.5.41)
13 PREM 4/17/3, Draft letter to President Roosevelt, 5.2.42
14 G. Kolko, *The Politics of War*, p. 283
15 FO 371/33145
16 W. Churchill, *The Grand Alliance*, p. 539
17 W. Hancock & M. Gowing, *British War Economy*, p. 546
18 R. W. Clarke, *Anglo-American Economic Collaboration*, p. 152
19 House of Commons, 16.5.47

Bibliography

Primary Sources

Public Record Office, Kew:
Admiralty (ADM)
Air Ministry (AIR)
Cabinet Office (CAB)
Dominions Office (DO)
Foreign Office (FO)
Home Office (HO)
Ministry of Information (INF)
Prime Minister's Office (PREM)
Treasury (T)
War Office (WO)

Private papers:

A. V. Alexander Papers	Churchill College, Cambridge
C. R. Attlee Papers	Churchill College, Cambridge
R. A. Butler Papers	Trinity College, Cambridge
Beaverbrook Papers	House of Lords Record Office
N. Chamberlain Papers	University of Birmingham Library
Chatfield Papers	National Maritime Museum, Greenwich
Hankey Papers	Churchill College, Cambridge
Lloyd George Papers	House of Lords Record Office

Secondary Sources

Adamthwaite, A., *France and the Coming of the Second World War 1936–1939* (London: Frank Cass, 1977)

Addison, P., 'Lloyd George and Compromise Peace in the Second World War', in Taylor, A., *Lloyd George: Twelve Essays* (London: Hamish Hamilton, 1971)

Addison, P., *The Road to 1945: British Politics and the Second World War* (London: Jonathan Cape, 1975)

Allen, H., *Who Won the Battle of Britain?* (London: Arthur Barker, 1974)

Amery, L., *My Political Life: Vol. 3 The Unforgiving Years 1929–1940* (London: Hutchinson, 1955)

Andrew, C., *Secret Service: The Making of the British Intelligence Community* (London: Heinemann, 1985)

Avon, Earl of, *Facing the Dictators* (London: Cassel, 1962)

Avon, Earl of, *The Reckoning* (London: Cassel, 1965)

Balfour, M., *Propaganda in War 1939–1945: Organisations, Policies and Publics in Britain and Germany* (London: Routledge and Keegan Paul, 1979)

Barker, E., *British Policy in South-East Europe in the Second World War* (London: Macmillan, 1976)

Barnett, C., *The Collapse of British Power* (London: Eyre Methuen, 1972)

Barnett, C., *The Desert Generals* (2nd edition) (London: Allen and Unwin, 1983)

Barnett, G., *The Audit of War: The Illusion and Reality of Britain as a Great Nation* (London: Macmillan, 1986)

Beck, P., *The Anglo–Argentine Dispute Over Title to the Falkland Islands: Changing British Perceptions on Sovereignty Since 1910* (Millennium: *Journal of International Studies* Vol. 12, No. 1)

Beck, P., *Research Problems in Studying Britain's Latin American Past: The Case of the Falklands Dispute 1920–1950* (Bulletin of Latin American Research Vol. 2, No. 2, May 1983)

Bell, P., *A Certain Eventuality: Britain and the Fall of France* (London: Saxon House, 1974)

Birkenhead, Earl of, *Halifax* (London: Hamish Hamilton, 1965)

Bond, B., *Chief of Staff: The Diaries of Lt-Gen Sir Henry Pownall, Vol. 1 1933–1940* (London: Leo Cooper, 1973)

Bond, B., *France and Belgium 1939–40* (London: Davis-Poynter, 1975)

Bond, B., *British Military Policy Between the Two World Wars* (Oxford: Oxford University Press, 1980)

Briggs, A., *The History of Broadcasting in the United Kingdom Vol. 3: The War of Words* (London: Oxford University Press, 1970)

Bullock, A., *The Life and Times of Ernest Bevin:*
Vol. I: *Trade Union Leader 1881–1940*
Vol. II: *Minister of Labour 1940–1945*
(London: Heinemann, 1960, 1967)

Burk, K., *Britain, America and the Sinews of War, 1914–1918* (London: Allen and Unwin, 1985)

Calder, A., *The People's War: Britain 1939–45* (London: Jonathan Cape, 1969)

Calder, A., and Sheridan, D., *Speak for Yourself: A Mass-Observation Anthology 1937–1949* (London: Jonathan Cape, 1984)

Calder, R., *The Lesson of London* (London: Secker and Warburg, 1941)

Campbell, J., *Nye Bevan and the Mirage of British Socialism* (London: Weidenfeld and Nicolson, 1987)

Carlgren, W., *Swedish Foreign Policy During the Second World War* (London: Ernest Benn, 1977)

Carlton, D., *Anthony Eden* (London: Allen Lane, 1981)

Carroll, J., *Ireland in the War Years* (Newton Abbot: David Charles, 1975)

Central Statistical Office, *Statistical Digest of the War* (London: HMSO, 1951)

Charmley, J., *Duff Cooper* (London: Weidenfeld and Nicolson, 1986)

Charmley, J., *Lord Lloyd and the Decline of the British Empire* (London: Weidenfeld and Nicolson, 1986)

Churchill, W., *The Second World War:*
        Vol. I: The Gathering Storm
        Vol. II: Their Finest Hour
        Vol. III: The Grand Alliance
(London: Cassel, 1948, 1949, 1950)

Clarke, R., *Anglo–American Economic Collaboration: British Economic Policy 1942–49* (London: Oxford University Press, 1982)

Colville, J., *The Fringes of Power: Downing Street Diaries 1939–1955* (London: Hodder and Stoughton, 1985)

Cooper, M., *The German Army 1933–1945: Its Political and Military Failure* (London: Macdonald and Jane's, 1978)

Cooper, M., *The German Air Force 1933–1945: An Anatomy of Failure* (London: Jane's, 1981)

Cowling, M., *The Impact of Hitler: British Politics and British Policy 1933–1940* (Cambridge: Cambridge University Press, 1975)

Cross, C. (ed), *Life with Lloyd George: The Diary of A. J. Sylvester 1931–45* (London: Heinemann, 1975)

Cross, J., *Sir Samuel Hoare* (London: Jonathan Cape, 1977)

Crozier, W., *Off the Record: Political Interviews 1933–1943* (ed A. J. P. Taylor) (London: Hutchinson, 1973)

Cruickshank, C., *The German Occupation of the Channel Islands* (London: Oxford University Press, 1975)

Day, D., *The Great Betrayal: Britain, Australia and the Onset of the Pacific War 1939–42* (North Ryde (NSW): Angus and Robertson, 1988)

Dennis, P., *Decision by Default: Peacetime Conscription and British Defence 1919–39* (London: Routledge and Keegan Paul, 1972)

Dilks, D. (ed), *The Diaries of Sir Alexander Cadogan, O. M., 1938–1945* (London: Cassell 1971)

Dilks, D., '"The Unnecessary War"? Military Advice and Foreign Policy in

Great Britain 1931–39', in Preston, A. (ed), *General Staffs and Diplomacy Before the Second World War* (London: Croom Helm, 1978)

Dilks, D., *The Twilight War and the Fall of France: Chamberlain and Churchill in 1940* Transactions of the Royal Historical Society, Vol. 28 [1978] pp. 61–86

Dimbleby, D., and Reynolds, D., *An Ocean Apart: The Relationship Between Britain and America in the Twentieth Century* (London: Hodder and Stoughton, 1988)

Dobson, A., *US Wartime Aid to Britain 1940–1946* (London, Croom Helm, 1986)

Donoughue, B., and Jones, G. W., *Herbert Morrison: Portrait of a Politician* (London: Weidenfeld and Nicolson, 1973)

Feiling, K., *The Life of Neville Chamberlain* (London: Macmillan, 1946)

Fest, J., *Hitler* (London: Weidenfeld and Nicolson, 1974)

Fisk, R., *In Time of War: Ireland, Ulster and the Price of Neutrality 1939–1945* (London: André Deutsch, 1983)

Foot, M., *SOE: The Special Operations Executive 1940–46* (London: BBC, 1984)

Gibbs, N., *Grand Strategy Vol. 1: Rearmament Policy* (London: HMSO, 1976)

Gilbert, M., *Churchill Vol. 5: 1922–1939* (London: Heinemann, 1976)

Gilbert, M., *Finest Hour: Winston S. Churchill 1939–1941* (London: Heinemann, 1983)

Gunsberg, J., *Divided and Conquered: The French High Command and the Defeat of the West, 1940* (Westport [Conn]: Greenwood Press, 1979)

Haggie, P., *Britannia at Bay: The Defence of the British Empire Against Japan 1931–41* (Oxford: Oxford University Press, 1981)

Hancock, W. and Gowing, M., *British War Economy* (London: HMSO, 1949)

Harman, N., *Dunkirk: The Necessary Myth* (London: Hodder and Stoughton, 1980)

Harris, K., *Attlee* (London: Weidenfeld and Nicolson, 1982)

Harrison, T., *Living Through the Blitz* (London: Collins, 1976)

Harvey, J., *The Diplomatic Diaries of Oliver Harvey 1937–1940* (London: Collins, 1970)

Hinsley, F., *British Intelligence in the Second World War: Its Influence on Strategy and Operations Vol 1* (London: HMSO, 1979)

Horne, A., *To Lose a Battle: France 1940* (London: Macmillan, 1969)

Howard, A., *RAB: The Life of R. A. Butler* (London: Jonathan Cape, 1987)

Howard, M., *The Continental Commitment* (London: Temple Smith, 1972)

Idle, E., *War Over West Ham: A Study of Community Adjustment* (London: Faber and Faber, 1943)

Irving, D., *Churchill's War: Vol. I: The Struggle for Power* (Bullsbrook [W. A.]: Veritas, 1987)

James, R. R., *Chips: the Diaries of Sir Henry Channon* (London: Weidenfeld and Nicolson, 1967)

James, R. R., *Anthony Eden* (London: Weidenfeld and Nicolson, 1986)

Jones, T., *A Diary with Letters 1931–1950* (London: Oxford University Press, 1954)

Kennedy, P., *The Rise and Fall of British Naval Mastery* (London: Allen Lane, 1976)

Kennedy, P., *The Rise and Fall of the Great Powers: Economic Change and Military Conflict from 1500 to 2000* (London: Unwin Hyman, 1988)

Kimball, W., *The Most Unsordid Act: Lend-Lease 1939–1941* (Baltimore: Johns Hopkins University Press, 1969)

Kimball, W., *Beggar My Neighbour: America and the British Interim Finance Crisis 1940–1941* (Journal of Economic History, Vol. XXIX, 1969)

Kimball, W., 'Churchill and Roosevelt: The Complete Correspondence Vol. 1: Alliance Emerging October 1933–November 1942' (Princeton: Princeton University Press, 1984)

King, C., *With Malice Towards None – A War Diary* (London: Sidgwick and Jackson, 1970)

Klein, B., *Germany's Economic Preparations for War* (Cambridge [Mass]: Harvard University Press, 1959)

Koch, H. (ed), *Aspects of the Third Reich* (London: Macmillan, 1985)

Kolko, G., *The Politics of War: The World and United States Foreign Policy, 1943–1945.* (New York: Random House, 1968)

Lampe, D., *The Last Ditch.* (London: Cassel, 1968)

Langer, W. and Gleason, S., *The Challenge to Isolation 1937–1940* (New York: Harper Bros, 1952)

Lawlor, S., 'Britain and the Russian Entry into the War', in Langhorne, R. (ed), *Diplomacy and Intelligence During the Second World War* (Cambridge: Cambridge University Press, 1985)

Lee, B., *Strategy, Arms and the Collapse of France 1930–40*, in Langhorne, R. (ed), *Diplomacy and Intelligence in the Second World War* (Cambridge: Cambridge University Press, 1985)

Lentze, J., *Bargaining for Supremacy: Anglo–American Naval Relations 1937–1941* (Chapel Hill [NC]: University of North Carolina Press, 1977)

Lewin, R., *Ultra Goes to War: The Secret Story* (London: Hutchinson, 1978)

Lewis, P., *A People's War* (London: Thames Methuen, 1986)

Louis, W., *Imperialism at Bay 1941–1945: The United States and the Decolonization of the British Empire* (Oxford; Oxford University Press, 1977)

Lowe, P., 'Great Britain and the Coming of the Pacific War 1939–1941' (*Transactions of the Royal Historical Society*, Vol 24 (1974), pp. 43–62)

Lukacs, J., *The Last European War: September 1939–December 1941* (London: Routledge and Keegan Paul, 1976)

McLaine, I., *Ministry of Morale: Home Front Morale and the Ministry of Information in World War II* (London: Allen and Unwin, 1979)

Macleod, R. and Kelly, D., (eds) *The Ironside Diaries 1937–1940* (London: Constable, 1962)

Macmillan, H., *The Blast of War 1939–1945* (London: Macmillan, 1967)

Marder, A., *From the Dardanelles to Oran: Studies of the Royal Navy in War and Peace 1915–1940* (London: Oxford University Press, 1974)

Marder, A., *Old Friends, New Enemies: The Royal Navy and the Imperial Japanese Navy, Strategic Illusions, 1936–1941* (Oxford: Oxford University Press, 1981)

Martin, B., *Friedensinitiativen und Machtpolitik im Zweiten Weltkrieg* (Dusseldorf: Droste Verlag, 1974)

Marwick, A., *The Home Front: The British and the Second World War* (London: Thames and Hudson, 1976)

Middlemass, K., *Diplomacy of Illusion: The British Government and Germany 1937–39* (London: Weidenfeld and Nicolson, 1972)

Milward, A., *War, Economy and Society 1939–1945* (London: Allen Lane, 1977)

Minney, R., *The Private Papers of Hore-Belisha* (London: Collins, 1960)

Mommsen, W. and Kettenacher, L., *The Fascist Challenge and the Policy of Appeasement* (London: Allen and Unwin, 1983)

Neave, A., *The Flames of Calais* (London: Cassel, 1965)

Nicolson, N. (ed), *Harold Nicolson: Diaries and Letters 1939–1945* (London: Collins, 1967)

Overy, R., *The Air War 1939–1945* (London: Europa, 1980)

Peden, G., *British Rearmament and the Treasury 1932–1939* (Edinburgh: Scottish Academic Press, 1979)

Pimlott, B., *Hugh Dalton* (London: Jonathan Cape, 1985)

Pimlott, B., *The Political Diary of Hugh Dalton 1918–40, 1945–60* (London: Jonathan Cape, 1986)

Pimlott, B., *The Second World War Diary of Hugh Dalton 1940–45* (London: Jonathan Cape, 1986)

Pratt, L., *East of Suez, West of Malta: Britain's Mediterranean Crisis 1936–1939* (Cambridge: Cambridge University Press, 1975)

Reynolds, D., *The Creation of the Anglo–American Alliance 1937–1941: A Study in Competitive Co-operation* (London: Europa, 1981)

Reynolds, D., 'Churchill and the British decision to fight on in 1940: right policy, wrong reasons', in Langhorne, R. (ed), *Diplomacy and Intelligence in the Second World War* (Cambridge: Cambridge University Press, 1985)

Reynolds, D., 'Roosevelt, Churchill and the Wartime Anglo–American Alliance, 1939–1945: Towards a New Synthesis', in Louis, W. and Bull, H. (eds), *The Special Relationship* (Oxford: Oxford University Press, 1986)

Roskill, S., *Hankey: Man of Secrets Vol. III: 1931–1963* (London: Collins, 1974)

Salmon, P., 'Crimes Against Peace: the case of the invasion of Norway at the Nuremberg Trials', in Langhorne, R. (ed), *Diplomacy and Intelligence During the Second World War* (Cambridge: Cambridge University Press, 1985)

Shakespeare, G., *Let Candles be Brought in* (London Macdonald, 1949)

Shay, R., *British Rearmament in the Thirties: Politics and Profits* (Princeton: Princteon University Press, 1977)

Smithies, E., *Crime in Wartime: A Social History of Crime in World War II* (London: Allen and Unwin, 1982)

Stafford, D., *Britain and European Resistance 1940–1945* (London: Macmillan, 1980)

Stammers, M., *Civil Liberties in Britain During the 2nd World War* (London: Croom Helm, 1983)

Stengers, J., 'Enigma, the French, the Poles and the British 1931–40', in Andrew, C., and Dilks, D. (eds), *The Missing Dimension* (London: Macmillan, 1984)

Stent, R., *A Bespattered Page?: The Internment of His Majesty's 'most loyal aliens'* (London: André Deutsch, 1980)

Stuart, C. (ed), *The Reith Diaries* (London: Collins, 1975)

Taylor, A., *The Origins of the Second World War* (London: Hamish Hamilton, 1961)

Taylor, A., *English History 1914–1945* (Oxford: Oxford University Press, 1965)

Taylor, A., *Beaverbrook* (London: Hamish Hamilton, 1972)

Taylor, T., *The Breaking Wave: The German Defeat in the Summer of 1940* (London: Weidenfeld and Nicolson, 1967)

Templewood, Viscount, *Nine Troubled Years* (London: Collins, 1954)

Terraine, J., *The Right of the Line: The Royal Air Force in the European War 1939–1945* (London: Hodder and Stoughton, 1985)

Thorne, C., *Allies of a Kind: The United States, Britain and the War Against Japan 1941–1945* (London: Hamish Hamilton, 1978)

Thorne, C., 'The Near and the Far: Aspects of Anglo–American Relations, 1919–1945', in *Border Crossings* (Oxford: Basil Blackwell, 1988)

Titmus, R., *Problems of Social Policy* (London: HMSO, 1950)

Wark, W., 'British Military and Economic Intelligence: Assessments of Nazi Germany Before the Second World War', in Andrew, C., and Dilks, D. (eds), *The Missing Dimension* (London: Macmillan, 1984)

Watt, D., *Succeeding John Bull: America in Britain's Place 1900–1975* (Cambridge: Cambridge University Press, 1984)

Webster, C. and Frankland, N., *The Strategic Air Offensive Against Germany 1939–1945*, 4 Vols (London: HMSO, 1961)

Young, R., *In Command of France: French Foreign Policy and Military Planning 1933–1940* (Cambridge [Mass]: Harvard University Press, 1978)

Index

Territorial Army 149
Thorpe, Jeremy 148
Times, The 156
Tizard, Sir Henry 204
Tobruk 175
Treasury
fears Britain's inability to pay for long war 7–8
'Gold and Exchange Reserves' paper 7

Ulster 189
'B Specials' 194
conscription not applied in 193
Home Guard not formed 193
plan to force into union with Eire 191–4 *passim*
United States 34–6, 173
armed forces in 1940 198
controls US dollars in GB 228
doubts about Britain's survival 199–200
economic and financial rise to power 14–16
inter-war isolation 18, 197–8
Japanese attack on 217, 226, 230
Neutrality Acts 36, 226
presidential election campaign, 1940 8–9

rearmament plans 198, 210
self-interest in supporting Allies 198, 210, 214–15
shift of power from Britain to 215
war effort, 1941–5 230–31
warships collect gold from South Africa 214
see *also* Anglo–American relations

Vickers shipyard, Barrow 142

Washington Naval Treaty, 1922 16–17
disadvantages for Britain 17–18
Weizacker, Herr von 114, 117
Welles, Sumner, peace mission 100–101
Weygand, Gen. 83
Wilkie, Wendell 9
Williams, Shirley 148
Wilson, Sir Horace 69
Windsor, Duke of 200
Wood, Kingsley 6–9 *passim*, 65, 67, 68, 73, 103, 206–7

Yugoslavia 229, 230
conquered by Germany 225, 229

A NOTE ON THE AUTHOR

After gaining first-class honors in history at Reading University, Clive Ponting spent two years researching British strategic policy in the 1930s before joining the civil service. He now writes on British politics and contemporary history and is an honorary research fellow at University College, Swansea. His first book, *The Right to Know*, was an account of his own trial under the Official Secrets Act in 1985, after he protested aspects of the Falklands war. He has also written two books about British government and a widely praised study of the 1964–1970 Labor government, *Breach of Promise*. He lives in West Wales.

ELEPHANT PAPERBACKS

American History and American Studies

Stephen Vincent Benét, *John Brown's Body*, EL10
Henry W. Berger, ed., *A William Appleman Williams Reader*, EL126
Andrew Bergman, *We're in the Money*, EL124
Paul Boyer, ed., *Reagan as President*, EL117
Robert V. Bruce, *1877: Year of Violence*, EL102
George Dangerfield, *The Era of Good Feelings*, EL110
Clarence Darrow, *Verdicts Out of Court*, EL2
Floyd Dell, *Intellectual Vagabondage*, EL13
Elisha P. Douglass, *Rebels and Democrats*, EL108
Theodore Draper, *The Roots of American Communism*, EL105
Joseph Epstein, *Ambition*, EL7
Paul W. Glad, *McKinley, Bryan, and the People*, EL119
Daniel Horowitz, *The Morality of Spending*, EL122
Kenneth T. Jackson, *The Ku Klux Klan in the City, 1915–1930*, EL123
Edward Chase Kirkland, *Dream and Thought in the Business Community, 1860–1900*, EL114
Herbert S Klein, *Slavery in the Americas*, EL103
Aileen S. Kraditor, *Means and Ends in American Abolitionism*, EL111
Leonard W. Levy, *Jefferson and Civil Liberties: The Darker Side*, EL107
Seymour J. Mandelbaum, *Boss Tweed's New York*, EL112
Thomas J. McCormick, *China Market*, EL115
Walter Millis, *The Martial Spirit*, EL104
Nicolaus Mills, ed., *Culture in an Age of Money*, EL302
Nicolaus Mills, *Like a Holy Crusade*, EL129
Roderick Nash, *The Nervous Generation*, EL113
William L. O'Neill, ed., *Echoes of Revolt: The Masses, 1911–1917*, EL5
Glenn Porter and Harold C. Livesay, *Merchants and Manufacturers*, EL106
Edward Reynolds, *Stand the Storm*, EL128
Geoffrey S. Smith, *To Save a Nation*, EL125
Bernard Sternsher, ed., *Hitting Home: The Great Depression in Town and Country*, EL109
Athan Theoharis, *From the Secret Files of J. Edgar Hoover*, EL127
Nicholas von Hoffman, *We Are the People Our Parents Warned Us Against*, EL301
Norman Ware, *The Industrial Worker, 1840–1860*, EL116
Tom Wicker, *JFK and LBJ: The Influence of Personality upon Politics*, EL120
Robert H. Wiebe, *Businessmen and Reform*, EL101
T. Harry Williams, *McClellan, Sherman and Grant*, EL121
Miles Wolff, *Lunch at the 5 & 10*, EL118

European and World History

Mark Frankland, *The Patriots' Revolution*, EL201
Clive Ponting, *1940: Myth and Reality*, EL202

ELEPHANT PAPERBACKS

Literature and Letters
Stephen Vincent Benét, *John Brown's Body*, EL10
Isaiah Berlin, *The Hedgehog and the Fox*, EL21
Philip Callow, *Son and Lover: The Young D. H. Lawrence*, EL14
James Gould Cozzens, *Castaway*, EL6
James Gould Cozzens, *Men and Brethren*, EL3
Clarence Darrow, *Verdicts Out of Court*, EL2
Floyd Dell, *Intellectual Vagabondage*, EL13
Theodore Dreiser, *Best Short Stories*, EL1
Joseph Epstein, *Ambition*, EL7
André Gide, *Madeleine*, EL8
John Gross, *The Rise and Fall of the Man of Letters*, EL18
Irving Howe, *William Faulkner*, EL15
Aldous Huxley, *After Many a Summer Dies the Swan*, EL20
Aldous Huxley, *Ape and Essence*, EL19
Aldous Huxley, *Collected Short Stories*, EL17
Sinclair Lewis, *Selected Short Stories*, EL9
William L. O'Neill, ed., *Echoes of Revolt: The Masses, 1911–1917*, EL5
Ramón J. Sender, *Seven Red Sundays*, EL11
Wilfrid Sheed, *Office Politics*, EL4
Tess Slesinger, *On Being Told That Her Second Husband Has Taken His First Lover, and Other Stories*, EL12
B. Traven, *Government*, EL23
B. Traven, *The Night Visitor and Other Stories*, EL24
Rex Warner, *The Aerodrome*, EL22
Thomas Wolfe, *The Hills Beyond*, EL16

ELEPHANT PAPERBACKS

Theatre and Drama
Robert Brustein, *Reimagining American Theatre*, EL410
Robert Brustein, *The Theatre of Revolt*, EL407
Irina and Igor Levin, *Working on the Play and the Role*, EL411
Plays for Performance:
  Aristophanes, *Lysistrata*, EL405
  Anton Chekhov, *The Seagull*, EL407
  Fyodor Dostoevsky, *Crime and Punishment*, EL416
  Georges Feydeau, *Paradise Hotel*, EL403
  Henrik Ibsen, *Ghosts*, EL401
  Henrik Ibsen, *Hedda Gabler*, EL413
  Henrik Ibsen, *The Master Builder*, EL417
  Henrik Ibsen, *When We Dead Awaken*, EL408
  Heinrich von Kleist, *The Prince of Homburg*, EL402
  Christopher Marlowe, *Doctor Faustus*, EL404
  The Mysteries: Creation, EL412
  The Mysteries: The Passion, EL414
  Sophocles, *Electra*, EL415
  August Strindberg, *The Father*, EL406